The Female Homicide Offender

❖

Prentice Hall's
Women in Criminal Justice Series

Series Editor:
Roslyn Muraskin, Ph.D

The Female Homicide Offender: Serial Murder and the Case of Aileen Wuornos
Stacey L. Shipley and Bruce A. Arrigo
ISBN: 0-13-114161-9

The Incarcerated Woman: Rehabilitative Programming in Women's Prisons
Susan Sharp
ISBN: 0-13-094067-4

It's A Crime: Women and Justice, 3e
Roslyn Muraskin
ISBN: 0-13-0482000-5

With Justice For All: Minorities in Criminal Justice
Janice Joseph and Dorothy Taylor
ISBN: 0-13-033463-4

The Female Homicide Offender

Serial Murder and the Case of Aileen Wuornos

❖

STACEY L. SHIPLEY, Psy.D.
North Texas State Hospital–Vernon

BRUCE A. ARRIGO, Ph.D.
The University of North Carolina–Charlotte

PEARSON

Prentice Hall

Upper Saddle River, New Jersey 07458

Library of Congress Cataloging-in-Publication Data

Shipley, Stacey L.
    The female homicide offender : serial murder and the case of Aileen
Wuornos / Stacey L. Shipley and Bruce A. Arrigo.
        p.   cm.
    ISBN 0-13-114161-9
        1. Women serial murderers—United States. 2. Wuornos, Aileen. 3.
Serial murders—Florida—Case studies. I. Arrigo, Bruce A. II. Title.
    HV6517 .S55 2003
    364.152'3'082—dc22   2003018283

Publisher: Stephen Helba
Executive Editor: Frank Mortimer, Jr.
Assistant Editor: Sarah Holle
Production Management: Mary Carnis
Production Editor: Linda Duarte,
    Pine Tree Composition, Inc.
Production Liaison: Barbara Marttine Cappuccio
Director of Manufacturing and Production:
    Bruce Johnson
Manufacturing Buyer: Cathleen Peterson
Creative Director: Cheryl Asherman
Cover Design Coordinator: Miguel Ortiz
Cover Designer: Steve Frim
Cover Image: Getty Images
Editorial Assistant: Barbara Rosenberg
Marketing Manager: Tim Peyton
Formatting: Pine Tree Compostion, Inc.
Printing and Binding: Phoenix Book Tech Park

Dedication

This book is dedicated with love and admiration to my parents, Carol and Robert Shipley, who always believed I would accomplish my dreams.

In memory of the victims of violent crime, both living and dead, may the study of offenders, including serial killers, help prevent future pain, devastation, and harm.

For all those who suffer from abuse, neglect, and abandonment, may we find a way to make things right by you; and may we find a way to make you whole, healthy, and healed.

Pearson Prentice Hall™ is a trademark of Pearson Education, Inc.
Pearson® is a registered trademark of Pearson plc.
Prentice Hall® is a registered trademark of Pearson Education, Inc.

Pearson Education LTD.
Pearson Education Singapore, Pte. Ltd.
Pearson Education Canada, Ltd.
Pearson Education—Japan
Pearson Education Australia PTY. Limited
Pearson Education North Asia Ltd
Pearson Educaçion de Mexico, S.A. de C.V.
Pearson Education Malaysia, Pte. Ltd

10 9 8 7 6 5 4 3 2
ISBN 0-13-114161-9

Contents

❖

The Female Homicide Offender

Serial Murder and the Case of Aileen Wuornos

Introductory Remarks
Roslyn Muraskin, Ph.D.
Women's Series Editor

Capital punishment is a controversial subject, yet it is a sentence that is administered in this country to both men and women alike. In particular, the women on death row are made to feel that they are a burden on society, in the hope that they will quietly disappear.

Who are these women who kill? Aileen Wuornos was one. In 1989, the body of Richard Mallory was discovered in the woods in Ormond Beach, Florida. He had been shot four times with a .22 caliber handgun. In the next 12 months, six more bodies of men were discovered. Each victim was of middle age and discovered near a highway. Also, each had been robbed of both money and valuables, and his car was stolen but found soon afterward. Moreover, each had been shot with a .22 caliber handgun.

According to the FBI, there were two female serial killers on the loose. The media reacted in a frenzy. In December 1990, the name Aileen Wuornos was brought to the forefront. At the time, she was 34 years of age. Arrested in January 1991, she confessed to the killing of these men in self-defense, claiming that they had all attempted to rape her.

Aileen Wuornos was a prostitute. She gave a "shocking, detailed confession at the behest of her lesbian ex-lover, and during her trial she was legally adopted by a well-meaning woman who claimed to receive her instruction from God" (www.crimelibrary .com/serial4/wuornos). What she was not was America's first female serial killer: over time, women have been murdering serially for as long a time as men. Aileen Wuornos was an interesting person. "She is both repellent and strangely pathetic" (ibid.).

Aileen Wuornos was executed by the state of Florida on October 9, 2002 at 9:47 A.M., being the forty-eighth U.S. woman to be executed in the last 100 years. She had requested to die, giving up all further appeals. Wuornos was born in Rochester, Michigan, in 1956. She was raised by her grandparents, having been abandoned by her mother as an infant. Her father was, according to the Associated Press, a convicted child molester who killed himself while serving time in a prison facility. Before the age of 13, Aileen Wuornos had been the victim of a rape, and by the time she had reached 15 years, she was already a prostitute. By the age of 30, she had been arrested for the robbery of a convenience store.

> In 1989 and 1990, Wuornos went on a killing spree, murdering and robbing six men in five counties, and earning the nickname of 'The Damsel of Death.' In custody, Wuornos confessed to a seventh murder. Although she initially claimed that she was raped by all the victims, and that each murder was a case of self-defense, Wuornos subsequently admitted that she killed them for money, in part to pay for an apartment to share with her lesbian lover. She also claimed to have 'hate crawling through my system' (Rostow, October 9, 2002, p. 1).

There were many who believed Wuornos to be severely psychotic, though she was found to be rational enough to resolve her own fate.

Stacey L. Shipley and Bruce A. Arrigo have put together a fantastic work in *The Female Homicide Offender: Serial Murder and the Case of Aileen Wuornos.* This book investigates "predatory homicide perpetrated by women" (Shipley & Arrigo, 2003, p. iv). Through their analysis of attachment theory, they set out to explain the killings by such women using Aileen Wuornos's case as the prime example. Who are these women who decided to kill in such a calculated, uncaring way? In the authors' words, "Attachment theory enables practicing psychologists and criminologists, as well as researchers and policy analysts, to understand the personality dynamics that exist in women who commit predatory homicide."

There have been numerous studies of the criminality of men, but it was not until 30 years ago that the study of women criminals was begun. Women have traditionally been placed in the role of victim; however, now we see them in a different light, that of the calculated murderer. It has been unusual to think of women as persons who commit murder in cold blood. In the following chapters, you will read about the literature on women and crime, women as offenders, the mental disorders of such women offenders, the use of psychopathy, and the application of attachment theory. This is the first time that an in-depth study of women as serial murderers has been presented in a thorough and an interesting manner. "Each chapter addresses an important dimension of the phenomenon under investigation. . . . [their] material endeavors to balance the criminological and psychological literature relevant to female-perpetrated predatory homicide. . . . the reader [becomes] better equipped to understand the nuances and complexities of women who murder where mental illness figures prominently in their analysis" (p. xvii).

It is the authors' contention that scholarly investigations must be based on definitive presuppositions. It is also their belief that "psychopathic female serial killers experience poor attachment with their primary caregivers" (p. xix). The authors surmise that "psychopathic and predatory female serial killers are not so much *victims* as they are cold, calculating offenders" (p. xix).

The authors show that historically, "civic leaders and moral crusaders have postulated that when women deviate substantially from their status as wife or mother, adopting instead a life of violent crime, they are deemed especially corrupt or evil" (p. 3). The idea has always existed that males were the aggressors and women the pacifists.

According to statistics from the Bureau of Justice, homicide is defined as causing the death of another person with no legal justification. *Murder* and *homicide* are terms used interchangeably: "predatory homicide perpetrated by women . . . [has as its] focus . . . *first-degree murder* rather than . . . manslaughter" (p. 13).

What is shocking to most is that women are not criminals who kill—at least not in the conventional view. According to Godwin, both the police and the courts have difficulty understanding that women *do* kill.

> What lies beyond the ken of most police officers are the outbursts of rabid violence staged by women, on their own accord, unconnected with any felony, and in response to the slightest provocations. In other words, actions hitherto reserved for only the most vicious of types of male bully. (Godwin, 1978, p. 127)

Godwin maintains that when women commit violence, they are "worse than their male counterparts: more bloodthirsty, more vicious, more unscrupulous, [and] more deadly than the male" (p. 113). Firearms are the choice of these females.

A study conducted in Stockholm, Sweden, indicates that "men with schizophrenia or major affective disorder were 4 times more likely to be convicted of a violent crime compared with men without a major mental disorder (schizophrenia, affective disorder, or paranoid state). *Women with a major psychiatric illness were 27 times more likely than those without a major psychiatric illness to be convicted of a violent crime*" (emphasis mine, p. 33). The conclusion reached is that women who kill are considered to be more mentally ill than their male counterparts.

According to the authors of this book, when there are issues of poor attachment made evident by the person's history, we can predict with some accuracy what will happen: a woman such as Aileen Wuornos falls in this category. Wuornos, in her own words, sometimes stretching the truth, explained what she is all about. During an interview in prison, she angrily declared, "Nobody is looking at my life. Nobody's looking at my life and . . . what's my life about" (p. 96). A study of her family history is presented, describing who Aileen Wuornos was and providing the reasons why she did what she did.

> Aileen's anger and aggression only grew in her teenage years. She was frequently thrown out of parties for being vulgar, being belligerent, and initiating fights. She had a short fuse and was easily provoked. In addition to using the drugs . . . Aileen began to drink vast quantities of alcohol, particularly beer. (p. 101)

Pregnant at age 14, she described her rapist in many different ways, including that he was an Elvis Presley look-alike.

The authors consider the following questions: "(a) Can childhood interactions with primary attachment figures be an important early marker of adulthood behaviors and personality development . . .? (b) Can the inhibition of early bonding or attachments and abandonment, as well as emotional, sexual, and physical abuse, lead to detachment, apathy, and lack of empathy for others? (c) Can hostility and aggression that becomes part of an individual's internal working model result in preemptive aggression and predatory murder?" (p. 109).

If a child does not develop trust and security from the primary caregivers, there is every indication that something will go wrong later in the child's life. And there we have the case of Aileen Wuornos. Aileen believed that she was evil, wicked, and worthless; that her life was filled with rejection and fright; and that there were no people whom she could trust.

Aileen became a runaway and a liar. She was hyperactive and impulsive, had poor learning skills, and failed to understand the consequences of her actions. The world owed Aileen Wuornos something, or so she believed. Thus, she stole, manipulated, and isolated herself from others, believing herself to be *the* focal point of the world while everything else revolved around her. In murdering the seven men, she actually believed herself to be the victim, not the perpetrator, of those crimes. She killed Richard Mallory with intent yet exhibited no fear for her own life.

In this work, the attributes of female serial killers are portrayed very realistically. Yet, how to recognize the symptoms and what to do once they are identified are matters that we somehow have not come to grips with, according to the authors. There is need for a working strategy to be used when we recognize who these women are. We can neither ignore them nor resort to execution (the easy way out). How to prevent such crimes from occurring is considered in one of the chapters. Aileen Wuornos "slipped through the cracks as a child. School personnel identified her need for treatment, and no one attended to those needs. Unfortunately, children with detached, neglectful, or abusive parents cannot count on their mothers or fathers to pursue or follow up on the provision of services. . . . mental health specialists . . . conscientiously must pursue programs that can benefit these children" (p. 139).

Accordingly, women who receive pathological treatment when young will act out in an aggressive manner later in life. Women have continuously been construed as the victims, but through the study of Aileen Wuornos and her life experiences, a better understanding of the females who commit homicides has been established. The authors discuss the kind of prison sentences that such females receive. Is the death penalty warranted when someone, such as Aileen Wuornos, suffers from psychiatric problems that are traced back to her early years? The authors state that the kind of punishment, that is, capital punishment, "warrants more detailed and thoughtful exploration as law and public policy analysts endeavor to protect the liberty interests of offenders while simultaneously ensuring the rights of an organized society" (p. 146).

Aileen's self-worth is examined by the authors of this book. No one stopped to intervene or to ask the right questions about her behavior. In her own words, "There's no sense in keeping me alive. This world doesn't mean anything to me" (Shipley & Arrigo as pointed out by Schneider, 2002).

Was the execution of Aileen the correct punishment? For many people, including her victims, the answer would be *yes,* but what should have been done for her? Could Aileen Wuornos have been saved somewhere along the line? Was there a complete breakdown of help for Wuornos? Was it society that failed, and could the destruction that she committed have been prevented? Which is better, death or serving the rest of one's natural life in a correctional facility? Or should there be treatment afforded to such offenders?

The story of Aileen Wuornos is intriguing. She was a sickening woman, but she was also a wretched person. On the one hand, it was her own belligerence that sealed her fate; on the other hand, she was an individual who never had a chance. Did she truly deserve to die in such a fashion? The woman who claimed that hate crawled through her system was, at her own request, executed.

Read this volume of ideas, theories, and suggestions. Then consider what the state of our criminal justice system is and whether it really is the best way to handle the guilty.

Introduction

This book investigates predatory homicide perpetrated by women. As such, this text does not consider female criminality as linked to justifiable and excusable homicide. In addition, this text excludes women who attribute their crimes to Battered Women's Syndrome or otherwise kill their abusive partners because they fear their lives are in danger. Although these homicides can still be considered criminal, the way that female offenders view these actions is an entirely different phenomenon beyond the scope of our immediate concern. Thus, in this text, we are particularly interested in understanding the phenomenon of female serial killers where the homicides are predatory, calculated, and seemingly without remorse.

To situate our analysis, the psychological construct of attachment theory is utilized. Attachment theory enables practicing psychologists and criminologists, as well as researchers and policy analysts, to understand the personality dynamics that exist in women who commit predatory homicide. Specifically, we narrow the focus to include women who kill who are diagnosed with antisocial personality disorder (ASPD) or its characteristic psychopathic traits. In general, the *Diagnostic and Statistical Manual of Mental Disorders,* Fourth Edition (APA, 1994), defines antisocial personality disorder as "a pervasive pattern of disregard for and violation of the rights of others occurring since age 15 years" (p. 645). Characteristics indicative of this disregard for and violation of others' rights include deceitfulness, impulsivity, irritability, aggressiveness, reckless disregard for safety of self or others, unsteady work behavior, irresponsibility with financial affairs, and a lack of remorse and empathy for others (APA, 1994). Individuals with this disorder must be at least 18 years of age.

WHY CONDUCT THIS STUDY?

Male criminality has been a topic of considerable academic research and of criminal justice policy debate for centuries. However, investigations of female criminality did not emerge until the 1970s. It is interesting that research on women and crime traditionally has neglected the more violent offenses. Indeed, as Wilbanks (1983, p. 302) observed, "The academic literature on female homicide offenders is sparse given the seriousness of the crime and the voluminous literature on women and crime in general." During the 1980s, an exploration into the etiology of the female homicide offender began to emerge (Mann, 1996). For example, several prison studies were conducted that examined the intelligence and psychology of female offenders, using assessment instruments administered within these penal institutions (Mann, 1996). However, this research was dramatically overshadowed by the idea of "victim precipitation," particularly in cases of spousal abuse. According to Wolfgang (1958, p. 252):

> The term victim precipitation is applied to those criminal homicides in which the victim is a direct, positive precipitator in the crime. The role of the victim is characterized by his having been the first in the homicide drama to use physical force directed against his subsequent slayer. The victim-precipitated cases are those in which the victim was the first to show and use a deadly weapon, to strike a blow in an altercation—in short, the first to commence the interplay of resort to physical violence.

In general, then, research involving women and crime has placed the female in the role of the victim. The majority of recent studies looking at women as offenders in criminal homicide also reflect a similar tendency. For example, the current literature on women who kill is almost exclusively related to women who claim to have killed their batterers (e.g., Egger, 2002; Hickey, 1997; Kelleher & Kelleher, 1998). Although the men are the actual homicide victims in these cases, the women are considered victims of alleged abuse that led to the homicide. Even though statistics reflect that women who kill are typically those being abused, these data are usually based on the self-reports of the offenders. Some researchers suggest that although many women act in defense of their lives, others use a popular defense (e.g., Battered Women's Syndrome) to murder with impunity. According to Thibault and Rossier (1992, p. 12), "Although some women may kill in the home in self defense, female killers in the home also plan to kill and kill because they want to."

For example, in a study conducted by Mann (1996), women who committed homicide in 1979 and 1983 began with the initial charge of first- or second-degree murder. However, almost two-thirds of the charges were reduced from murder charges to a lesser charge such as manslaughter, and less than half of the women obtained prison terms (Mann, 1996). This research is as suggestive as it is provocative. Indeed, it provides insight into women who kill not as a defense but for other, more complex reasons. Accordingly, we argue that these "other reasons" must be the basis for future research if the phenomenon of female predatory homicide is to be adequately explained.

As a society, we typically view women as caretakers: passive and gentle. Whereas aggressive, violent behavior is expected in men, Western culture has great difficulty in perceiving women as *cold-blooded killers*. Rarely are women thought to commit a murder for personal or material gain, with little or no regard for human life. Bell and Fox (1996) expressed the need to move the current focus of female killers from the battered woman phenomenon to the wider and more difficult questions posed by a woman who kills an innocent third party. They proposed this concentration of research as necessary both for feminist discourse on violent women and for reforming laws affecting female killers.

Brownstein, Spunt, Crimmins, Goldstein, and Langley (1994) maintained that historically, research on female homicide offenders has focused on battered women who kill their abusers, while coming to terms with the growing number of women who kill for other reasons. These researchers concluded that "detailed, personal accounts of homicides by women need to be studied in order to better understand this phenomenon" (1994, p. 99). Indeed, careful exploration into the backgrounds and family dynamics of female offenders can make it possible to understand what motivates a woman to commit predatory homicide.

In particular, Brownstein et al. (1994) explored the impact of drugs on women who kill. They found that the cases of women in their sample in which illicit substances were excessively used did not result in the women becoming violent. The authors therefore noted that the homicides might have been related to the drugs in some way, but not from a "drug-induced violent outburst" (Brownstein et al., 1994, p. 99). Consequently, these investigators argued that more qualitative research was needed: studies that described the circumstances and characteristics of the homicides to better understand women as lethal offenders. It is interesting that as a cohort, women with ASPD have nearly 10 times the rate of lifetime drug and alcohol disorder, contrary to the general population. Regrettably, women who kill and who are diagnosed with a mental disorder (specifically, ASPD or psychopathy) are neglected in current research.

Accordingly, the current study addresses the more complex question of how women diagnosed with ASPD or with psychopathic personality traits experience their crime. ASPD is the mental disorder most closely related to the criminal mind phenomenon or the psychopathic personality (Hillbrand, Kozmon, & Nelson, 1996). Individuals with these characterological traits generally do not take into consideration the pain and suffering of others. They are primarily concerned with their own personal or material gain as generated from a particular situation. For example, the taking of a human life could be an acceptable price to pay for a love interest, a monetary award, or an act of revenge. Whereas the experience of a woman who kills in protection of herself or her children previously has been explored, little is known about women with ASPD (psychopathy) who engage in the act of homicide. Indeed, what life experiences allow her to stretch the boundaries of gender, morality, and the law? What is there about her family, friends, and ongoing social interactions that enables her to take a human life without remorse? These and similar queries have not received much attention (qualitative or otherwise) in the relevant criminal justice and psychological literature to date.

Despite the strong correlation that exists between violent crime and ASPD (psychopathy) (e.g., Arrigo & Shipley, 2001), little is known about the impact of ASPD on women who kill. These women are considered an anomaly by many researchers and by society at large. This book aims to rectify the paucity of research on female predatory homicide, drawing attention to the phenomenon of ASPD and its impact on and relation to the act of predatory murder. In particular, by way of an instrumental case study (the story of Aileen Wuornos), we provide a richly textured and experientially based analysis within the context of attachment theory. In addition, our investigation demonstrates the power of early attachment on the adult detachment of a woman who committed predatory homicide. As such, we focus on a previously under-examined area of female homicide behavior.

Society continues to focus on seemingly *senseless* violence in men. However, Mann (1996) explained that women do not go unaffected by the violence that occurs around them. Citing Murray Straus, she stated that "Female assaults grow out of the same cultural and structural roots as male violence" (Mann, 1996, p. 2). Currently, the statistical numbers of women who commit murder diagnosed with ASPD (psychopathy) are small when compared with their male counterparts. However, as women are reared in more violent and neglectful homes, their propensity for violence will likely increase.

Approximately 1 of every 10 persons arrested for homicide in the United States is a woman (Brownstein et al., 1994). In addition, the number of women involved in the killing of strangers or persons to whom they are not emotionally connected is also on the rise (Pollock, 1999). However, neither frequency distributions nor empirical research reflects the tremendous impact that murder has on society when committed by women. Thus, we contend that by exploring the antecedents and life histories of predatory female homicide offenders, it may be possible to predict and prevent future acts of lethal criminality.

OBJECTIVE AND METHODS

In this book we employ an instrumental case study design and utilize attachment theory to better comprehend the predatory homicidal actions of one woman (Aileen Wuornos) with ASPD (psychopathy). In addition, this text aims to provide a more complex conceptualization of what motivates these women to kill and how their life experiences and attachment styles impact their crimes. Given these objectives, we contend that our investigation will considerably extend the knowledge about the phenomenon of female serial killers.

To facilitate our inquiry, we rely on detailed and in-depth data collection methods. This approach enables us to present and analyze themes and to make interpretations or assertions about the personality structure of women who commit predatory homicide. This qualitative approach to female serial killing allows us to explore several questions previously unanswered in the relevant literature. For example, why do some women commit criminal homicide and view their transgressions without remorse or affect (feeling)? Can the motivating factors behind these murders be attributable to material gain? Can female serial killers experience their crime with a sense of exhilaration or thrill? How do some women come to value money or revenge more than the taking of a human life? In what way do the poor or unhealthy early childhood attachments of girls toward their primary caregivers create detachment for them from others in adulthood? Is it possible for a woman to have pro-social adult attachments toward some individuals and yet possess a complete lack of global respect for human life?

Our instrumental case study method adds depth and humanness to the overwhelming empirical research on women and crime. Indeed, our approach allows themes to emerge from individual experiences in order to then interpret them within larger social and psychological theories (Creswell, 1998). Thus, the case study method allows the reader to proceed from a very broad to a very narrow understanding, rather than trying to comprehend the phenomenon under consideration from a reductionistic, presupposed category or model. Moreover, given the paucity of research on female serial killers diagnosed with ASPD (psychopathy), our method of inquiry permits the sample investigated to be smaller, and it makes possible a more personal analysis of the life experiences of women who engage in lethal crime.

We also note that the dearth of empirical scholarship on the phenomenon of female predatory homicide underestimates the impact of these crimes for society. Arguably, the justification for the absence of more statistical analysis is linked to the limited number of documented cases of female serial killers. However, in research that follows the natural science paradigm, nominal numbers indicate something that is inconsequential or not worthy of further analysis. As a result, this group of women has not been systematically identified for purposes of ongoing empirical investigation. Instead, gender-role stereotypes inappropriately are utilized, resulting in the misidentification of these women and their criminal behaviors in current studies. To remedy this situation, we contend that, at this point, studying female serial killers necessitates a descriptive method of analysis. Indeed, as Mann (1990, p. 176) observed, statistical data on murder do "not provide sufficiently nuanced profiles of offenders and their victims, excluding many important details specific to each situation." Clearly, then, a case study research design can come much closer to describing the phenomenon under consideration.

In addition, the research that has explored women with ASPD tends to accept the categories and hypotheses created by investigations on men and then generalizes them to women. However, according to Rutherford, Alterman, Cacciola, and Snider (1995), the psychometric properties of ASPD are weak for women when compared with those for men. Although their study did not critically analyze the diagnostic validity or accuracy of ASPD for women, the case study methodology they employed sought to explore the life of one woman to better understand the development of her symptoms and behaviors. Moreover, as Baskin and Sommers (1993, p. 559) noted, "Unique characteristics of female offender subsamples generally have been masked by the tendency to view women in purely gender-linked, generic terms." As a result, these investigators concluded that little has been learned about the nature of females' involvement in specific types of crimes. We agree. Accordingly, we employ an instrumental case study approach and apply this method to an investigation of female-perpetrated predatory homicide in which attachment disorder in childhood gives rise to ASPD (psychopathy) in adulthood.

ORGANIZATION OF THE BOOK

The Female Homicide Offender: Serial Murder and the Case of Aileen Wuornos is divided into eleven chapters. Each chapter addresses an important dimension of the phenomenon under investigation. In addition, the material endeavors to balance the criminological and psychological literature relevant to female-perpetrated predatory homicide. In this way, the reader is better equipped to understand the nuances and complexities of women who murder when mental illness figures prominently in the analysis.

In Chapter 1 we review the literature on women and crime. Relevant statistics are presented, and the limitations of these data are delineated. In addition, various theories regarding female criminality and aggression are discussed. Other factors affecting female offending, including childhood victimization, broken homes, substance abuse, race/ethnicity, Premenstrual Syndrome (PMS), and mental illness are explored.

In Chapter 2 we narrow our investigation and focus on women as homicide offenders. Arrest trends for murder by women versus men and the likely social factors influencing those developments are reviewed. The contradictory role of women as murderers versus caretakers/mothers is assessed. In addition, empirical and related investigations examining the phenomenon of women as perpetrators of violence, including various explanations for this phenomenon, are described. The profile of the female serial killer and different typologies of the same are discussed. Prevalent traits among these typologies are identified and consolidated.

In Chapter 3 we explore the presence of mental illness among female homicide offenders. The relationship between violence and psychiatric disorders among women is examined. The role that mental illness plays in female-perpetrated homicide is evaluated. Also, empirical data specifying the number and type of psychiatric disorders among women are supplied. The impact that mental illness has on the disposition of women who kill is reviewed, mindful of how gender-role stereotypes impact the analysis.

In Chapter 4 we systematically explore antisocial personality disorder (ASPD) and psychopathy. The relationship between these two psychiatric/psychological constructs is delineated. The diagnostic criteria for ASPD are described. The development of ASPD/ psychopathy from various psychological perspectives is presented. Also, the impact that abuse and neglect have on a person's symptomotology is discussed. The effects that gender has when diagnosing ASPD (psychopathy) are considered as well.

In Chapter 5 we focus our investigation on the relationship between ASPD (psychopathy) and homicide. The context in which the two phenomena seem inseparably linked is delineated. Meloy's (1992) research on predatory violence and psychopathy, and empirical investigations on psychopathic males and murder are presented. In addition, Eronen's (1995) work on psychiatric illness in women and homicide is systematically reviewed. Several suggestions for future research in the area of ASPD (psychopathy) and female-perpetrated murder are outlined.

In Chapter 6 we examine the literature on attachment theory as developed by the psychiatric/psychological research community. The phenomenon is described on the basis of the decisive work of Ainsworth et al. (1978). Studies exploring attachment styles/patterns over the life course are examined, and differences between childhood and adult attachment are enumerated. The classification of adult attachment disorder is delineated. Also, empirical and related literature exploring adult attachment disorder and psychopathology (i.e., personality disorders) is discussed. The relationship between insecure attachment styles and psychopathy is reviewed. In addition, several observations concerning reactive attachment disorder are presented. Finally, the neurobiology of attachment, emphasizing the work of Schore (1991, 1994) is specified.

In Chapter 7 we discuss relevant methodological issues informing our assessment of Aileen Wuornos and her life story. Several observations regarding the instrumental case study approach are presented. Also, the viability of this method versus quantitative and other qualitative approaches is reviewed. Justifications for our selection of the Aileen Wuornos case are enumerated, and the limits of our methodology are delineated.

In Chapter 8 we present the life narrative of Aileen Wuornos. A chronological sequencing of personal, interpersonal, familial, and social events is provided. In addition, the circumstances surrounding her first murder are disclosed. The forensic evidence and Aileen's confession also are described.

In Chapter 9 we analyze and interpret the data. Aileen Wuornos's behavioral, cognitive, and affective states are identified. Also, the personality traits and motivational factors she exhibited, as linked to her attachment patterns, are reviewed. There is a description of her ratings/scores on the Attachment Disorder Symptoms Checklist and the Psychopathy Checklist Revised. Her murderous actions are assessed, mindful of Meloy's (1992) work on predatory aggression. Summary observations on the relationship among insecure attachments, psychopathy, and predatory violence are supplied, and naturalistic generalizations are delineated.

In Chapter 10 we discuss the implications of our analysis. The domains of forensic/ correctional psychology, law and public policy, and criminal justice administration and management specifically are explored. Also, a summary of the book and what each chapter endeavored to accomplish is supplied.

In Chapter 11 we reflect of the ethics of crime, mental illness, and justice, especially when the criminal justice and mental health systems seemingly fail to assist persons in profound distress. The role of the media in fashioning a culture of violence is reviewed. Also, the contributions of radical or Marxist criminology are speculatively discussed. The philosophy and practice of restorative justice are provisionally applied to the case of Aileen Wuornos. Finally, the responsibility of society in helping to create the psychopathic female serial killer is discussed.

PRESUPPOSITIONS

All scholarly investigations are based on certain presuppositions or convictions, and our research is no exception to this established practice. In particular, we believe that psychopathic female serial killers experience poor attachment with their primary caregivers. Moreover, we maintain that these offenders do not express the kind or type of remorse found among women who kill their batterers, especially since women who murder serially are so detached from others that might harm them. In addition, our preexisting knowledge regarding ASPD leads us to conjecture that psychopathic women who engage in predatory homicide are irritable and aggressive because many of their most basic needs went unmet when they were children. Relatedly, we assume that these women feel entitled, acting as if the world owes them something because of their early experiences of emotional, financial, and social deprivation. Given these suppositions, we propose that psychopathic and predatory female serial killers are not so much *victims* as they are cold, calculating offenders. To the extent that these women murder for personal profit, material gain, or are unable to control their rageful impulses, we maintain that their homicidal actions are not the result of victim-precipitated murder.

All of these convictions and assumptions were identified and discussed prior to the actual investigation of Aileen Wuornos, her life story, her behavior, and her personality structure. Having reviewed these presuppositions, we then set them aside. Indeed, we allowed the phenomenon to present itself through the case study materials, exploring its relationship to attachment theory as we carefully synthesized, analyzed, and interpreted the data.

1

Women and Crime

❖

INTRODUCTION

This chapter explores the pertinent literature regarding female criminality. Many stereotypes and myths surround a woman's role in crime—specifically, homicide. The research presented in this chapter draws attention to several themes that help explain the lack of scholarship on female-perpetrated, predatory homicide. In addition, the chapter contextualizes the need for and the importance of such applied investigations. Although the commentary that follows is not exhaustive, it does demonstrate some of the issues affecting society's understanding of female criminality.

Chapter 1 begins by examining the extent of female crime, including relevant statistics pertaining to the crime rates for women versus that for men. In addition, observations on the rate of female property crime versus violent crime are supplied. These statistics cover important trends on women and offender behavior, revealing the magnitude of female criminality. Some of the limitations pertaining to these data are also examined.

Also described in the chapter are various theories of female criminality. Historically, criminological theory has focused on investigating men, and thus the perceptions of women in crime have been colored mostly by stereotypes. Various biological, socioeconomic, psychological, and feminist-inspired perspectives of the female offender are offered. In particular, the work of Lombroso, Freud, Thomas, Pollack, Adler, and Chesney-Lind are delineated, showing the progression of thought in understanding female criminality. Theories of aggression pertaining to women and the relative impact of this behavior for female criminality are also elucidated. The chapter concludes by examining other factors affecting female offending, including childhood victimization, broken homes, substance abuse, race/ethnicity, Premenstrual Syndrome (PMS), and mental illness.

THE EXTENT OF FEMALE CRIME

The extent of female crime is consistently obscured relative to the incidence, severity, and awareness of male criminality (e.g., Flowers, 1994; Naffine, 1987; Rafter, 2000). This is particularly the case when studying violent crime perpetrated by women. Indeed, other, nonviolent offenses characteristically have been viewed as more traditionally female (e.g., prostitution). This situation notwithstanding, female crime is increasing, is more hetero-geneous and, consequently, is in need of systematic research.

According to Flowers (1994), the Federal Bureau of Investigation's (FBI) Uniform Crime Reporting Program is the most significant source for identifying and evaluating female offenders. The FBI's *Crime in the United States: Uniform Crime Reports* (UCR) documents data that were gathered from a nationwide statistical effort of over 16,000 city, county, and statewide law enforcement agencies reporting crimes known to them (FBI, 1997). During 1996, these law-enforcement organizations accounted for 95 percent of the total population established by the Bureau of the Census.

However, Mann (1996) indicated that the UCR failed to provide data on gender and race, citing this failure as a serious drawback. In addition, Spunt, Brownstein, Crimmins, and Langley (1997) explained that national crime statistics have only limited utility as they offer minimal information about the homicide offender and victim. They reported that "Face-to-face interviewing with women who kill would seem to have great potential for obtaining insight into the feelings and perspectives of these women and the many dif-ferent facets of female-perpetrated homicide" (Spunt et al., 1997, p. 294). Despite the ob-vious shortcomings of the UCR, researchers studying female criminality have relied on it for computing female homicide rates (Mann, 1996). Accordingly, we utilize the UCR to determine the extent of female crime as of 1996.

In 1996, there were an estimated 729,900 persons (both men and women) arrested for violent crimes, which include murder, forcible rape, robbery, and aggravated assault. Women accounted for 15.1 percent of all violent crime arrestees. In 1996, women were responsible for an estimated 10.3 percent of all murder and nonnegligent manslaughter ar-rests, 9.7 percent of all robbery arrests, 17.9 percent of aggravated assault arrests, and only 1.2 percent of forcible rape arrests.

In addition, women accounted for 27.9 percent of all property crimes for 1996 (FBI, 1997). Property crimes include burglary, larceny-theft, motor vehicle theft, and arson. Women composed an estimated 11.3 percent of all burglary arrests, 33.8 percent of larceny-theft arrests, 13.6 percent of motor vehicle theft arrests, and 14.9 percent of arson arrests. Currently, women play a larger role in property crimes than in violent crimes. We note, however, that this finding is not to minimize their role in violent crimes in which physical or emotional injury to other persons is imminent.

The UCR is divided into two parts: Part 1—Crime Index offenses (both violent and property crimes), and Part 2—nonindex offenses, consisting of 21 less serious crimes. The nonindex offenses include crimes such as other assaults, vandalism, fraud, embezzle-ment, prostitution and commercialized vice, drug abuse violations, and runaways. In 1996, women accounted for an estimated 20.3 percent of other assaults arrests, 13.8 per-cent of vandalism arrests, 41.7 percent of fraud arrests, 44.7 percent of embezzlement arrests, 60 percent of prostitution and commercialized vice arrests, 16.7 percent of drug-abuse violations arrests, and 57.3 percent of runaways (FBI, 1997).

According to the UCR, among the Crime Index offenses, larceny-theft arrests were the highest (33.8 percent). For nonindex offenses and arrests overall, prostitution and commercialized vice arrests were the highest (60 percent). Both of these figures suggest that there is some validity to the notion that women are most likely to be prostitutes or *shoplifters* if they are engaging in criminal activity. However, women are certainly engaging in a number of other crimes, albeit less frequently.

Baskin and Sommers (1993) theorized that gender-based stereotypes have resulted in little knowledge about women's involvement in certain types of crimes, specifically violent crimes. In addition, they maintained that the paucity of research and information about this area stems from the persistent belief that women's participation in crime, particularly violent crime, is insignificant. These researchers also pointed out that the UCR should be broken down further into geographic regions, sex, and race to obtain a more accurate picture of increases or decreases in crime rates. For example, in 1987 women's arrests for aggravated assault and robbery had increased by 17.6 percent from 1978. However, in New York City, a more dramatic growth was noted. Women's arrest rates for aggravated assault and robbery were 47 percent and 75.8 percent, respectively (Baskin & Sommers, 1993).

In more recent years, whereas arrests for some crimes are increasing, others are decreasing. According to the UCR (FBI, 1997), from 1992 to 1996, every violent crime had some percentage of decrease for males. However, for women in all age groups, the percentage of increase or decrease for violent crime arrests was as follows: murder and non-negligent manslaughter −12.4 percent, forcible rape −15 percent, robbery +2.1 percent, aggravated assault +28.8 percent, burglary +1.0 percent, larceny-theft +4.5 percent, motor vehicle theft +3.6 percent, and arson +9.3 percent. Overall, for women of all ages, there was a total increase of +22.8 percent for violent crimes and +4.2 percent for property crimes. These statistics lend support to the belief that female criminality is on the rise (Pollock, 1999).

THEORIES OF FEMALE CRIMINALITY

How do we account for these rising trends in female criminality? One response is to assess what we know theoretically about female criminality. As a historical matter, research regarding criminal behavior is almost exclusively focused on men. Indeed, the view that women are gentle and passive is antithetical to the perception of a criminal. Moreover, in those instances when women have stepped outside society's imposed gender roles, typically they have been labeled mentally ill (Showalter, 1985). In addition to this stigma, civic leaders and moral crusaders have postulated that when women deviate substantially from their status as wife or mother, adopting instead a life of violent crime, they are deemed especially corrupt or evil (e.g., Pollock, 1999; Scull, 1989). Not only do these women lose their liberty, but they also frequently are denied their femininity (Smart, 1977). It is interesting that the masculinity of the worst male criminal rarely, if ever, has been called into question.

As previously noted, whereas the role of women in violent crime (specifically murder) has received little research attention, offenses such as prostitution and shoplifting traditionally have been viewed as female phenomena. Many theories of female criminality reflect the position of women in society during the time of the theory's conception (Naffine, 1987). For example, during the end of the nineteenth century, Cesare Lombroso and William Ferrero were among the first researchers to undertake the scientific study of female criminality. Lombroso held a more physiologically based position of female crime. The skeletal remains of female offenders (focusing on the brain, face, jawbones, and cranium) were examined for atavism. Atavism is defined as the possession of physical anomalies that resemble more primitive genetic traits. Lombroso and Ferrero determined that women were biologically predisposed to being criminals. Although these researchers postulated that fewer females than males were born criminals, women who were born criminals were depicted as

> even more immoral and menacing than male criminals . . . less compassionate and sensitive to pain, while possessing jealousy and capable of vengeful behavior. These "ladylike" characteristics tend to be mitigated by common female attributes such as weakness, piety, maternity, and insufficiently developed intelligence. . . . Women are simply overgrown adolescents who when bad, are far more frightening than men. These women lack maternal affection, illustrating their degeneracy and masculinity. (Flowers, 1994, p. 92)

In addition, Lombroso maintained that "the born female criminal makes up for what she lacks in relative numbers by the excess vileness and cruelty of her crimes" (Smart, 1977, p. 33). "Her maternal sense is weak because psychologically and anthropologically she belongs more to the male than to the female sex" (cited in Smart, 1977, p. 33). Lombroso also identified the "occasional" female criminal. This more common type of female offender committed crimes as a result of "male persuasion, higher education (preventing marriage and inducing want), and excessive temptation" (cited in Flowers, 1994, p. 92). Women were thought to be particularly materialistic and in many cases unable to resist clothing or other goods available in stores. Today, the work of Lombroso and Ferrero largely has been rejected as lacking sufficient theoretical and methodological rigor to warrant additional consideration (Pollock, 1999).

Sigmund Freud was a physician and psychoanalyst. His theories on the unconscious greatly influenced the psychological approach to female criminality (Flowers, 1994). He believed that females were biologically inferior to males (Arrigo, 2004). In particular, he asserted that female offenders were passive, narcissistic, and masochistic as a result of a masculinity complex or as a consequence of penis envy (Freud, 1933/1968). Freud believed that women were unable to resolve the oedipal conflict, leaving them less in control over their impulses. As such, they were motivated by sentiments of "jealousy, immorality, emotionalism, and bad judgment" (Flowers, 1994, p. 67). In addition, Freud believed that anatomical deficiencies (e.g., relative size, strength, dexterity) predisposed women to immorality (Arrigo, 2004).

William I. Thomas (1923/1969) linked the social environment to a woman's proclivity for criminality (Flowers, 1994). He believed that many gender differences were a result of social and cultural influences rather than biological differences, although biology was seen as playing an important role. Indeed, Thomas argued that female criminality was a socially induced pathology, steeped in instinctive processes rather than biologically predetermined states. In his later work, Thomas asserted that the *wish* or desire for new experiences significantly impacted female criminality (Pollock, 1999). More specifically, he maintained that *wishes,* as derived from biological instincts, could be socialized to achieve appropriate goals. For example, Thomas alleged that the intense need to give and feel love frequently led women to adopt criminal patterns of behavior, especially in relation to sexual offenses (e.g., prostitution) (Smart, 1977).

Through a comprehensive survey of American, British, German, and French literature, Pollack (1950) theorized that female crime was predominantly sexually motivated, whereas male crime was more economically motivated. The one exception to this theory was thought to be crimes of passion. In addition, Pollack explained the "masked" or hidden nature of female criminality. As he indicated, crime statistics fail to show the true extent of female offending as "criminal statistics are probably the least reliable of all statistics because they undertake to measure something which is designed to escape observation and thus escape measurement" (Pollack, 1950, p. 150). Pollack maintained that women are drawn to crimes that are easily concealed and rarely reported. For example, as the caretakers of children or the sick, women have easy access to abused youth, the infirmed, or the elderly (Pollock, 1999). According to Flowers (1994), proponents of the hidden nature of female crime cite infanticide, prostitution, and illegal abortions as evidence of female criminality with low reportability rates.

Pollack also argued that the nature of women's biological makeups led them to be deceitful (e.g., faking arousal and orgasm; concealing menstruation), whereas men were biologically forced to "show the true state of [their] feelings" (Pollack, 1950, p. 151). As a result, Pollack argued that women were both biologically and culturally more powerful in the area of concealment. Thus, female criminality often went undetected (Pollack, 1950). Finally, Pollack believed that female criminals, when detected, were treated far more leniently by the criminal justice apparatus. In short, he maintained that the system demonstrated a paternalistic regard for women.

Other more recent theorists assert that it is not sexual motivation but, rather, economic need or blocked opportunities that breed female criminality. These socioeconomic theorists contend that when legitimate means of reaching social goals are not available, illegitimate ones (i.e., criminal activity) become available (e.g., Chesney-Lind, 1998; Flowers, 1994; Pollock, 1999). To illustrate, Datesman, Scarpitti, and Stephenson (1975) found that perception of blocked opportunity more precisely influenced female delinquency than male delinquency. In addition, Cernkovich and Giordano (1979) surveyed 1,355 female and male high school students, finding that blocked opportunity was the best predictor of delinquency for both sexes.

The work of Adler (1975) and Simon (1975) are credited with the *female emancipation theory* of female criminality (see also, Adler & Simon, 1979). This theory postulates that the rise in female crime is a result of the Women's Liberation Movement or increased opportunities (Edwards, 1986). Adler was the keynote speaker at the 1976 National Conference on Women and Crime held in Washington, D. C. (Godwin, 1978). In commenting on this issue, she suggested that "Although males will commit by far the greater number of absolute offenses, females are surpassing them in rates of increase for almost every major crime." Moreover, as she stated, "It is apparent, that [women] are no longer willing to be second-class criminals, limited to 'feminine' crimes of shoplifting and prostitution, but that they are making their gains noticeable across the offense board" (cited in Godwin, 1978, p. 114).

Adler's theorizing on female criminality is also significant for other reasons. She argued that a correlation existed between the Women's Liberation Movement and technology, suggesting that the combination of both made the capacity for violent crimes perpetrated by women more compatible with those of men (Adler, 1975). Moreover, she argued that "A frail woman with a pistol is just as threatening to a bank teller as a burly man" (cited in Godwin, 1978, p. 115). She explained that many female criminals were indifferent to the women's movement and that some women committed offenses regardless of the opportunities gained from it.

Many scholars have taken exception to the notion of female emancipation as causing increased female offending. Speaking at an annual meeting of the American Association for the Advancement of Science in the 1970s, Denmark stated that

> The female offender, whether acting by herself or with others, is not typically the emancipated intellectual striving for civil liberties. Her crime is rarely an assertion of civil rights, or an unconscious attempt at achieving her own or others' rights. She may feel dominated by men or even wish to imitate men or obtain male approval for her actions. (cited in Godwin, 1978, p. 128)

However, Blum and Fisher (1978) indicated that female crime rates (and murder rates) come closer to their male counterparts in countries where women have been the most liberated (e.g., countries in Western Europe and the United States). In addition, these researchers demonstrated that female crime rates differ the most from their male counterparts in countries where little freedom for women exists.

Simon (1975) also addressed the way in which female criminality was akin to male offending. For example, she suggested that "women have no greater store of morality than do men. Their propensities to commit crimes do not differ but, in the past, their opportunities have been much more limited" (Flowers, 1994, p. 71 Simon, R. J., 1975, p. 48). Also, Simon (1976) argued that any increase in female crime was mostly due to property offenses rather than violent crime. Unlike Adler (1975), Simon (1976) maintained that elevations in female offending primarily would occur in the area of property and white-collar criminality rather than violent offending (Vold, Bernard, & Snipes, 1998).

Notwithstanding the progressive positions taken by Adler and Simon, many feminists were outraged by their insistence that a correlation existed between women's liberation and crime. Indeed, part of the frustration for feminists and mainstream liberals was that masculinization theory (Adler) and opportunity theory (Simon) contradicted the myth that the equalization of the sexes diminished crime (Godwin, 1978; Naffine, 1987). In addition, critics contended that many female offenders represented minority, poor, undereducated, and unemployed groups—constituencies that did not benefit from the increased opportunities afforded to women by the Liberation Movement (Flowers, 1994). Therefore, as critics observed, the liberation effect could not have contributed even remotely to the rates of criminality for disenfranchised women.

A number of radically inspired feminist theories have challenged the liberal position and the social structure within which the liberal-feminist viewpoint operates. For example, radical feminists look at the function of patriarchy in society and the subservient roles that women play in relation to it (e.g., Messerschmidt, 1986, 1997). They suggest that individuals are socialized within "core gender identities" (Vold et al., 1998, p. 278). Marxist feminists tie the patriarchy of society to the economic structure of capitalism (Messerschmidt, 1986). Men are thought to control the economy and, as such, many of the property crimes committed by women are related to the unequal distribution of resources (Lynch, Michalowski, & Groves, 2000). Thus, definitions of law and crime are related to maintaining male dominance.

Socialist feminists added a focus on natural reproductive differences in men and women (Jurik, 1999). They maintained that because of menstruation, pregnancy, childbirth, nursing, and menopause, women historically had been at the mercy of their biology. Commenting on the sexual division of labor, socialist feminist theorists argued that women naturally were more involved with child care, whereas men worked outside the home (e.g., Daly & Chesney-Lind, 1988; Dobash & Dobash, 1979; Klein, 1973; Smart, 1976). However, with the invention of birth control methods, women were able to take more control of their bodies and obtain more diverse statuses in society. In addition, Messerschmidt (1986, 1997) argues that men are socialized into more violent and dominating roles. And finally, postmodern feminists demonstrate how discourse or language is used to define or name certain women as *criminals* (Wonders, 1999). A more thorough examination of the various radically inspired feminist positions is beyond the scope of this chapter. Clearly, however, these various strains of critical thought tell us a great deal about the various ways in which female criminality can be interpreted.

One line of radical feminist scholarship warranting some particular attention includes the work of Meda Chesney-Lind (1998). She contends that factors such as economic marginalization and victimization lead women to crime. To illustrate, she indicates that a disproportionate number of female criminals have histories that include drug-using parents, violent partners, childhood sexual abuse, and rape. Moreover, she explains how "criminal roles [represent] a form of caretaking" (Chesney-Lind, 1998, p. 110). This caretaking is demonstrated when a mother steals or prostitutes herself to feed her children, believing there are no other options. As such, Chesney-Lind argues that, in most cases, women offenders are socialized into exploitation. With no marketable skills and little education, these women find themselves structurally dislocated. Given the abusive and victimizing experiences that women endure, she questions "not why women murder but rather why so few murder" (Chesney-Lind, 1998, p. 98).

AGGRESSION/FEMALE VIOLENCE

The debate over whether men are typically more violent than women has traditionally led to aggression studies. Recently, increasingly sophisticated research methodologies have enabled investigators to analyze more closely the relationship between women and aggression. The following subsection briefly examines the literature, demonstrating some of the differences between male and female aggression. In addition, the correlation between aggression and acts of violence also is tentatively examined.

Many theories about women's roles in crime relative to those of men stem from the notion that men are biologically more aggressive and more prone to violence. Commenting on the phenomenon of aggression, Berkowitz (1964, p. 104) defines it as "behavior whose goal is the injury of some person or object," whereas anger is viewed as "the emotional state resulting from a frustration presumably creating a readiness for aggressive acts" (see also, Frodi, Macaulay, & Thome, 1977, p. 635). However, as Blackburn (1998, p. 158) notes, "Violent crime . . . constitutes only a small part of the phenomenon of aggression, which covers the intentional infliction of harm more generally." Thus, understanding aggression, particularly as it is linked to women and criminality, entails closer scrutiny.

Eagly and Steffen (1986) undertook a meta-analytic review of sex differences in relation to aggression, finding that differences were inconsistent across studies. For example, whereas men were more likely to aggress in situations that produced pain or physical injury, the differences were less pronounced when it came to aggression leading to social or psychological harm. In addition, the investigators found that women more than men perceived that engaging in aggressive behavior would produce harm to the target as well as to themselves. Along these lines, the researchers noted that women believed more so than their male counterparts that they would experience guilt and anxiety following their aggressive conduct (Eagly & Steffen, 1986). This finding is consistent with studies indicating that empathy is a characteristic of women more so than men (Frodi et al., 1977). Thus, Eagly and Steffen (1986) theorized that sex differences were a function of the perceived consequences of aggression, learned from gender roles.

Campbell, Muncer, and Gorman (1992) argued that aggression for women was more appropriately attributable to an expressive act or a cathartic discharge of anger. In addition, the researchers found that men were more likely to use instrumental aggression explained as "a way to obtain or exercise power to gain social rewards" (Campbell et al., 1992, p. 125). Their study also indicated that female criminals were likely to use instrumental aggression, viewing it, however, as a legitimate means to obtain what they wanted.

Other researchers have speculated on the social meaning of aggression when applied to men versus women. For example, Fry and Gabriel (1994, p. 165) stated that "a reluctance to focus on female aggression may be a reluctance to consider similarities between women and men" (p. 165). In addition, they suggested that aggressive and violent behavior in men is valorized, whereas in women it is pathologized. Thus, Fry and Gabriel (1994) concluded that aggression was a male-gendered category; one that was not amenable to understanding feminine identity and the existence of women as synonymous with motherhood and pacifism.

In 1977, a review of 314 articles on aggression revealed that 54 percent of the studies were conducted only on men, whereas 8 percent were conducted only on women (Frodi et al., 1977). Commenting on these studies, Bjorkqvist (1994) indicated that the well-known testosterone aggression link, often leading to violence, was found to be weak. This link was based on animal data, ignoring the more complex dimensions of human behavior. Psychosocial history and cognitive factors were thought to play a greater role, impacting (and inhibiting) aggression levels (Bjorkqvist, 1994). Whereas males consistently have been found to use more physical means of aggression than their female counterparts, women are more likely to use verbal, social, or other indirect means of aggression than are men.

What constitutes "indirect" means of aggression has caused some debate. The definition most commonly used refers to when "the target is attacked, not directly, but circuitously, and the aggressor can thereby remain unidentified and avoid counterattack" (Bjorkqvist, 1994, p. 183). Thus, researchers maintain that women are capable of physical aggression; however, they typically fear the retaliation of a larger male (Bjorkqvist, 1994; Frodi et al., 1977).

Frodi et al. (1977) argued that when aggression is seen as pro-social or justified, women may act just as aggressively as their male counterparts. These investigators also discovered that for the majority of male and female aggression studies, men were much more likely to be the targets of aggressive behavior. In addition, consistent with subsequent research (Eagly & Steffen, 1986), women were more inclined to feel guilt, anxiety, or fear over their aggressive acts, causing them considerable discomfort and inhibiting them from admitting responsibility (Frodi et al, 1977). However, we note that with women diagnosed with antisocial personality disorder (ASPD) or otherwise considered psychopathic, feelings such as these are less likely to be embodied (e.g. Gacono, 2000).

Bettencourt and Miller (1996) examined the factor of provocation in gender differences and aggression, using a meta-analysis. In particular, they explained that under essentially neutral conditions, men were more aggressive. However, when women were provoked, they acted slightly more aggressively than men. Moreover, the investigators determined that women were more vulnerable to insensitivity or condescending behaviors than physical provocation (e.g., being bumped in a bar). In this study, the victims of violence were almost exclusively intimates; this is a condition that researchers postulate as necessary if provocation is to induce aggressive conduct. Finally, through her meta-analysis of gender differences in aggression, Hyde (1984) found that within-gender differences were far more significant than the variability between genders. She also stated that socialization and cultural norms changed, causing gender differences to shrink.

OTHER FACTORS AFFECTING FEMALE CRIMINALITY

In addition to specific criminological theories, other factors bear some relationship to female criminality. For example, female deviance or criminality is frequently associated with broken homes. A broken home is defined as a place "in which one or both parents are absent due to desertion, divorce, separation, or death—thereby depriving the child or children of the benefits of a complete, stable family environment" (Flowers, 1994, p. 72). In a study on 66 convicted female felons, Cloninger and Guze (1970a) found that 65 percent of these women reported at least one parent permanently absent from the household before the person was 18 years of age. Research has shown this factor to be more prevalent in female delinquents than in their male counterparts (e.g., Chesney-Lind, 1998; Chesney-Lind & Sheldon, 1992). In addition, the U.S. Department of Justice (1992), Bureau of Statistics, found that more than half of the women living in jail or prison in 1989, lived with only one or neither parent as they were growing up (see also, Pollock, 1999).

This special report also uncovered that more than 4 in 10 women incarcerated suffered from some form of childhood victimization. Moreover, Flowers (1994) indicated that there is a strong correlation between female sex offenders and childhood sexual abuse. Indeed, studies consistently find a strong relationship between female runaways, prostitution, and sexual abuse (e.g., Chesney-Lind, 1998). Thus, as Baskin and Sommers (1993) summarized it,

> typically, then, the chain of events leading to criminalization is described as beginning with child physical or sexual abuse; this produces a vicious cycle that includes running away, institutionalization, return to the dysfunctional family, and ultimately street deviance, for example, prostitution and drug use. (p. 561)

Another factor linked to female criminality involves women who are abused by significant others. Abusive couples are not a rare occurrence (Dibble & Straus, 1980). Researchers estimate that 2 million husbands, as compared with 1.8 million wives, have endured at least one serious form of spousal abuse (Pollock, 1999, pp. 30–32). In addition, recurring sexual, physical, and mental abuse by boyfriends or husbands is reported by the overwhelming majority of women who kill their significant others (Flowers, 1994). In 293 murder cases reviewed by Mann (1996) for which the victim/offender relationship was known, 47.8 percent involved partners in relationships: married, lovers/living together, separated, homosexual lovers, or former lovers. According to the U.S. Department of Justice (1994), a 1991 study revealed between 50 percent and 80 percent of women surveyed in correctional institutions around the country reported being victims of domestic violence. Statistics such as these have led some investigators to conclude that there is a direct causal relationship between victimization and subsequent offending (e.g., Arnold, 1990; Chesney-Lind, 1998).

Some researchers have also found that women who use or abuse drugs or alcohol are much more likely to be involved in criminal activity (Mann, 1996; Rosenbaum, 1987). This finding includes the commission of serious felony behavior. Indeed, as Steele (cited in Flowers, 1994, p. 32) noted,

> chronic use of alcohol and the taking of hallucinogenic drugs can cause severe distortion of mental functioning with delusional thinking and the lowering of the threshold for the release of violence in many forms, including child abuse, homicide, and suicide.

Baskin and Sommers (1993) reported that abusing drugs reduces a woman's options to pursue other income-producing positions, thus leaving illegal activities as her only viable outlet by which to generate money for drug consumption. Some research has shown that criminal behavior precedes drug use; however, other investigators have found that the two occur concurrently as the female emerges into the stage of adolescent antisocial behavior (Arrigo, 2004; Baskin & Sommers, 1993). In addition, 8 of 10 female convicts in state prison used drugs at one time, and one-third were under the influence at the time of their most recent offense (Pollock 1999).

Race and ethnicity is yet another important factor affecting female criminality. In the relevant literature, race and ethnicity appear to have differential influences, depending on the type of crime. For example, white and non-Hispanic women are disproportionately represented in runaways and prostitution (Flowers, 1994). However, black and Hispanic women are overrepresented in violent crimes, arrests, and incarcerations (Baskin & Sommers, 1993; Mann, 1996).

In addition, some research suggests that minority women are more likely to experience contact with police officers, to be arrested, and to be subjected to further processing through other stages of the criminal justice system (e.g., courts and prisons) then are other nonminority women (Flowers, 1994). For our purposes, this trend is of concern, especially when the alleged crime is homicide. The issue of race, gender, and crime is examined further in the subsequent chapter on women homicide offenders.

Some investigators have explored the biological effect of the menstrual cycle on female criminality. Studies reveal that female violence frequently occurs during certain stages of the menstrual cycle—the 4 days preceding menstruation and the first 4 days of menstruation (Shah & Roth, 1974). Dalton (1961) conducted a provocative study on the relationship between menstruation and female crime. Over a 6-month period, she interviewed 156 new prisoners who had committed their crime in the last 28 days and were incarcerated at an English women's prison. In fact, Dalton discovered that 49 percent of these women had committed their crimes during either the 4 premenstrual days or the first 4 menstrual days.

Studies linking menstruation and premenstrual syndrome (PMS) to female criminality often refer to increased irritability, tension, and aggression as precipitating factors. This association is most often made with female-perpetrated homicide. Otto Pollack (1950) made reference to a woman's *generative* phases (e.g., menstruation, pregnancy, and menopause), arguing that they were frequently accompanied by psychological disturbances leading to female crime (Smart, 1977). More recently Dalton (1982) emphasized the role of hormonal imbalance in her explanation of the role of PMS in female-perpetrated violence.

The perception of mental illness in female offenders is another critical factor influencing theories of female criminality. Historically, women who commit offenses, particularly those considered violent, are viewed as more pathological than their male counterparts. "Women who 'resort' to violence are frequently considered 'sick' rather than willful" (Edwards, 1986, p. 80). Phillips and DeFleur (1982) suggested that women who commit crimes are viewed as psychiatrically disordered as a result of gender typescripts. In other words, the stereotypes for women and the stereotypes for criminals do not produce a combined stereotype of the female criminal (Phillips & DeFleur, 1982). Instead, a woman can be described only as mentally ill when she deviates so far from her gender role (Showalter, 1985). Thus, in this context, women who commit crimes are exhibiting masculine characteristics, indicating to clinicians that the woman is mentally unhealthy (Phillips & DeFleur, 1982). Clearly, this is a function of gender-role stereotypes rather than any empirical data. Indeed, the most reliable and valid research indicates that mental illness is a factor in only a small percentage of female crimes (Arrigo, 2004).

We note, however, that certain crimes reveal some relationship to specific psychiatric disorders. For example, violent crimes and child maltreatment bear some association with depression, schizophrenia, and psychosis (Flowers, 1994). In addition, violent crimes, especially homicide, are linked to personality disorders like ASPD (psychopathy). In Chapter 3, we explore in greater detail the association between female homicide offenders and psychiatric illness.

CONCLUSIONS

This chapter broadly examined the phenomenon of women and crime. We highlighted important data on the offenses that women commit, emphasizing the extent of female criminality. As we indicated, female-perpetrated offending is on the rise. To partially explain this reality, we selectively reviewed several relevant theories of female criminality. These accounts represent very different frames of reference (e.g., biological, psychoanalytic, economic, radical) that help deepen our regard for women and crime. We also reviewed several studies on aggression, outlining important gender differences between and within male and female cohorts, and factors linked to their respective perceptions of and attitudes toward violence. The chapter concluded by tentatively examining several correlates of female criminality. These included such things as childhood victimization, broken homes, substance abuse, race/ethnicity, Premenstrual Syndrome, and mental illness.

What is significant about this chapter, especially in regard to female serial killers, is that definitions of women (and their concomitant behavior) do not exist in a vacuum. Indeed, it is simply inadequate to fully interpret women as artifacts of prevailing sociopolitical norms, values, and practices, wherein they are rendered passive, helpless, submissive creatures abdicating unfettered responsibility for their choices and/or actions. The theoretical literature on women and crime has evolved too much, the aggression studies on gender differences are too revealing, and the research on the correlates on female offending is too compelling. However, what remains to be seen is whether when controlling for the type of offense (i.e., homicide), any more significant information about the nature of female criminality emerges. This issue is squarely addressed in Chapter 2.

2

Women as Homicide Offenders

❖

INTRODUCTION

This chapter explores the phenomenon of women as homicide offenders. According to Holmes and Holmes (1994, p. 2), homicide (or murder) is defined as the unlawful killing of a human being with malice aforethought. In addition, the Uniform Crime Reports classifies murder and nonnegligent manslaughter as the willful killing of one human being by another (FBI, 1997, p. 13). The Bureau of Justice Statistics for the U.S. Department of Justice identifies homicide as causing the death of another person without legal justification or excuse (cited in Holmes & Holmes, 1994, p. 2). This definition includes the crimes of murder, nonnegligent manslaughter, and negligent manslaughter (Arrigo, 2004). Moreover, Rush (1991, p. 147) indicates that homicide is "any willful killing." Given these sundry definitions, we note that the words *murder* and *homicide* can be used interchangeably. Accordingly, this is how they function throughout this chapter. However, for purposes of our investigation of predatory homicide perpetrated by women, the focus is on *first-degree murder* rather than on manslaughter. The elements of first-degree murder include premeditation and deliberation. In other words, the act of murder must have been considered before its commission—even if only for a moment—and the act itself must not have been impulsive (Holmes & Holmes, 1994).

In this chapter we provide arrest trends for homicides committed by women versus men, as well as the possible social factors affecting those trends. Moreover, the contradictory role of women as murderers rather than as caretakers/mothers is explored. We also note that few studies appear in the relevant literature focused on women as perpetrators of violence. As such, the chapter examines the various reasons for this trend, including such things as gender-role stereotypes and the feminist reluctance to focus on women as victimizers. In addition, theories linked to the "mad" versus "bad" dichotomy and to the "deadlier species" hypothesis are described as a way to account for the phenomenon of female homicide offenders.

The chapter also presents the profile of the female homicide murderer, emphasizing such components as race/ethnicity, the role of drugs and alcohol, age, socioeconomic status, ecological circumstances, weapons, victims, and motives for the crime. In addition, typologies of female homicide offenders developed by a number of researchers are delineated. These typologies categorize the various women murderers on the basis of factors such as mental state, victims, and motives. The chapter concludes by illustrating different patterns among the typologies for purposes of identifying what the prevalent traits are among murderesses.

THE NATURE OF FEMALE HOMICIDE

When examining the UCR arrest trends from 1987 to 1996, the percentage of change for murder and nonnegligent manslaughter for all women was 19.5 percent (FBI, 1997). It is interesting, however, that the arrest trend for women under 18 years old was +18.9 percent (FBI, 1997). This discrepancy appears to be a function of age or possibly different social factors for this age group.

A look at the same arrest trends from 1995 to 1996 reveals that the arrests of women taken as a whole decreased by 2.7 percent. However, women under 18 years of age saw no appreciable change in the arrests for murder and nonnegligent manslaughter. In 1996, the female age group with the most arrests for murder or nonnegligent manslaughter was 30 to 34 years old with 228 arrests, followed closely by women age 25 to 29 with 220 arrests. The age group with the fewest arrests for this crime was the under-10-years-of-age cohort with one arrest, closely followed by ages 10 to 12 years old with two arrests (FBI, 1997).

According to Egger (2002), homicide rates can show dramatic fluctuations from year to year based on sociodemographic variables such as age, race, sex, time, and social change. In addition, Holmes and Holmes (1994) maintain that these statistics are often misleading, vague, and contradictory. As such, they are not necessarily useful for policy making. Indeed, researchers can (and sometimes do) hold their own biases for such factors as gender, interfering with more objective data collection and analysis (Hickey, 1997).

Another difficulty facing the study of women as homicide offenders is that this behavior is contrary to the gender-role stereotypes of females as docile caretaker/mother figures. "Women are usually described as emotional, gullible, submissive, passive, illogical, sneaky, unambitious, dependent, gentle, and childlike" (Phillips & DeFleur, 1982, p. 438). Goetting (1988b) investigated why considerable research attention is given to women as victims of violence, whereas virtually no scholarly reviews are given to violent women. She explained this in the context of gender stereotyping, arguing that "traditional female role expectations accommodate the woman as victim, but not as the perpetrator of violence" (Goetting, 1988b, p. 3). In addition, Wilbanks (1983, p. 152) pointed out that when males commit crimes, their actions are often attributed to economic factors and inadequate socialization, whereas for women, their illicit transgressions are often accounted for because of alleged sickness, weakness, frailty, and vulnerability. This assessment is consistent with stereotypic gender-based representations of women.

According to Godwin (1978), sadistic cruelty in women is the most shocking to society because it directly contradicts the more conventional and "purer" view of a woman's nature. He further suggested that the police and the courts have had a difficult time reacting to the female criminal. As he explained,

> What lies beyond the ken of most police officers are the outbursts of rabid violence staged by women, on their own accord, unconnected with any felony, and in response to the slightest provocations. In other words, actions hitherto reserved for only the most vicious of types of male bully. (Godwin, 1978, p. 127)

Observations such as these draw attention to how gendered expectations regarding feminine (acceptable) and nonfeminine (unacceptable) behavior informs institutional (criminal justice) interpretations of and responses to female criminality.

As the previous chapter suggested, questions about stereotypic portrayals of women as offenders were challenged, especially in the theoretical literature on female criminality. Blum and Fisher (1978) attributed the critique of the stereotyped, one-dimensional view to the onset and rise of feminism. They suggested that as more women occupied professional roles (including the status of academic scholar), a new set of investigators with a different set of assumptions conducted and disseminated the vast majority of research on female homicide offenders. Today, as a result, the previously oversimplified perceptions of murderesses are increasingly being challenged (Hickey, 1997). For example, we note that the trend in female homicide literature during the 1990s overwhelmingly placed the woman in the victim role (Egger, 2002). Many feminist scholars have worked tirelessly to bring the histories of victimization, battering, and neglect to society's attention (e.g., Chesney-Lind, 1998). The current research in this area mostly investigates the female homicide offender who kills an abusive spouse. Admittedly, these studies are reflective of a large percentage of murderesses; however, the shift in research changes the sexist focus to a victim focus. From our perspective, this modification, although certainly legitimate, does not adequately account for all women who engage in predatory acts of serial killing.

Bell and Fox (1996) expressed the need to move the debate on women who kill from its current focus on battered women to the more difficult and thorny question of accounting for cases in which victimization does not figure so prominently, if at all, in the analysis. For example, more research could be conducted on women who murder for no apparent motive or who kill for personal profit or instrumental gain. Bell and Fox (1996) suggested that far too many feminist scholars have remained silent on these types of cases because they are relatively rare occurrences and because the victimization perspective is easier, in some respects, to investigate and document. Moreover, attention drawn to the isolated, sensationalized cases of female serial killers can compromise the tragedy and grief that victims, relatives, and other loved ones endure in the face of murder (Hickey, 1997).

A related issue concerning the literature on female-perpetrated homicide is determining what position is most appropriate with respect to the phenomenon of female violence. Bell and Fox (1996) explained this dilemma, drawing attention to the important strides made by the feminist critique without, at the same time, reflecting on its own very real (or potential) limits. In short, the issue amounts to "dividing an emerging feminist consensus on how to confront male violence by posing the difficult question of how to come to terms with violent or abusive women" (p. 485). Moreover, these commentators stated that if feminists continued to remain silent in relation to female-perpetrated murders that ostensibly were motiveless, that were based on personal profit, or that were designed to produce instrumental gain, then many of the most challenging issues for feminist theory would be avoided. For example, when the victim of a woman's murderous actions is a child or is another female, the difficulties in accurately explaining the assailant's behavior are exacerbated when the prevailing theoretical model indicates that the *offender* is a victim. Indeed, as Bell and Fox (1996, p. 485) asserted, "unambiguously discreditable" female killers are largely ignored by feminist discourse. This posture undermines the overall literature on women and murder and, regrettably, does a disservice to those persons who are victims of some female-perpetrated homicides.

Another component to the debate on women who murder deals with the old "mad" versus "bad" taxonomy and the new "bad" versus "victim" dichotomy. The latter perspective, popularized by much of the feminist-inspired and critical literature, identifies the female homicide offender as either extremely deviant or as playing the role of the victim. The former approach, traceable to the research of the nineteenth century and early-to-mid twentieth century, regards the female homicide offender as either mentally ill or *evil.* Several investigators have expounded on these two classifications.

For example, Blum and Fisher (1978) indicated that, in general, women who kill are seen as "good" versus "bad," as "mothers" versus "whores," or as "the gentler sex" versus "the more deadly species" (p. 188). These alternatives are quite revealing when applied to the phenomenon of female criminality. Indeed, in relation to murderesses, they are defined as "deviant and bad, since they . . . abandoned their natural feminine roles [and] betrayed their womanhood" (Blum & Fisher, 1978, p. 189).

Perhaps most interesting in the previous comments is the *deadlier sex* hypothesis. Pollack (1950) observed that women were more murderous than men in some specified contexts. Godwin (1978, p. 113) expressed the conviction that society irrationally dichotomized female killers, believing that once women committed violence, they became "worse than their male counterparts: more blood thirsty, more vicious, more unscrupulous, [and] more deadly than the male." The poet Tennyson perpetuated the deadlier species theory by stating that

> The woman criminal is the panther of the underworld. She can follow relentlessly through the jungle day after day, she can wait her time, she can play with her victim and torture him in sheer wantonness, and she can pile cruelty upon the act of killing as does the panther, but never the lion. (cited in Godwin, 1978, p. 114)

We also note that there has been a long-standing association between women and crimes of cunning and deceit (Bell & Fox, 1996). Godwin (1978) discussed the sexual power that women can have over men. In particular, he postulated that if women were held accountable for all of the homicides they set in motion by using men as their murder "weapon" (actually committing the act), then the murder rate for women would greatly increase. Once again, we are drawn to the importance of how women are defined (i.e., bad, mad, victimized, violent) and the manner in which this helps to explain (or excuse) their homicidal actions.

THE PROFILE OF THE FEMALE HOMICIDE OFFENDER

The summary profile for the typical female homicide offender is that of a "single, thirty-one-year-old, unemployed African American mother with less than a high school education who has been arrested in the past" (Mann, 1996, p. 164). This profile notwithstanding, women who kill represent a heterogeneous group with varying characteristics and manifold circumstances. Mann's profile is based on statistical data derived from other empirical studies. In what follows, we provide a composite description of various offender characteristics for the female killer.

Race/Ethnicity

There is a large disparity in the racial or ethnic composition of female homicide offenders. In particular, research consistently has found that the majority of homicide perpetrators and their victims are African American (Goetting, 1988b; Mann, 1990, 1996; Wolfgang, 1958). In fact, black women rank second in frequency of arrests for murder and nonnegligent homicide in the United States (Mann, 1990; Wolfgang, 1958). Wolfgang was the first to look at black women who kill in an empirical context (see also, Cole, Fisher, and Cole,1968; Mann, 1986, 1990, 1996; Wilbanks, 1983). The rate of homicide offending for African American women has been compared with that of white males (Mann, 1990). However, Farr (1997) found that first-degree murderesses on death row were most likely to be white.

Approximately 78 percent of all women who kill are African American (Holmes & Holmes, 1994; Mann, 1990, 1996). Mann's 1990 study consisted of 296 females from six cities with high homicide rates. The racial makeup of her sample was as follows: 77.7 percent black, 12.8 percent white, and 9.5 percent Hispanic. According to Baskin and Sommers (1993), the rate of arrests for black and Hispanic females is significantly higher than for white females. In Goetting's (1988b) study of 136 female homicide offenders in Detroit, she found that 93.4 percent of those arrested for homicide and their victims were black. This much higher than average percentage was the result of sampling from an urban, predominantly black population, with an extremely high homicide rate. Another study by Goetting (1988a) looked at a population of 15 female homicide offenders whose murderous acts occurred between 1982 and 1983. The racial makeup for these women consisted of the following: 11 (73.3 percent) were black, and the remaining 4 (26.7 percent) were white. Given these investigations, we note that despite some discrepancies between arrest rates for white and Hispanic females, black females disproportionately have experienced higher rates of homicide offending as reported in the published research.

Mann (1996) reported that nonwhite female homicide offenders were more likely to be mothers. African American women usually killed alone, whereas white or Hispanic women were more likely to have accomplices. In addition, when comparing white and African American women killers, members of the former group were more likely to murder members of the latter group. Moreover, when comparing Hispanic and white female killers, members of the former group were more likely to murder individuals of the latter group. Notwithstanding these racial/ethnic differences, Mann (1996) indicated that most homicides were committed intraracially.

The Role of Drugs and Alcohol

Brownstein et al. (1994) explored the impact of drugs on women who kill. They found that the cases in which substances were used in excess did not result in the woman's becoming violent. Thus, these investigators concluded that the homicide may have been related to drug or alcohol use; however, it was not the result of a drug-induced violent outburst. Brownstein et al. (1994) also noted that in cases in which people were killed as a result of a violent, drug-induced outburst, alcohol was the substance of choice.

Goetting (1987) reported that alcohol was a significant component of marital homicide when wives were the perpetrators. Researchers consistently have found that female criminality is viewed as a result of various *victim* roles, such as substance abuser, battered woman, or single, poverty-stricken parent (Arnold, 1990; Baskin & Sommers, 1993). Mann (1996) determined that Southern female killers were slightly more likely to have been drinking just prior to their offense than their non-Southern female counterparts. However, 58.6 percent of the murders were committed by non-Southern women when drugs (other than alcohol) were used immediately preceding the crime. In addition, Mann found that female homicide offenders were more likely to kill intimates than were their male offender counterparts. When controlling for drug consumption among women murderers, though, nonusers rather than users were significantly more likely to kill intimates, and users, rather than nonusers, were more likely to kill strangers.

Wolfgang (1958) found that alcohol was present in 64 percent of homicides. In addition, he noted that prior to the murder, both the offender and the victim had been drinking in 44 percent of the cases. Cole et al. (1968) conducted psychiatric evaluations on 112 homicide cases at the California Institution for Women. They found that alcohol was related to 50 percent of the murders, that narcotics were linked to 10 percent of the crimes, and that neither alcohol nor narcotics were associated with 44 percent of the offenses. Baskin and Sommers (1993) found that the earlier the onset of a woman's criminal career, the more likely it was that her illicit conduct was not directly related to drugs. Rather, the drugs became a part of the lifestyle. Conversely, for women whose onset of criminal behavior emerged later in the life cycle, the more likely that their illicit conduct was related to drug addiction (Baskin & Sommers, 1993). Finally, in reviewing 215 female-perpetrated homicides, Spunt et al. (1997) determined that two-thirds of the murders were drug related. One-third of the homicides were not connected to illicit substances in any way.

Women with ASPD have nearly 10 times the rate of lifetime drug and alcohol abuse disorder than does the general population (Mulder et al., 1994). Eronen, Hakola, and Tiihonen (1996) studied 693 Finnish homicide offenders. They found that severe alcohol dependence in relation to ASPD greatly increased the likelihood of homicidal behavior. The relationship between ASPD and women who kill is more thoroughly examined in Chapter 4.

Age

Typically, female homicide offenders are older than their male counterparts (Mann, 1990, 1996; Wilbanks, 1983). For example, Wolfgang (1958) found that 51.4 percent of black female homicide offenders were between 25 to 39 years of age, whereas the majority of male offenders were between 15 to 24 years of age. Bunch et al. (1983) determined that the average age for women who kill was 29.3. In his sample, Goetting (1986) found that female homicide offenders had a mean age of 34.1. In addition, some researchers have indicated that the average age for convicted white female homicide offenders is 40.7, compared with 39.0 for convicted nonwhite murders (Hewitt & Rivers, 1986). Segall and Wilson (1993) reported that the average age of all murderesses is 38.9 years. Overall, notwithstanding some minor discrepancies, the ages for women who kill range from the late twenties to the early forties.

Socioeconomic Status

Mann (1990) found that unemployment or employment in lower-status jobs for black women who murdered was commonplace. In addition, she reported that the black women who killed frequently were poverty-stricken, suggesting a connection between economic status and homicide. She concluded that the combined disadvantages of being poor, black, and female were so devastating that the person's elevated stress level contributed to homicide (Mann, 1990).

Goetting (1988b) reported that out of 107 female offenders for whom information on formal education was available, 45.8 percent had completed at least 12 years of schooling. Overall, however, a relatively low degree of formal education was reflected among female homicide offenders as compared with the general population of the United States. Over three-quarters, or 76.9 percent, of the women in the sample were unemployed (Goetting, 1988b). Researchers have concluded that homicide offenders typically suffer from and are adversely affected by their low socioeconomic conditions (Goetting, 1988a, 1988b; Mann, 1996).

Ecological Circumstances

Ecological circumstances are also thought to influence female-perpetrated homicide. In 1979 and 1983, Mann (1996) conducted a descriptive study that included 296 females arrested for homicide in six cities: Atlanta, Baltimore, Chicago, Houston, Los Angeles, and New York. Her investigation supported other research on women who kill, indicating that the murder typically took place in the residence of the offender, in that of the victim, or in their mutual domicile (Goetting 1987; Mann, 1996; Wolfgang, 1958). Indeed, the home appears to be the most dangerous place for female-perpetrated homicides, since the crime takes place there 70.4 percent of the time. More specifically, murders occur in the mutual domicile of the victim/offender 42.3 percent of the time. In addition, the residence of the offender is more frequently the murder site than is the home of the victim (Mann, 1996).

Wolfgang (1958) and Blum and Fisher (1978) found that females most often committed murder in the kitchen, where the weapon of choice was a knife. Both Totman (1978) and Goetting (1989) determined that the bedroom was the most common homicide location. In Mann's (1996) study, the living room/family room/den or *social areas* were the most frequent murder sites, followed by the bedroom and the kitchen.

The home was not the only location wherein female-perpetrated homicides occurred. For instance, in McClain's (1982) study on African American female murderers, 29 percent of the crimes took place on the street. This finding was supported by Mann

(1996), whose investigation found that 20 percent of the murders took place at outside taverns, as well as on streets, in alleys, and in yards.

When controlling for time, research generally supports the fact that homicides occur on the weekends, particularly Saturday nights (Goetting, 1987; Mann, 1996; Wolfgang, 1958). Some investigators have found that during the summer months, murders occur more frequently, whereas other researchers find that there is no seasonal variation. Mann (1996) found that alcohol and drug users were more likely to kill on the weekends (59.4 percent), whereas nonusers were more likely to kill on weekdays (66.7 percent).

Weapons

Some research has shown that most female homicide offenders attack their victims in the home, with household instruments such as knives or poison (Daniel & Harris, 1982). However, in the past two decades, the trend increasingly has moved toward guns. In Mann's (1996) study, Southern women were significantly more likely than non-Southern women to use firearms in the homicides they committed (60.1 percent versus 39.9 percent). Non-Southern women were the most likely to use knives and varied from their Southern female counterparts in their use of methods, relying upon such techniques as beating/stomping, drowning, or suffocating. Mann suggested that this variation could be the result of the victim's age (i.e., generally under the age of 25), with a high percentage of children being represented in this cohort. Along these lines, Daniel and Harris (1982) reported that the death instrument employed was related to the age of the victim. For example, an adult victim usually was assailed by a weapon (e.g., firearms), whereas a child could be murdered by a variety of other methods, given the youth's relative lack of size and strength.

Clearly, firearms are the number one choice of weapon utilized by female killers (Daniel & Harris, 1982; Goetting, 1988b; Holmes & Holmes, 1994; Mann, 1996; Wilbanks, 1983). Wilbanks (1983) reported that 57.5 percent of females used guns compared with 64.6 percent of males. He regarded a firearm as the great equalizer of the sexes. In addition, murderesses were more likely than males to use a knife (27.6 percent to 19.1 percent) (Wilbanks, 1983). Some researchers also have pointed out that the image of a female electing to poison her victim as the preferred approach to murder is a myth (Godwin, 1978; Wilbanks, 1983). Moreover, the use of fatal elixirs seems to have given rise to the popular (though misguided) belief that women are more undetectably cruel, fancying a lengthy death for their victims (Godwin, 1978). However, prior to the advent of sophisticated techniques for postmortem forensic analysis, the use of poison was much more common in female-perpetrated homicides (Godwin, 1978).

Victims

Most women kill people known to them, usually husbands or male lovers (Blum & Fisher, 1978; Farr, 1997; Goetting, 1987; Mann, 1996). According to Flowers (1994, p. 74), "Women in prison for murder are almost twice as likely to have killed a spouse, ex-spouse, or other intimate than [they are to have killed] other family members." However, research indicates that there has been a decline in the number of women who commit homicides against male significant others and a rise in the number of women who kill strangers (male and female) and other nonrelated individuals (Spunt et al., 1997). For example, a study conducted by Bunch et al. (1983) found that only 33.3 percent of the female homicide offenders knew their victims well. These investigators suggested that sampling from a prison population may have had an impact on the frequency distributions for the majority of acquaintance or stranger homicides. The investigators claimed that crimes against friends or relatives tended to be passion-based offenses that could be treated by the system more leniently. As such, these crimes would not necessarily be represented in a prison population.

Overall, African American males were found to be at the greatest risk in female-perpetrated domestic homicide (Holmes & Holmes, 1994; Mann, 1996). Frequently, these men have arrest records, including substantially more arrests for violent crimes than victims in the nondomestic cases (Egger, 1994, 2002; Mann, 1996). In addition, African American males also are more likely to have been drinking prior to their deaths. Research further indicates that there were more female and white victims in nondomestic murders and that the victims were younger than those killed by sexual intimates (Holmes & Holmes, 1994; Mann, 1996). Farr (1997) examined the cases of 35 women on death row and determined that white females were most likely to kill spouses or other relatives, whereas black females were most likely to kill acquaintances. We also note that the victims of nondomestic female homicide offenders are frequently incapacitated when slain (e.g., helpless or asleep) (Farr, 1997).

Studies indicate that the killing of one's parents or siblings is rare among women (D'Orban & O'Connor, 1989). For example, D'Orban and O'Connor studied 17 female parricides (the killing of parents). The parricides consisted of 14 matricides (killings of mothers) and 3 patricides (killings of fathers). These researchers found that most female matricides were perpetrated by "single, socially isolated women in mid-life, living alone with a domineering mother in a mutually dependent but hostile relationship" (p. 27). Out of 111 female homicide offenders at the California Institution for Women in 1965, Cole et al. (1968) found that only 1 had killed her father. Patricide remains a rare occurrence for females.

Overall, murder is considered an intragender and intraracial crime; however, female offenders are the exception with respect to gender. For example, Wilbanks (1983) found that women seldom killed other females. In addition, while investigating the prevalence of female-perpetrated homicide during a 2-year period (1982–1983) in Detroit, Michigan, Goetting (1988a) determined that there were only 15 cases of women killing other women. In this study, she noted that the age range of the female killer was between 19 and 45 years. Only 11.1 percent of her sample of 136 homicide offenders committed intragender murder. As a result, she determined that female-on-female homicide was a rare phenomenon. According to the U.S. Department of Justice, 260 out of the 2,760 women (9 percent) who were victims of homicide in 1992 were murdered by other women (cited in Mann, 1996). Clearly, then, men are by far the victim of choice for both male- and female-perpetrated murder.

The offender profile that Mann (1996, p. 124) offered with respect to the typical female-on-female homicide was that of a "single, unemployed, African American mother about twenty-eight years of age with less than a high school education, who usually killed an acquaintance, unassisted, in a residence on a weekend." Mann also reported that women who characteristically kill strangers do so for economic gain, often with an accomplice, and most likely with a gun. The murder of friends or acquaintances routinely occurs alone and frequently with victim provocation.

When women kill other women, almost half of their victims are their children or stepchildren (Goetting, 1988a). A study conducted by D'Orban found that in 80 percent of the cases of female homicide, the assailant murdered someone in their family (cited in Holmes & Holmes, 1994). In 50 percent of those cases, the victim was one of the murderess's children. In addition, investigators report that psychosocial stressors, which include abandonment by the husband or the loss of economic resources to ensure her and her baby's survival, can trigger these homicidal actions (Flowers, 1994). Moreover, risk factors such as the child's sex, birth order, and age can put the child at greater or lesser risk for victimization.

The mother's age in relation to that of her children or to pregnancy also can be a risk factor, contributing to a woman's murderous conduct. For example, the younger the mother is, the greater the risk; however, the older the mother is at the point of conception, the lower the risk (Holmes & Holmes, 1994). Divorced mothers have the greatest likelihood of killing their children, followed by single mothers, and finally, married mothers (Hickey, 1997). In some cases, the suicide of the mother immediately follows the murder of her offspring. Holmes and Holmes (1994) maintained that this behavior can be thought of as an act of love by the woman who believes that the world is a terrible place in which she no longer wants herself or her child to live.

Infanticide ("the killing of an infant soon after birth") is almost entirely a female phenomenon (Flowers, 1994, p. 84). In 1992, 254 children under the age of 1 were killed, followed by 408 of ages 1 to 4 and by 126 of ages 5 to 9 years old respectively (Arrigo, 2000). "Women who kill their infants or young children usually are severely disturbed, suffer from extreme bouts of depression and many experience delusions" (Flowers, 1994, p. 85). Edwards (1986) maintained that women who commit infanticide are regarded as sick. In addition, she pointed out that mothers who kill their infants are generally treated quite leniently, whereas mothers who neglect their children are treated as monsters.

Motives

When a crime as incomprehensible as murder occurs, particularly by a female, typically the first response is to ask *why?* Although some homicides appear to have no obvious reason, women who frequently murder have both their motives and the consequences of their behavior tied to men (Wilson, 1991). Moreover, as with men, it is important to note that female killers view their actions as the solution to a problem.

Women rarely commit murder while perpetrating other felonies (Farr, 1997; Goetting, 1988b; Holmes & Holmes, 1994; Wilbanks, 1983). Women who kill are frequently in situations in which the victim, usually a male, precipitated the violence by being the first to use physical force (e.g., strike a blow or threaten with a weapon); thus, the female perpetrator reacts to her victimization (Spunt et al., 1997). Often, these women have been battered or have otherwise suffered some kind of ongoing abuse from the person that they eventually kill. There is a low incidence of victim precipitation with female victims. Goetting (1988a) suggested that in part, this low incidence can be explained by the large number of children who fall into this category, posing no serious physical threat to the offender. As we explained in the Introduction, our focus is not on battered women who kill but on predatory homicide perpetrated by women. As such, pursuing any other literature not directly germane to this cohort of female killers is decidedly beyond the scope of the present inquiry.

Spunt et al. (1997) conducted a series of interviews with 215 female homicide offenders incarcerated or on parole in New York to examine the various circumstances, including motives, under which women commit murder. They suggested that any particular homicide may have more than one motive associated with it. Indeed, they argued that the traditional procedure of law enforcement and homicide researchers to offer a single code when identifying the circumstance of a killing hid the complexity involved in murder. To substantiate their position, Spunt et al. (1997) determined that from each homicide, only 33 percent could be identified by a single motive. Thus, the majority of homicide events had a combination of at least two motives. The motives identified in their study included self-defense, harassment of subject by victim, psychiatric condition, the need to obtain drugs or money for illicit substances, the need to obtain money not for drugs, angry retaliation, jealousy, discipline or scare tactic, or motive missing. Overall, the investigators concluded that 67 percent of these homicide cases had more than one plausible motive associated with it.

In a study by Goetting (1988b), out of the 133 homicide cases in which information regarding motive was available, 54.9 percent were a result of a domestic argument or confrontation, and 15.8 percent were in a quarrelsome milieu. Of this 15.8 percent, the overwhelming majority (14.3 percent) involved friends, neighbors, or acquaintances, whereas 1.5 percent involved strangers. With respect to Goetting's (1988b) analysis, another 9.8 percent of the cases were based on self-defense; 5.3 percent took place in the context of a burglary, robbery, or theft; and 4.5 percent were attributed to impatience with a small child. In addition, 3.8 percent resulted from revenge, 2.3 percent from psychotic reactions, and 1.5 percent by insurance benefits. In an additional 1.5 percent of the cases, the victim was left unattended, and in one case the death was accidental.

In Mann's (1990) study of black female homicide offenders, she found that the most common motive given by the offenders was self-defense (41.7 percent), followed by accident (12.2 percent), and then by emotional reasons (11.7 percent). These emotional reasons included anger, jealousy, and revenge. Wolfgang (1958) also found self-defense as the most frequently reported motive by offenders. The research on motives provides considerable variability. For example, in McClain's (1982) study, anger and revenge were reported as the most frequent motives in 44.4 percent of the cases. In Weisheit's (1984) inquiry, anger and revenge represented 30 percent of the reported cases. In both instances, psychological reasons were given 35.5 percent and 40 percent of the time respectively for second- and third-degree female murders. Anger was the most commonly cited motive in Goetting's unpublished manuscript (cited in Mann, 1990). Self-reports from female homicide offenders generally give motives that render them *not responsible*. However, the reliability of these reasons is questionable.

TYPOLOGIES OF FEMALE HOMICIDE OFFENDERS

Another strategy for understanding the motives of women who kill is to create typologies or categorizations for the motives. For example, Holmes and Holmes (1994) created a general typology of homicide offenders for both male and female killers. Certain murders fit the *depressive* classification. Ordinarily, they are under the care of mental health professionals but are not psychopathic. Frequently, these offenders are without criminal records. They may believe that life is not worth living, and so they commit suicide, taking a loved one with them. These individuals view this behavior as a display of love. Women who kill their children are often in this category.

The *mysoped,* or sadistic child offender, is another category that is identified in the general typology developed by Holmes and Holmes (1994). This offender relates the murder, especially toward children, with sexual gratification. Many infamous male killers, such as Ottis Toole and Henry Lucas, ostensibly fall into this category (Egger, 2002). However, women rarely are placed within this classification.

The *sexual* killer is frequently a serial killer (Holmes & Holmes, 1994). These individuals commonly associate erotic violence and homicide with their own sexual gratification (Arrigo, 2004). Thus, they are likely to be serial offenders (Hickey, 1991; Holmes & Holmes, 1994). Once again, women are less commonly identified in this category.

The *psychotic* killer represents one who is out of touch with reality. Typically, the individual sees or hears voices (visual or auditory hallucinations) and believes that he or she has been commanded to commit a crime. For example, Joseph Kallinger, "the Shoemaker," alleged that a voice commanded him to kill everyone in the world (cited in Holmes & Holmes, 1994). This category of murderer is related to mental illness and, as such, could correspond with many views of female criminality.

The typology that is the specific focus of our inquiry is the so-called (female) *psychopathic* killer. Holmes and Holmes (1994) suggested that this category encompasses many of the other types of killers. For example, serial killers frequently are in this classification (e.g., Ted Bundy and John Gacy). In explaining the psychopathic murderer, Holmes and Holmes indicated that

> A psychopathic individual has a character disorder that results in his or her being unable to experience feelings of social responsibility, guilt, shame, empathy, sorrow, or any of the other "normal" feelings that generally result when one has harmed another person. (Holmes & Holmes, 1994, p. 14)

This type of killer is self-focused and is concerned only with his or her own feelings. We note that a more thorough discussion on the relationship between psychopathy and homicide in female offenders is detailed in Chapter 4. This material explores female homicide offenders who possess severe ASPD traits, receive this diagnosis, or are psychopathic.

In addition, Holmes and Holmes (1994) categorized murderers who kill as a result of an organic or a brain disorder that predisposed them to violence. In addition, they classified killers who were mentally retarded. Finally, they discussed professional hit killers. Although each of these categories could be given a great deal of attention, they go well beyond the limits of the present study.

Holmes and Holmes (1994) also created a typology of female killers. Although relatively rare in comparison with their male counterparts, female homicide offenders do exist (Egger, 2002; Hickey, 1997). In part, Holmes and Holmes attributed society's reluctance to accept the notion that women engage in acts of predatory homicide to the misguided conviction that they were incapable of this violence. However, as the researchers asserted, "reality . . . betrays tradition" (Holmes & Holmes, 1994, p. 116). Accordingly, their classifications included visionary, comfort, hedonistic, power-seeking, and disciple female killers. Each of these types is discussed in the following sections.

Visionary—The visionary killer hears voices or sees visions that command the person to murder an individual or a group of people. They are compelled to offend, frequently driven by either demonic or godlike forces. According to Holmes and Holmes (1994), an insanity defense can be an effective strategy with this type of murderer.

Comfort—This type of female serial killer murders for material gain (e.g., insurance money, business interests). Victims usually are intimates or people known to the assailant (e.g., a husband, a lover, or children). Most female serial killers fit this category.

Hedonistic—Holmes and Holmes (1994) indicate that hedonistic killers are the least understood in terms of women homicide offenders. They kill for sexual reasons, because they make a connection between murder and sexual gratification (Arrigo, 2004).

Power-Seeking—Typically these murderesses are attempting to gain some form of control or power in their lives. To illustrate, consider the nurse who repeatedly takes a patient to the brink of death only to restore the person to life. She may eventually tire of this, kill the person in question, and move on to the next patient (Holmes & Holmes, 1994).

Disciple—These female homicide offenders have "fallen under the spell of a charismatic leader and kill upon command" (Holmes & Holmes, 1994, p. 120). The woman's motivation to kill comes from the leader, and her reward is pleasing this figurehead. For example, Susan Atkins and the other women of Charles Manson's *family* were disciple killers (Arrigo, 2004).

Other typologies regarding female homicide offenders have been developed, including women on death row. In Farr's (1997) study, 35 women awaiting execution were identified as follows: Cold Calculators, Black Widows, Explosive Avengers, Robber-Predators, Accommodating Partners, or Depraved Partners. Among the 35 women in the sample, 42.8 percent were women of color (11 African American and 4 Latinas), and 57.2 percent were white.

Cold Calculators were described as women who would ruthlessly kill their loved ones for financial gain. In this category, 8 of 10 female serial killers were white. "These women typically were characterized as heterosexually promiscuous, coldhearted and ruthless, and as conning and enlisting other men to help them with their murderous plans" (Farr, 1997, p. 264).

Black Widows (all 3 were white) "were sentenced to death for the serial murders of their husbands, lovers, and other kin" (Farr, 1997, p. 264). Motives for their behavior included financial gain, but in some instances, there appeared to be no motive. These women typically used poison as their preferred method for committing murder. Typically, the media portrays these women as seductive and cunning.

Explosive Avengers were assigned masculine qualities or were considered lesbians. Farr (1997) reported that in these cases, homicidal premeditation was far from clear. Their crimes seemed to be impulsive or motivated by passion. The ethnic makeup for this category included 5 African Americans, 2 Latinas, and 3 white women.

Robber-Predators were found to engage in murder "while committing or covering up financial gain, felonies, robbery or . . . theft" (Farr, 1997, p. 264). This type of killer is commonly seen in men. Robber-predator killers accounted for 4 of the offenders in Farr's sample. Three women were African American, and 1 was Latina.

Accommodating Partners (2 women of color and 1 white woman) were described as individuals who resigned themselves to perpetrating homicidal actions that were created by a boyfriend or husband (Farr, 1997).

Depraved Partners (4 out of 5 were white) were considered "another side of female evil, that of the highly charged, (hetero)sexual, violence-loving young woman who linked up with an evil, murderous male partner to commit serial murders, often involving the kidnapping and torture of young White women" (Farr, 1997, p. 264). Generally speaking, Farr viewed white female homicide offenders on death row as coldhearted, manipulative, and seductive. He perceived women of color as explosive, hotheaded, and impulsive, who were prone to behavior motivated by rage or revenge.

Typologies based on the personality structures of female killers also have been generated. For example, in a study undertaken by Cole et al. (1968), the personality styles of 111 female homicide offenders at the California Institution for Women were explored. As such, these investigators identified 6 behavioral pattern categories. These categories included the masochistic, the overtly hostile violent, the covertly hostile, the inadequate, the psychotic, and the amoral.

The *masochistic* type generally is perceived as stable, has a good reputation, and sometimes is overly religious. However, this offender type tends to involve herself with abusive, unstable, chaotic partners (Farr, 1997). Typically, after years of exposure to violent abuse, this female killer murders impulsively, fearing for her safety.

The *overtly hostile violent* category of women is characterized as "emotionally unstable, aggressive, impulsive, and active" (Cole et al., 1968, p. 2). These women have a history of violence, usually attacking their victims with the intent to harm but not to kill. They are capable of a sense of loss; however, generally they do not possess a sense of guilt.

The *covertly hostile* murderess often chooses to kill children rather than to retaliate against an abusive male partner. Usually, the homicide is the product of one impulsive, angry blow.

The *inadequate* type of female murderess generally has few coping skills, a low self-esteem, limited intelligence, little emotional response, and complete dependence on a dominant male partner. Her primary concern is pleasing her partner. She is frequently ordered to participate in the homicide act and shows little remorse over the incident.

The *psychotic female* homicide offender is officially diagnosed as psychotic, particularly with paranoid schizophrenia. Typically, the murder takes place after continuous, strong urges to kill or during a severe psychotic episode (Farr, 1997). For example, the woman may have experienced auditory *command* hallucinations, telling her to kill.

The *amoral* group commits deliberate, premeditated homicides for either personal or material gain. Individuals in this group have lengthy histories of antisocial behavior, and frequently they have criminal records (Farr, 1997). In the Cole et al. (1968) study, their general level of functioning and ability was above the rest of the sample. A significant amount of manipulation and self-interest is common within this collective. In addition, this female killer type appears to have no conscience or empathy, treating others as objects (Farr, 1997). From our perspective, this category of female offender appears to match the focus of the present inquiry: women with ASPD traits/diagnosis or psychopathy.

In Wilson's *Good Murders and Bad Murders* (1991), he offers a more informational perspective on female homicides, describing them as Alpha, Beta, and Omega offenders. Overall, his categorizations emphasize the victim/offender relationship. Each of these offender types is described in the following paragraphs.

The *Alpha* female uses violence only to protect herself or others from possible harm. There is no intent to kill without the threat of violence by the victim. Examples of this offender include the woman who assails her batterer or the woman who kills a stranger as she defends herself from a rape. This offender murders only for what she perceives as self-preservation. She lacks the culpability that occurs in a Beta relationship.

The *Beta* female usually kills for reasons such as jealousy and hatred. This offender type emphasizes provocation that is a result of extreme passion and leads to impulsive actions (Wilson, 1991). Other motives surrounding an emotional investment in a typically unstable personal relationship are common. This female killer differs from the Alpha offender in that she contributes to the fighting and unrest in her relationship. Although she is sometimes the victim, the Beta killer also plays the role of the victimizer in personal (intimate) relationships. She may also victimize other nonintimates because of a close association with them.

The Beta female frequently establishes a love/hate relationship with the victim. This type of female homicide offender creates a confusing picture of who the aggressor is. In addition, she typically "offers a confusing 'face' to law enforcement" (Wilson, 1991, p. 158). In addition, the Beta female assailant may be adept at manipulation and lying. Wilson offered the example of Glenn Close's role of Alex in the (1987) film, "Fatal Attraction." In the motion picture, Close is a rejected lover who cannot control her passion for the married man who left her. Her injurious behavior is directed at herself as well as at her lover and his wife (Arrigo, 2004). The actions of the Beta female are not in self-defense; rather, they stem from uncontrolled jealousy and the like.

The *Omega* female exemplifies detachment (Wilson, 1991). Greater deception toward and less personal attachment with the victim are common. These homicide offenders are sexually provocative and use sex or eroticism to gain leverage in personal endeavors. The Omega female displays a considerable self-centeredness, shows little compassion or empathy, and deliberately commits homicidal acts or various beguiling behaviors. Despite opportunities for a loving relationship with some victims, these females categorically disregard this kind of emotional attachment. However, according to Wilson (1991), they may express some sentiment towards or investment in another person or cause.

For the Omega female, the victim's suffering is incomprehensible. Indeed, this type of killer feels only contempt for the party harmed. Wilson (1991) further explains that Omega women will hurt those who choose to cross her. We contend that this typology resembles the female homicide offender with ASPD traits/diagnosis or, more specifically, with the characteristics of psychopathy. In addition, we note that the coldness exhibited by this female killer does not take years to develop. Indeed, as Wilson (1991) observes, a child can display this kind of behavior. He offers the following vignette in support of this position:

Mary Bell, a girl of 11 years with an angelic face and apparent behavior to match, hardly qualified for the calloused deeds of strangling two small boys. But Chief Inspector James

Dobson could not disregard certain incriminating episodes that helped to establish his culprit's identity. On August 7, the day of Brian Howe's burial, Dobson made these remarks: "I watched her (Mary Bell) as she stood in front of the Howe's house while the coffin was brought out. . . . That was when I knew I couldn't risk another day. She stood there laughing, laughing and rubbing her hands. I thought, My God, I've got to bring her in or she'll do another one." (adapted from Wilson, 1991, p. 168)

Wilson further indicates that the little girl's motivation was difficult to ascertain because she lied frequently and intelligently. However, he describes the awkwardness of her logic. In addition, he reports that she genuinely seemed to enjoy the aftereffects of the murders.

Finally, Bell and Fox (1996) present three familiar stories of women who kill. The authors describe how all three representations of women are problematic for feminist discourse. The first story is derived from the *Lady Macbeth* model of female criminality. This perspective maintains that women must be more depraved than men as a result of the profound evil that ostensibly led them away from their femininity. Female murderers are considered monsters. As the researchers state, "They have violated not just moral or legal codes but a code of nature under which women naturally nurture rather than destroy" (Bell & Fox, 1996, p. 472).

Shakespeare's classic murderess, Lady Macbeth, further elucidates this notion of "antimother":

I have given suck, and know how tender 'tis to love the babe that milks me: I would, while it was smiling in my face, have plucked my nipple from his boneless gums and dashed the brains out. Lady Macbeth, *Macbeth*, I. (cited in Blum & Fisher, 1978, p. 189)

The second narrative chronicle by Bell and Fox (1996) is the *Pygmalian* model. This story depicts the woman as a fool. She will do anything for love and commits a murder to please or solidify her relationship with her male partner.

The third and final account presented by Bell and Fox (1996) portrays the woman *killer as mad*. She possesses a long and charted history with female criminality. In this story, the woman must be insane to steer so far from the behavior that society expects of her.

It is not surprising, then, that many of the aforementioned typologies have noticeable similarities. For instance, one categorization seems to be that of the *psychopathic* homicidal female who is detached, is cold, lacks empathy for her victim, and is considered a *monster* by society. Cole et al.'s (1968) amoral killer, Wilson's (1991) Omega female, Holmes and Holmes's (1994) psychopathic killer, and Bell and Fox's (1996) Lady Macbeth model all fit this characterization. From our perspective, this categorization most closely resembles women with ASPD or, more specifically, women with a psychopathic personality.

Another example is the description of the female homicide offender who is unstable, emotional, impulsive, and jealous, typically reacting violently with the intent to harm but not to kill. Cole et al.'s (1968) Overtly Hostile Violent designation, Wilson's (1991) Beta female, and Farr's (1997) Explosive Avenger all appear to fit this classification. These characteristics closely resemble symptoms of the psychiatric diagnosis of borderline personality disorder. Indeed, according to the *Diagnostic and Statistical Manual of*

Mental Disorders, Fourth Edition (APA, 1994, p. 629), "Borderline Personality Disorder is a pattern of instability in interpersonal relationships, self-image, and affects (emotions), and marked impulsivity."

Still another classification includes the female who seemingly kills for a male partner. She experiences low self-esteem, is a fool for love, is in a relationship with a dominant male, and has little remorse for her victim. Her main goal is to please her partner. Every researcher for whom a typology was presented had a category to fit this general grouping. Cole et al.'s (1968) Inadequate schema, Holmes and Holmes's (1994) Disciple type, Bell and Fox's (1996) Pygmalian model, and Farr's (1997) Accommodating Partner and Depraved Partner types fit this general categorization.

In addition, the cold-hearted, calculating murderess—a woman who kills for financial gain with no regard for her victims—is another general category. Holmes and Holmes's (1994) Comfort Killers and Farr's (1997) Cold Calculators and Black Widows types exemplify this grouping. Both Wilson's (1991) Alpha female and Cole et al.'s (1968) Masochistic type represent another category of women who kill in self-defense, usually fearing the taking of their lives from abusive male partners.

Finally, a common general classification for female homicide offenders is that they are mentally ill, sick, or psychotic. Both Holmes and Holmes's (1994) and Cole et al.'s (1968) psychotic killers, Holmes and Holmes's (1994) Visionary female killer designation, as well as Bell and Fox's (1996) Female Madness story, all represent the strong conviction that women who commit homicide should be psychopathologized.

CONCLUSIONS

In this chapter, we explored the literature on female homicide offenders. The preceding review was not exhaustive; however, it was relevant for comprehending the phenomenon of women who kill. In particular, we described arrest trends for female-perpetrated homicide, as well as the social factors influencing those trends. Moreover, we canvassed some of the prominent gender-based stereotypes regarding female predatory homicide offenders. Then, too, we generally examined an array of perspectives that define women who kill as mad, bad, victimized, and violent. We note that although these categorizations are not mutually exclusive, they give us some sense of how murderesses have been interpreted in the scholarly community in the face of their criminal conduct.

In addition, we reviewed the profile of the female homicide offender, mindful of relevant sociodemographics that contextualize and inform our appreciation for this type of murderer. Relatedly, we delineated a number of typologies developed in the scientific literature. These typologies highlight different personality and behavioral dimensions of the female killer. We concluded the chapter by identifying a number of similarities across these respective classification schemas.

Clearly, Chapters 1 and 2 told us a great deal about women who commit crime, including the offense of murder; however, this book is uniquely interested in how mental illness (specifically ASPD/psychopathy) factors into the analysis. As such, exploring what we know about psychiatric disorders and female criminality (i.e., homicide) is important to our overall enterprise. This is the specific project to which we are directed in the subsequent chapter.

3

Mental Disorders in Female
Homicide Offenders

❖

INTRODUCTION

This chapter examines the association between violence (specifically homicide) and mental disorders found among women. The discussion is limited to harmful conduct toward others (e.g., partners, children), consistent with our focus on female killers. The commentary that follows is not exhaustive. Rather, we highlight those empirical and related studies that further our regard for this often misunderstood phenomenon.

We begin by generally discussing violence potential and psychiatric disorders. This review is important because it provides an important context within which the subsequent analysis on women, crime, and mental illness can be evaluated. The balance of the chapter delineates the role that psychiatric disorders play in female-perpetrated homicide. In particular, we review the various perspectives describing murderesses and their link to mental illness. Along these lines, empirical data are given, specifying the number and type of psychiatric disorders found among homicidal women. The chapter concludes by briefly outlining the impact that mental illness has on the disposition of female murderers, mindful of how gender-role stereotypes (i.e., women killers as sick or victims) do a disservice to society's understanding of women and of the criminal acts they commit.

VIOLENCE AND PSYCHIATRIC DISORDERS

According to Monahan (1998), the relationship between violence potential and mental disorders is documented in Greek and Roman literature, dating back to the fifth century BCE. Moreover, as he explained, the public's perception that a disproportionate number

31

of the mentally disordered are violent has continued since then to the present time in all cultures. For example, in 1984, the California Department of Mental Health polled 1,500 adults. Respondents were asked whether or not they agreed with the following statement: "A person who is diagnosed as schizophrenic is more likely to commit a violent crime than a normal person" (cited in Monahan, 1998, p. 92). Sixty-one percent of those polled indicated that they definitely or probably agreed with this statement.

In Monahan's (1998) study, he found that there was a greater-than-chance relationship between mental disorder and violent behavior. Moreover, he postulated that psychiatric illness might be a statistically significant risk factor for the occurrence of violence (see also, Arrigo, 2004). However, previous research conducted by Swanson, Holzer, Ganju, and Jono (1990) found that 90 percent of those with mental disorders were not violent. In response, Monahan (1998, p. 97) suggested that "Compared to the magnitude of risk associated with the combination of male gender, young age, and lower socioeconomic status . . . the risk of violence presented by mental disorder is modest." In addition, he noted that the presence of psychosis added significantly to the likelihood of violent behavior.

As noted before, Swanson et al. (1990) found an association between a major psychiatric disorder and violent conduct. These investigators sampled individuals from the community, using a data set of 10,000 American adults from Baltimore, Maryland; Los Angeles, California; and Durham, North Carolina. Their analysis was based on the National Institute of Mental Health's Epidemiological Catchment Area (ECA) study (Reiger, Myers, et al., 1984; Robins & Regier, 1991). The participants were interviewed using the Diagnostic Interview Schedule (DIS) to establish the presence of a major mental illness as defined by the criteria in the DSM-III (APA, 1980). In order to measure violence, five items on the DIS were used. Four of these items were criteria for antisocial personality disorder, and one of the items was part of the criteria for a diagnosis of alcohol abuse or dependence. A participant was considered violent if he or she endorsed one of the five questions and if the behavior occurred during the year preceding the interview.

The results of the Swanson et al. (1990) study indicated that those who met the criteria for schizophrenia, major depression, mania, or bipolar disorder were approximately six times more likely to self-report violent behavior in the past year as compared with persons not diagnosed with a mental disorder. The prevalence of violence for individuals diagnosed with alcoholism was 25 percent compared with 12 times that of those not receiving a diagnosis. In addition, the prevalence for those meeting the criteria for abusing drugs (35 percent) was 16 times that of individuals with no diagnosis.

A study by Link, Andrews, and Cullen (1992) supported the ECA data. These researchers examined rates of arrest and self-reported violent behavior (including hitting, fighting, using weapons, and hurting someone badly) for 400 New York City adults (Monahan, 1998). Those individuals who had never been in a psychiatric hospital or who had no contact with mental health professionals were compared with samples of former mental health patients from the same area (Link et al., 1992; Rice & Harris, 1997). Several demographic and related variables such as age, gender, educational level, ethnicity, socioeconomic status, family structure (e.g., children), homicide rate of the census tract where the participant lived, and the subjects' need for approval were controlled for in the study (Link et al. 1992; Monahan, 1998).

Frequently, the patient samples were two to three times as violent as the never-treated sample. In addition, the investigators found a significant relationship between violence and mental patient status, even when many demographic factors were taken into account (Link et al., 1992). However, when controlling for recent symptomatology, the differences between the respective group rates for violence disappeared. In this study, almost all of the measurable differences in violent behavior were accounted for by active psychotic symptoms that were experienced by the participant (Link et al., 1992; Monahan, 1998). Thus, some researchers conclude that these and similar findings suggest that the relationship between mental disorder and violent crime is causal, and that active psychotic symptoms create the effect (Link et al., 1992; Rice & Harris, 1997).

Link and Stueve (1994) reanalyzed the data from Link et al's (1992) research to better understand the link between psychotic symptoms and violence. They explained their results by exploring the principle of "rationality-within-irrationality." They described this phenomenon as follows:

> The principle of rationality-within-irrationality posits that once one suspends concern about the irrationality of psychotic symptoms and accepts that they are experienced as real, violence unfolds in a "rational" fashion. By rational we do not mean reasonable or justified but rather understandable. (Link & Stueve, 1994, p. 143)

Illustrations of the rationality-within-irrationality phenomenon are discernible. For example, hallucinations and delusions may be experienced as real; thus, individuals who succumb to such occurrences may feel threatened by those whom they attack.

Relying upon a longitudinal prospective research design, Hodgins (1992) engaged in a 30-year follow-up on 15,117 individuals born in Stockholm, Sweden, in 1953. Mental disorder was estimated through hospital records, and violent behavior was estimated through police records. Men with schizophrenia or major affective disorder were 4 times more likely to be convicted of a violent crime compared with men without a major mental disorder (schizophrenia, affective disorder, or paranoid state). Women with a major psychiatric illness were 27 times more likely than those without a major psychiatric illness to be convicted of a violent crime (Hodgins, 1992; Monahan, 1998).

We also note that several studies question the idea that major psychiatric disorders cause crime and violence (e.g., Rice & Harris, 1997). Indeed, the majority of individuals with a major mental illness who commit a crime engage in this behavior prior to being 18 years of age (Hodgins, 1992; Rice & Harris, 1997). Thus, many of their offenses occur before the symptoms of their psychiatric disorders are even present (Rice & Harris, 1997). This realization calls into question the idea that mental disorders cause violent behavior in psychiatrically disordered offenders.

Additional studies have considered whether, and to what extent, psychiatric illness causes violence. For example, Teplin, Abram, and McClelland (1996) interviewed jail detainees with schizophrenia, major affective disorder, and alcohol or drug use disorders, using the DIS. This study examined whether or not the subjects were more frequently arrested for violent offenses than detainees with no mental disorder. In a 6-year follow-up, even when controlling for other risk factors, none of the disorders were related to an increased number of arrests for violent offenses. Thus, as in the conclusions reached by Rice and Harris (1997), the association between psychiatric illness and violent conduct does not appear to be completely resolved.

WHAT ROLE DO MENTAL DISORDERS PLAY IN HOMICIDE?

Typically, prison psychiatrists regard women who murder as more mentally ill than their male counterparts (Blum & Fisher, 1978). Indeed, some investigators have found female offenders as a group to have higher prevalence rates for psychiatric disorders than similarly situated male offenders (Daniel & Harris, 1982). Frequently, women criminals are viewed as less threatening and less responsible for their actions (Phillips & DeFleur, 1982). In particular, women are perceived as committing a crime stemming from mental illness or someone else's influence, whereas men are believed to possess a cognitive or rational motive for their offender behavior (Phillips & DeFleur, 1982).

Goetting (1988b, p. 3) addressed the issue of gender bias in diagnosing. As she asserted, a considerable amount of data available on women who kill consists of "psychological and psychiatric interpretations that seem to be designed to sensationalize rather than to inform." In addition, she maintained that sociological perspectives on homicidal women were largely ignored. Elsewhere, Goetting (1998a) suggested that whereas many explanations were offered for male homicide (e.g., economic or inadequate socialization), women as perpetrators of violence were far too routinely defined as sick.

Similar interpretations for the female homicide offender are found within the relevant literature. For example, Wilczynski (1997, p. 419) stated that with respect to murder, "men are bad and normal [while] women are mad and abnormal." Indeed, as we explained in the previous chapter, many researchers theorize that women who kill experience serious psychological and psychiatric disorders (Cole et al., 1968; Daniel & Harris, 1982; D'Orban, 1979). However, the association between mental illness and female criminality remains indeterminate and complicated.

Daniel and Harris (1982) suggested that the actual prevalence rate of mental disorders in female criminals is masked, especially since the majority of studies are conducted with incarcerated women. Moreover, they hypothesized that in these studies, nonconvicted women or those channeled through the mental health system do not represent a viable cohort subject to exploration and testing. For example, in England, 64.3 percent of women versus 30 percent of men who commit filicide (the killing of children) use a psychiatric plea, requiring the proof of an abnormal mental state (Wilczynski, 1997). Wilczynski further argued that women are much more likely than men to receive shorter sentences and to benefit from more lenient, treatment-oriented methods. Moreover, their sentences usually involve the intervention of psychiatry and social work much more frequently than do their male counterparts, who typically end up in prison. Mothers were less likely than fathers to be convicted of murder and sentenced to prison, receiving instead probation or psychiatric dispositions (Wilczynski & Morris, 1993).

In order to examine the role of mental disorders in females who commit homicides and other crimes, Daniel and Harris (1982) conducted their study in a psychiatric facility. The investigators compared the demographics, medical and psychiatric disorders, and previous criminal activity of female offenders charged with murder with another group of women charged with an array of different crimes. Women charged with murder and referred to a large state hospital in Missouri for pretrial psychiatric examinations from 1974 to 1979 were compared with all other female offenders admitted for evaluation during the same 5-year period. Each of the evaluations was mandated by the court in order to determine whether or not the alleged offender was competent to stand trial and whether she was criminally responsible for the identified offense (Daniel & Harris, 1982).

The sample for the Daniel and Harris (1982) study consisted of a total of 66 women. Twenty-two (33.3 percent) of these individuals were charged with murder and 44 (66.6 percent) were charged with other crimes. A history of prior hospitalization revealed that 77.3 percent of the women in the homicide group and 63.6 percent of women in the non-homicide group had at least one significant psychiatric hospitalization.

A comparison was made among the distribution of psychiatric diagnoses for both groups (Daniel & Harris, 1982). Schizophrenia was the primary diagnosis in 31.8 percent of homicidal women compared with 18.2 percent of the nonhomicide group. No women in the homicide group were found to have an affective disorder, whereas 13.6 percent of the nonhomicide cohort was diagnosed with this mental health condition. Personality disorders were the primary diagnosis in 31.8 percent of the homicide cohort compared with 27.3 percent for the nonhomicide group. The rates for alcoholism were 9.1 percent for the homicide group versus 6.8 percent for the nonhomicide cohort. Whereas 15.9 percent of the nonhomicide group was diagnosed as mentally retarded, only 1 or 4.5 percent of the homicide group received this diagnosis. Organic brain syndrome with psychosis was diagnosed in 9.1 percent of the homicide cohort versus 6.8 percent for the nonhomicide group. No mental disorder was found in 13.6 percent of the alleged female homicide offenders compared with 6.8 percent of the nonhomicide group. Overall, these researchers found that 19 (85.4 percent) of the 22 women charged with murder had at least one mental disorder, with 9 (41 percent) diagnosed as having psychosis. In addition, personality disorders had high prevalence rates in both the homicide and the nonhomicide groups.

The Daniel and Harris (1982) study also examined the type of diagnosed psychiatric disorder in relation to the homicide victim. Out of 14 women charged with murder of adults, 7 experienced personality disorders, 2 were diagnosed with alcoholism, and 2 suffered from schizophrenia. In addition, 3 women were not found to possess an identifiable mental disorder. The majority of the female offenders (7 out of 8, or 87.5 percent) charged with the murder of a child were diagnosed with psychosis. Five of the 7 women had prominent paranoid hallucinations involving the child victim. In particular, Daniel and Harris (1982, p. 265) noted that many of these women responded to the "perceived threat from the persecuting child."

Additional studies exploring the relationship between mental illness and female homicide draw attention to familial murder. For example, psychosis is frequently diagnosed in women who commit infanticide and parricide (Arrigo, 2000). In D'Orban and O'Connor's (1989) study on female parricides, 70 percent of the 17 women sampled had a history of inpatient or outpatient psychiatric care. Eleven patients had a history of suicide attempts. Moreover, the investigators found that out of the 17 parricides, 6 were schizophrenic, 5 experienced psychotic depression, 3 suffered personality disorders, and 1 was alcoholic.

In addition, whereas 78 percent of D'Orban and O'Connor's (1989) female matricides were diagnosed with a psychotic illness, 3 out of 14 were not. Of the 3 matricide cases, 2 were found to have no psychiatric diagnoses, and 1 case was identified with antisocial personality disorder. Moreover, mental illness was not directly related to the parricides for 7 women (D'Orban & O'Connor, 1989).

Related studies indicate that mothers who kill their children are frequently psychotic (Edwards, 1986). These women are perceived as sick rather than willful. Indeed, the perception is that these offenders are "victims, mad, irresponsible, hormonally disturbed and non-dangerous" (Wilczynski, 1997, p. 425). This point of view is widespread not only for women who commit filicide but also for women in general. Thus, some researchers contend that the sick perception of female-perpetrated filicide fits into the medicalization of female violence (Arrigo, 2004; Showalter, 1985; Wilczynski, 1997). This view maintains that there must be some form of pathology for a woman to commit such heinous crimes. In short, she must be suffering from a mental illness.

Although many of the studies on the subject of female violence (including homicide) and psychiatric illness are dated, there is some empirical research that examines relevant medical and psychiatric factors. For example, in their evaluation of 95 females, the factors that Climent, Rollins, Ervin, and Plutchik (1973) found to be most related to violent behavior included loss of one's mother before 10 years of age, severe parental punishment, neurological disorders in family members, dyscontrol syndrome, and access to weapons. Moreover, in a study conducted by Sutker, Allain, and Geyer (1978, p. 1142), they compared violent female criminals with nonviolent criminals. The investigators concluded that "women who murdered could be said to be more defensive, less in touch with impulses to action, more socially conforming, and more removed from a stereotyped definition to femininity (p. 1142)."

Research examining the prevalence of mental disorders in incarcerated female offenders typically cites high rates of substance abuse disorders and personality disorders (Gunn, 1993; Jordan, Schlenger, Fairbank, & Caddell, 1996). For example, a study conducted at the Institute of Psychiatry in London found that substance abuse and personality disorders were the most common diagnoses among prisoners, with only 1 percent to 2 percent being psychotic (Gunn, 1993). In another study, female felons ($N = 805$) entering prison in North Carolina were assessed for psychiatric disorders (Jordan et al., 1996). These inmates were also found to have high rates of substance abuse and dependence, as well as antisocial and borderline personality disorders compared with other women in the community.

It is interesting that in the Jordan et al. (1996) inquiry, white women had higher rates of diagnosed mental illness than did African American women. The researchers suggested that this phenomenon could reflect the notion that only the most deviant or disturbed of white women was likely to be incarcerated, compared with minority women.

Jordon et al. (1996) also considered the effect of co-occurring disorders. Specifically, ASPD and drug abuse/dependence were highest among women from urban areas, whereas alcohol abuse/dependence was the highest among women who grew up in small towns. ASPD was the most prevalent among the women with the least education. All of the women were more likely to have had exposure to traumatic events than other women in the community. Overall, these researchers concluded that "convicted women felons have high rates of those disorders that include acting out and engaging in illegal behaviors. . . . We speculate that these disorders may be contributing factors in the criminal behavior that [led to their] incarceration" (Jordan et al., 1996, p. 518).

Bell and Fox (1996) examined the issue of women who kill an innocent third party rather than an abusive man, utilizing the single case of Susan Christie. On March 25, 1991, in North Ireland, Susan Christie cut the throat of Penny McAllister, the wife of

Susan's lover. She then inflicted superficial wounds upon herself. Christie claimed that she did not remember anything about committing the homicide. Although she was charged with murder, Christie was convicted of manslaughter on the basis of diminished responsibility. According to Northern Irish law, diminished responsibility is a partial defense that permits the court to take into account factors that normally underlie sentencing decisions, specifically, the presence of a psychiatric illness at the time of the offense (Bell & Fox, 1996). The legal construct of diminished responsibility also plays a role in American and English law (Arrigo, 2004).

Diminished responsibility provides an opportunity for the defense to call expert psychiatric witnesses, thus allowing evidence of the circumstances surrounding the homicide into the case. This evidence is normally excluded in more structured defenses. However, Bell and Fox (1996) warn that the lack of structure permits the woman's perspective to be shaped by stereotypes of her criminality. It is not surprising that this includes the role of mental illness in crafting the female offender's identity.

The basis for Susan Christie's diminished responsibility defense was linked to depression, allegedly produced by a number of stressors in part caused by the husband of the deceased. Bell and Fox (1996) note that Christie's legal claim was likely to have been received well by mental health professionals. Indeed, as the investigators explained, depression is a diagnosis that is more liberally applied to female offenders.

The defense counsel focused on the alleged psychological abuse inflicted upon Christie by her lover, portraying him as cold and calculating. In contrast, her defense team constructed an image of Christie as passive, naive, and seemingly helpless. As Bell and Fox (1996, p. 481) depict her, Christie "appeared blonde, frail, tearful and virginal, thus fitting the requisite feminine stereotypes." The defense lawyer, Kelly J., painted this picture, conveying it through the following question put to the jury: "Can you conceive of a girl . . . a comparatively innocent young girl . . . carrying out this vicious murder, this vicious act of killing if she had not taken leave of her senses?" (Kelly J., Trial Transcript 1992, p. 13, as cited in Bell & Fox, 1996, p. 481).

More generally, Bell and Fox (1996) maintained that both the prosecution and the defense teams use gender stereotypes either to convict women or to help set them free. What is problematic here is that the stereotypes prevail, absent a more genuine consideration of the women's circumstances, experiences, and histories. Indeed, whereas a diminished responsibility defense built on a gender-based mental disorder "arguably allows the woman's voice to be heard, her story is not her own, but is mediated by medical and legal experts" (Bell & Fox, 1996, p. 481).

In the United States today, existing legal standards do not allow the diagnosis of antisocial personality disorder or psychopathy to reduce the culpability of a female homicide offender. Moreover, this diagnosis is most frequently applied to men (Gacono, 2000). Thus, the receptivity of mental health professionals and society at large to the role of ASPD/psychopathy and their relative influence on female-perpetrated homicide is questionable at best. This is especially the case, given the paucity of research on the subject to date.

Some researchers maintain that the continued portrayal of female homicide offenders as only mentally ill, specifically as psychotic or as victims of battered women's syndrome, "avoids the social causes of female violence, and denies the rationality and agency of the offender" (Wilczynski, 1997, p. 425). For example, Wilczynski (1997) argued that women who kill their children are labeled as mad and hormonally unbalanced under the assumption that all women are *natural* mothers. Moreover, she asserted that society's view that motherhood is joyful and fulfilling for all women ignores the reality that many women do not experience this phenomenon in this way. Gender stereotypes regarding motherhood can impact female homicide offenders. Thus, it follows that some female killers can benefit from gender-role stereotypes in that these offenders are viewed as blameless victims (Gordon, 1988).

Those women who do not fit either the sick or the victim (i.e., psychopathic female homicide offender) stereotypical gender role may be treated more severely by society and the criminal justice system. Failing to acknowledge the potential need to administer justice in this way raises some significant questions about our fundamental understanding of women, crime, and social control. Indeed, as Wilczynski (1997) notes,

> The "moral gatekeeping" involved in rewarding "good" women and penalizing "bad" women reinforces all women's position of subordination. It also represents a more subtle but in some ways inherently more coercive and dangerous system of social control than is provided for men by the criminal justice system. (p. 426)

Thus, the current view of female-perpetrated homicide tells the story only of those women who fall into the stereotypic categories of women as assigned to them by men. We argue that these include the designations of victim or psychotic, classifications that are incomplete. What is perhaps most troublesome is that even when women clearly do not fit into these categories, some will claim that they do for purposes of a criminal defense, including the mitigation of penal or societal sanctions (Bell & Fox, 1996). Moreover, mental health professionals are frequently nonreceptive to diagnosing psychiatric disorders in women, especially those women that do not neatly or seamlessly fit established gender roles (i.e., the woman as passive, nurturer, mothering) (Bell & Fox, 1996).

These ideological and practical problems notwithstanding, this book squarely examines the application of a diagnostic category disproportionately applied to men (ASPD/psychopathy), arguing for its utility in relation to female homicide offenders. In this context, the subsequent chapter investigates what we know about predatory homicide committed by women diagnosed with antisocial personality disorder or possessing a psychopathic personality. Our aim is to tell the story of these women as best we can from their own perspectives, in order to highlight the unique experiences of these offenders.

CONCLUSIONS

This chapter explored the literature on mental disorders in female homicide offenders. To access the pertinent research, we reviewed several empirical studies on violence potential and psychiatric illness. Overall, although there does appear to be some relationship between mental disorder and crime, specifying what that association is remains unclear and subject to debate. Canvassing this material was important to our enterprise, since it provided a context within which to assess the phenomenon of female-perpetrated murder.

The balance of the chapter specifically addressed a number of facets regarding psychiatric illness and women who kill. Admittedly, the research in this area is limited and somewhat dated; however, what we do know indicates that female offenders find that their criminal transgressions are often interpreted as the product of victimization or mental illness. Although we agree that these assessments are relevant to understanding some female killers, regrettably, they are incomplete. In particular, we are concerned that these gender-role stereotypes do a disservice to women and their agency, reducing their identity to conventional portrayals consistent with masculine categories assigned to women by men. Such classifications potentially undermine society's appreciation for women and compromise the justice system's ability to adequately and appropriately respond to female criminality, including homicide.

We note that the incidence of criminal and violent behavior is essentially a diagnostic criterion of ASPD (Swanson et al., 1990). The relationship between ASPD/psychopathy and violence in men is a strong one (Gacono, 2000). However, systematic investigations of women in this area are sparse. Both the prevalence of gender bias in psychiatric diagnoses and the lack of research interest in these women—given their relatively small sample sizes—have contributed significantly to the paucity of information on this topic. These limits notwithstanding, the next two chapters explore what we do know about women who kill and who are diagnosed with antisocial personality disorder and/or who possess psychopathic traits. In particular, Chapter 4 assesses the literature on the ASPD-Psychopathy continuum. Chapter 5 reviews the empirical and related studies on homicidal women with this diagnosis and/or with these personality characteristics. We contend that exploring both sets of research moves us that much closer to the world of Aileen Wuornos, her psychological makeup, and the crimes she committed.

4

Understanding Antisocial Personality Disorder and Psychopathy

❖

INTRODUCTION

Despite all of the research focus on psychotic disorders and violence, ASPD and substance abuse disorders increase the likelihood of violent behavior significantly (Arrigo, 2004; Swanson et al., 1990). Moreover, investigators have noted that violence is essentially a diagnostic feature of this psychiatric condition (Swanson et al., 1990). Various studies have used the Diagnostic Interview Schedule (DIS) to determine DSM diagnoses and have specifically used the diagnostic sections for ASPD to determine self-report information about the violent behavior of respondents (Regier, Myers, et al., 1984; Swanson et al., 1990). There is a strong connection between ASPD and violence. However, some confusion exists about the connection between ASPD and psychopathy as clinical constructs (Gacono, 2000). As such, Chapter 4 attempts to clarify the continuum between ASPD and psychopathy.

In particular, we discuss the development of the ASPD diagnosis and the psychopathy construct in order to shed some light on the relationship between these overlapping psychiatric conditions. Additionally, the diagnostic criteria for ASPD are supplied as a way to better understand this phenomenon. We also discuss the development of ASPD/psychopathy from the psychodynamic, cognitive, behavioral, and biological perspectives. More specifically, the impact of abuse and neglect are analyzed, focusing on how symptoms of the disorder may develop. We conclude the chapter by examining the effects that gender has on diagnosing ASPD (psychopathy). This approach is consistent with the concerns raised in the previous chapter, where we explained how stereotypical and related assumptions about women inform the association between violence and mental illness.

WHAT IS SEVERE ASPD AND PSYCHOPATHY?

The construct of *psychopathy* has a long history with changing personality patterns and clinical characteristics dating back the past two centuries (Arrigo & Shipley, 2001; Millon, Simonsen, & Birket-Smith, 1998). In the late 1700s, Pinel observed that some of his patients engaged in impulsive acts that caused self-harm (Millon et al., 1998). These individuals were able to comprehend the irrationality of what they were doing, and their reasoning abilities did not appear to be impaired. He described these individuals as suffering from *manie sans delire* (insanity without delirium; Dinges, Atlis, & Vincent, 1998; Millon et al., 1998). In the early 1800s, Benjamin Rush documented confusing cases that were described by clarity of thought along with moral depravity in behavior (Millon et al., 1998). Rush has been credited as the first person to initiate what has become a long-standing practice of social condemnation for those labeled *psychopathic*.

Cleckley's work, *The Mask of Sanity* (1941), marked the beginning of the modern clinical construct of psychopathy. It has remained relatively stable to the present day (Hart & Hare, 1998). Cleckley developed his description of the psychopath on the basis of observations of white, middle-class male patients who were inpatients of a psychiatric facility (Dinges et al., 1998). Hart and Hare (1998) summarize the essential features of Cleckley's psychopath:

> Interpersonally, psychopaths are grandiose, arrogant, callous, superficial, and manipulative; affectively, they are short-tempered, unable to form strong emotional bonds with others, and lacking in empathy, guilt or remorse; and behaviorally, they are irresponsible, impulsive, and prone to violate social and legal norms and expectations. (p. 25)

According to Lykken (1995), Cleckley viewed moral feelings or the human conscience as learned, and he believed that the learning process was directed and reinforced by emotional sentiments. In addition, Cleckley contended that if normal human emotions were diminished, the development of morality or socialization would be jeopardized. Ultimately, he found that normally socializing experiences were ineffectual with psychopaths. However, some critics argue that psychopaths are capable of experiencing genuine emotions such as anger, satisfaction, and self-esteem (Lykken, 1995).

Cleckley's conceptualization of the psychopath focused on the patient's intrapersonal characteristics. These were defined as "inferred, nonobservable, processes . . . such as lack of judgment, impulsivity, an inability to feel remorse or guilt, an inability to learn from punishment, and rationalizing or blaming others for one's behavior" (Dinges et al., 1998, p. 463). Thus, his focus was not on the person's criminal history.

The psychiatric diagnoses for sociopathic personality disturbance, namely, antisocial reaction (APA, 1952) and the DSM-II diagnosis of ASPD (APA, 1968) employed the majority of Cleckley's original features of the psychopath, adding some criminal behaviors to the diagnostic criteria (cited in Dinges et al., 1998). The diagnosis of ASPD began to emphasize criminal acts and inappropriate interpersonal behaviors with the publication of the DSM-III (APA, 1980) and the DSM-III-R (APA, 1987). In addition, the inclusion of conduct disorder or the participation in criminal acts such as truancy, theft, and vandalism before 15 years of age were required in order to receive the diagnosis of ASPD as an adult (Dinges et al., 1998; Forth & Mailloux, 2000). Some critics noted that this *purer* conceptualization of psychopathy in the ASPD diagnosis made it too behaviorally based, neglecting persistent personality traits (Dinges et al., 1998).

From this criticism, Hare (1980) developed the Psychopathy Checklist (PCL), followed by a current, revised version the PCL-R (Hare, 1991) to operationalize the concept of psychopathy based on the primary features of Cleckley's original criteria.

> A focus on behavioral symptoms (e.g., irresponsibility, delinquency) to the exclusion of interpersonal and affective symptoms (e.g., grandiosity, callousness, deceitfulness, shallow affect, lack of remorse) may lead to over diagnosis of psychopathy in criminal populations and under diagnosis in noncriminals. (Hart & Hare, 1998, p. 23)

However, we note that few criminal behaviors are among the diagnostic criteria used within this instrument. Instead, there are many other personality-based items.

The original PCL (Hare, 1980) consisted of a 22-item rating scale, which was shortened to 20 in the PCL-R (Hare, 1991). A 3-point scale is used to score items (0 = item does not apply; 1 = item applies somewhat; 2 = item definitely applies). The total scores range from 0 to 40, and they represent the extent to which an individual matches the classic psychopath. A score of 30 or higher on this checklist indicates psychopathy (Hart & Hare, 1998). A more extensive explanation of the PCL-R is given in Table 4.1, which accompanies. Some researchers postulate that the most current DSM-IV diagnosis of ASPD should focus on observable behaviors, since clinicians cannot effectively evaluate interpersonal and affective characteristics (Hart & Hare, 1998; Robins, 1978). According to Dinges et al. (1998), the DSM-IV criteria for ASPD consist of more objective criteria. In addition, the new emphasis on early-onset delinquency as a critical element for the disorder differentiates ASPD from adult antisocial behavior or other mental illnesses (Hart & Hare, 1998). In part, the criteria for the DSM-IV's interpretation of ASPD were based on the results of empirical research (Hart & Hare, 1998).

TABLE 4.1   Items on the Psychopathy Checklist–Revised (PCL-R)

Factor 1—Interpersonal/Affective	Factor 2—Social Deviance	Additional Items
Glibness or superficial charm	Need for stimulation	Promiscuous sexual
Grandiose sense of self	Proneness to boredom	behavior
Pathological lying	Parasitic lifestyle	Many short-term relation
Conning or manipulative quality	Poor behavioral controls	ships
Lack of remorse or guilt	Early behavioral problems	Criminal versatility
Shallow affect	Lack of realistic, long-term	
Callousness or lack of empathy	goals	
Failure to accept responsibility	Impulsivity	
for one's own actions	Irresponsibility	
	Juvenile delinquency	
	Revocation of conditional	
	release	

According to the current psychiatric diagnostic schemata, antisocial personality disorder (ASPD) takes the place of earlier labels such as psychopathy, sociopathy, and dyssocial personality (Lykken, 1995). Hart and Hare (1998) referred to psychopathy as a personality disorder with specific interpersonal, affective, and behavioral symptoms. Although ASPD is the current DSM-IV diagnosis most closely encompassing the characteristics of psychopathy, PCL-R scores are used to find a diagnosis (not from the DSM-IV) of psychopathy. The DSM-IV criteria for ASPD are as follows:

301.7 Antisocial Personality Disorder

I. There is a pervasive pattern of disregard for and violation of the rights of others occurring since age 15 years, as indicated by three (or more) of the following:

1. failure to conform to social norms with respect to lawful behaviors indicated by repeatedly performing acts that are grounds for arrest.

2. deceitfulness, as indicated by repeated lying, use of aliases, or conning others for personal profit or pleasure.

3. impulsivity or failure to plan ahead.

4. irritability and aggressiveness, as indicated by repeated physical fights or assaults.

5. reckless disregard for safety of self or others.

6. consistent irresponsibility, as indicated by repeated failure to sustain consistent work behavior or honor financial obligations.

7. lack of remorse, as indicated by being indifferent to or rationalizing having hurt, mistreated, or stolen from another.

II. The individual is at least age 18 years.

III. There is evidence of Conduct Disorder with onset before age 15 years.

IV. Occurrence of antisocial behavior is not exclusively during the course of Schizophrenia or a Manic Episode. (APA, 1994, pp. 649–650)

Researchers have found that the empirical relationship between the PCL-R scores and an ASPD diagnosis or symptoms to be quite large (approximately $r = .55$ to .65) with fair to good diagnostic agreement, even with forensic subjects (Hare, 1980; Hart & Hare, 1998). However, the prevalence rates for those determined to have ASPD compared with psychopathy are different. For instance, using the DSM criteria, 50 percent to 80 percent of offenders and forensic patients are diagnosed with ASPD, whereas only approximately 15 percent to 30 percent of those same individuals meet the PCL-R criteria for psychopathy (Hare, Hart, & Harpur, 1991; Hart & Hare, 1998). Many researchers criticize the most recent DSM-IV diagnosis for confounding ASPD with criminality in general (Hare et al., 1991; Hart & Hare, 1998).

Whereas the vast majority (about 90 percent) of criminals classified by the PCL-R as psychopathic are diagnosed with ASPD, only about 30 percent of those with the diagnosis of ASPD can qualify as psychopathic. Thus, the American Psychiatric Association recommends that inferences measured by the PCL-R be drawn when diagnosing ASPD in forensic settings. Failure to do this may produce inaccurate diagnostic classifications (APA, 1994, p. 647).

It is important to understand the difference between diagnosing someone with ASPD or characterizing the person as psychopathic. However, the development of these respective psychiatric conditions also impacts the individual's symptomatology. Accordingly, the next section discusses various models of development, the way that they purport to measure ASPD (psychopathy), and the way that various symptoms of the disorder occur in the diagnosed individual.

THE DEVELOPMENT OF THE ASPD (PSYCHOPATHY) CONTINUUM

The development of ASPD is explained primarily from psychodynamic, cognitive, behavioral, and biological models (Comer, 1995). According to Gabbard (1990), psychodynamic theorists postulate that this disorder begins with a lack of parental love in infancy. Thus, these children form a lack of trust in other human beings. Individuals who develop ASPD react to such early neglect by becoming emotionally detached and learning to relate to others through manipulation, power, and destructiveness (Gabbard, 1990).

Ultimately, psychodynamic theorists maintain that ASPD is caused by a tremendous failure of the superego, that part of the psyche that comprises the "moral precepts of our minds as well as our ideal aspirations" (Brenner, 1973, p. 35; Comer, 1995), thus resulting in a lack of conscience and morality. Whether the cause is from parental loss, rejection, excessively punitive actions, or inconsistent punishment by parents, the psychopathic individual has little opportunity to maintain close relationships or identification with his or her parents (Widom, 1998). According to the psychodynamic perspective, the individual failed to develop an adequate conscience, resulting in poor behavioral controls (Widom, 1998).

Childhood abuse, neglect, and the witnessing of violence are factors identified by many scholars as integral to the development of psychopathy/ASPD (Widom, 1998). For example, researchers have found that individuals with rather than without ASPD are more likely to experience family conflict, separation, neglect, alienation, violence, and poverty (Farrington, 1991; Luntz & Widom, 1994). In addition, the parents of these individuals are more likely to have ASPD, creating a lack of trust toward their parents and in relationships more generally (Comer, 1995). The American Psychiatric Association's *Diagnostic and Statistical Manual of Mental Disorders* (1994) suggests that child abuse or neglect can increase the chances that conduct disorder (CD) during adolescence will evolve into ASPD during adulthood.

Widom (1998) explained that abuse or neglect encourages the development of coping styles that are adaptive in an abusive home setting; however, they would not be prosocial in an adult in other relationships. For example, the youth might develop characteristics such as a lack of realistic, long-term goals; being manipulative or conning; pathological lying; or superficial charm in order to cope in his or her abusive family (Widom, 1998). In addition, impulsive behavioral styles, leading to poor school performance, also could stem from the child's home environment. Thus, as Widom (1998 p. 160) explains, "Adaptations that may be functional at one point in development (avoiding an abusive parent or desensitizing oneself against feelings) may later compromise the person's ability to draw upon the environment in a more adaptive and flexible way."

In addition, Widom (1998) notes that bodily changes related to the development of antisocial behavior can also occur from the adolescent's abuse or neglect. For instance, desensitization from pain and anxiety could occur from repeated experiences of being beaten. Widom postulated that this desensitization could result in the child's becoming less emotionally and physiologically responsive to the needs of others. Moreover, the child may become nonresponsive to conditioning by punishment as seen in the psychopath (Forth & Mailloux, 2000).

Some cognitive theorists maintain that those diagnosed with ASPD are extremely slow in acquiring moral principles and rationality (Comer, 1995; Kagan, 1986). Thus, they are thought to reflect upon the position of others only after they have considered their own perspective. Frequently, the feelings of others are not considered at all by these individuals (Widom, 1998). In addition, persons diagnosed with ASPD seem not to learn from experience or to appreciate the consequences of their actions, particularly upon others (Comer, 1995). Yet, other cognitive theorists contend that persons with ASPD hold beliefs that minimize the relevance or importance of other people's needs (Levenson, 1992).

Many behavioral theorists suggest that the symptoms of ASPD are taught through modeling, particularly from parents who have ASPD or engage in antisocial behaviors (Comer, 1995). Following this perspective, "each generation learns to be violent by being a participant in a violent family" (cited in Widom, 1998, p. 160). Other behaviorists believe that antisocial actions are inadvertently taught at home by the parents, reinforcing a child's aggressive behavior (Patterson, 1986).

Some research suggests that ASPD (psychopathy) may be associated with biological variables, and twin and adoption studies help substantiate the notion that the relationship is partly due to genetic factors (Comer, 1995; Dahl, 1993). For example, the autonomic and central nervous systems of persons with ASPD appear to respond more slowly than do those without the disorder (Comer, 1995; Raine, 1998). The plurality of electroencephalogram (EEG) slow waves, decreased skin conductance, and low arousal in those individuals with ASPD (psychopathy) are used as measures supporting the biological theories (Arrigo, 2004; Comer, 1995; Raine, 1998). These biological factors have all been supported by the thrill-seeking and related behaviors frequently undertaken by those with ASPD (psychopathy) to increase the person's autonomic and central nervous system activity (Raine, 1998). We also note that chronic underarousal may lead to sensation-seeking behavior by those with ASPD (psychopathy) (Comer, 1995; Raine, 1998).

In addition, some investigators suggest that those with ASPD have frontal lobe functional deficits or problems in the region of the brain controlling inhibition, resulting in impaired impulse control and perseveration (Linnoila, 1998). However, critics maintain that ASPD is a socially defined construct that is inappropriately studied from a biological perspective (Rutter, 1998). Thus, these commentators maintain that "it is clearly unacceptable to equate breaking the law with individual disorder or psychopathology" (Rutter, 1998, p. 115).

Children with both conduct disorder (CD) and attention-deficit hyperactivity disorder (ADHD) seem to have an increased risk of adult development for ASPD (APA, 1994). CD is defined as "persistently high levels of fighting, lying, bullying, vandalism, and other antisocial behaviors during childhood or adolescence. . . . ADHD refers to developmentally inappropriate levels of attention problems, motor hyperactivity, and impulsive behaviors" (Lahey & Loeber, 1998, p. 51). Although these childhood disorders are related to adult

ASPD, the likelihood of this diagnosis in adulthood is much greater with the combination of these other psychiatric conditions (Lahey & Loeber, 1998). However, critics contend that several methodological problems plague this research, making their conclusions suspect. Thus, according to Lahey and Loeber (1998), no firm conclusions can be drawn without further investigating the association between these childhood disorders and ASPD.

The various explanations for ASPD (psychopathy) are not mutually exclusive. For example, Lykken (1995) found that these individuals experience less anxiety than others and, therefore, are less likely to learn a number of socially desirable behaviors that stem from their desire to avoid or decrease the anxiety created by others' disapproval. Comer (1995) further explained that psychopathic people cannot learn from feelings of anxiety or from empathy for other people because they do not experience these feelings. Psychopathic individuals tend to "tune out" threatening or emotional situations, either by slow-wave cortical activity (electrical activity in the brain) or by way of a learned response from living with continuous abuse (Comer, 1995, p. 599; Hare, 1980). There are many other complex and detailed theories regarding the development of ASPD as a disorder. Some of these include prenatal and postnatal hormones, neurotransmitter turnover, and head trauma. We note, however, that these conceptualizations are all well beyond the scope of the present inquiry.

GENDER AND ASPD (PSYCHOPATHY)

Although the prevalence rates of ASPD for women versus men are dramatically different, several characteristics must exist in women and men for the finding of an ASPD diagnosis. Individuals with ASPD show a pervasive pattern of disregard for and the violation of the rights of others (APA, 1994). Although an age limit of 18 years is necessary for the diagnosis of ASPD, those with this psychiatric condition display patterns of criminal behavior before the age of 15. Some examples include "truancy, running away from home, initiation of physical fights, forced sexual activity, physical cruelty to animals or people, deliberate destruction of property, fire setting, and frequent lying and stealing" (Comer, 1995, p. 592).

According to Comer (1995), persons with the diagnosis of ASPD are typically irresponsible with money, although skillful at obtaining personal gain from the manipulation of others, rationalizing that the victims were weak and deserved to be conned. Moreover, those with this disorder are impulsive, deceitful, and unable to work consistently at a job. Vaillant (1994) characterized those with ASPD as irritable and aggressive, often initiating physical altercations.

Investigators also note that there is a strong association between ASPD and alcoholism, as well as other substance-related disorders (Comer, 1995). Alcohol abuse and dependence in those with ASPD generally begins at an early age. The high degree of comorbidity between ASPD and substance-related disorders has an impact on those diagnosed with ASPD and violent behaviors such as homicide (Arrigo, 2004). Indeed, the continued use of substances, in conjunction with the diagnosis of ASPD, correlates with an increase in violent behavior (Mohanan, 1998). This relationship is further examined elsewhere in this chapter. However, in the remainder of this section, we explore several related aspects of gender and ASPD (psychopathy).

Prevalence Rates

Approximately 1.5 percent to 3.5 percent of the adult population is diagnosed with ASPD, and the figures for men are 3 times greater than for women (APA, 1994). In addition, men are more frequently diagnosed, regardless of race, age, socioeconomic status, and the like (Mulder et al., 1994). Gacono and Meloy (1994) suggest that the prevalence rates of ASPD for women in incarcerated populations tend to range between 40 percent to 60 percent as compared with 60 percent to 80 percent for men. ASPD is disproportionately represented in correctional populations, especially for males.

Salekin, Rogers, and Sewell (1997) examined the construct of psychopathy in 103 female offenders, using various instruments, including the PCL-R. Compared with previous research using male samples (Hare, 1991), low prevalence rates of psychopathy were found. Sixteen percent scored above the cutoff of 30 designated by Hare, compared with 25 percent to 30 percent generally found in male offender samples. In addition, somatization disorder was negatively correlated with the measures of psychopathy. Historically, somatization disorder has been referred to as hysteria and is defined as "a polysymptomatic disorder that . . . is characterized by a combination of pain, gastrointestinal, sexual, and pseudoneurological symptoms" (APA, 1994, p. 445). However, the prevalence rate of ASPD among female offenders is 56 percent (Salekin et al., 1997). These investigators found that this percentage, although somewhat lower than most male rates, was similar to those found in a few male samples.

Arguably, the most comprehensive study of women with ASPD is the Epidemiological Catchment Area (ECA) project (Reiger, Myers, et al., 1984). This was the largest community-based study of psychiatric disorders, examining the relationship between psychiatric disorders and violence in the United States. In this investigation, a representative sample of adult household residents taken from five metropolitan cities (New Haven, Baltimore, St. Louis, Raleigh-Durham, and Los Angeles), were surveyed (Reiger, Myers, et al., 1984). Between 1980 and 1983, 3,000 to 5,000 household residents in each city were given structured diagnostic interviews. The primary instrument utilized for purposes of interviewing was the Diagnostic Interview Schedule (DIS).

As Chapter 3 explained, the DIS is used to establish DSM diagnoses. In addition, the DIS items used to determine violent behaviors were contained in the diagnostic section for ASPD (items 1–4) and item five of the alcohol abuse or dependence disorder (Swanson et al., 1990). In relation to ASPD, three important issues were extracted from these data: (a) ASPD was on the rise for both women and men, although the rate of increase was greater in women (Robins, Tipp, & Przybeck, 1991); (b) ASPD was often a comorbid phenomenon, co-occurring with other psychiatric disorders such as drug abuse, anxiety, and depressive disorders; and (c) women with ASPD had fewer symptoms than men.

One-month prevalence rates for mental disorders were determined from 18,571 persons interviewed in the first set of community samples from all five sites of the ECA study. Overall, ASPD was found in 0.5 percent of the population (Regier, Boyd, et al., 1988). The male rate of the disorder (0.8 percent) was 4 times that of the female rate (0.2 percent) (Regier, Boyd, et al., 1988). For both men and women, ASPD was predominantly found in the under-45-year-old age group. The male groups, ages 18 to 24 years, had a rate of 1.5 percent compared with 1.2 percent of males, ages 25 to 44 years. A significant decrease was noted with male rates of 0.2 percent and 0.1 percent respectively for those in the 45 to 64 age group and the 65 years and older groups. Although the

2 youngest female groups (i.e., 18 to 24 and 25 to 44) had rates of 0.4 percent and 0.3 percent respectively, no women over 44 years of age were diagnosed with ASPD (Regier, Boyd, et al., 1988). Overall, men had significantly higher rates of substance use disorders and ASPD, whereas women had significantly higher rates of affective, anxiety, and somatization disorders.

Whereas the ECA data were drawn from individuals in the community, rates of ASPD are higher among incarcerated populations (Jordan et al., 1996). In a 1996 study by Jordan et al., almost the entire population of women entering a North Carolina prison ($N = 805$) were assessed to determine the rates, risk factors, and outcomes of specific psychiatric disorders among women in prison. The Composite International Diagnostic Interview (CIDI), a modification of the DIS, was the main assessment instrument. In addition, in order to ensure validation, structured clinical interviews were used to diagnose a mental disorder. We note, however, that the CIDI does not have a section that assesses ASPD. As such, the items in the DIS evaluating ASPD were used in the clinical interviews (Jordan et al., 1996). The results of the study indicated that female convicts had higher rates of substance abuse and dependence, borderline personality disorder, and ASPD compared with the women in the ECA study (women in the community).

Although rates of ASPD for women are significantly lower than for male prisoners, the rates are elevated among female offenders (Jordan et al., 1996). ASPD was the most prevalent among the 18 to 25 age group with a rate of 4.7 percent for Caucasian women and 3.8 percent for African American women. The rates for women ages 26 to 50 were 2.6 percent for Caucasian women and 1.5 percent for African American women. The investigators maintained that the higher rates for (non-Hispanic) whites for most disorders suggested that only the most deviant or disturbed of these women were likely to be incarcerated. However, some researchers contend that African American women may be incarcerated for less serious offenses with fewer signs of psychopathology (Jordan et al., 1996).

Sociodemographic characteristics were examined in relation to various disorders. ASPD and drug abuse/dependence had the highest prevalence rates for those women who grew up in urban areas. ASPD was also found to have the highest rates among those with the least education (Jordan et al., 1996). The authors indicated that this outcome was to be expected, since the criteria for ASPD (e.g., truancy, fighting, and trouble with authority figures) greatly increased the chances of expulsion.

Compared with a North Carolina community population, ECA ($N = 1,007$), the likelihood of convicts having a substance abuse disorder or ASPD were 5 to 25 times greater (Jordan et al., 1996; see also, Rutherford, Alterman, & Cacciola, & Snider, 1995). Moreover, Jordan et al. (1996) maintained that many prisoners will experience comorbid ASPD and substance abuse disorders, thereby aggravating antisocial or illegal behaviors. Comorbidity of ASPD and depression with incarcerated women is substantial. Researchers speculate that women with ASPD in the community act out their distress, also lowering their rates of anxiety disorders (Jordan et al., 1996).

ASPD: A Diagnosis Designed for Men

Rutherford et al. (1995) conducted a study evaluating the differences in prevalence rates, short-term reliability, and internal consistency for the diagnosis of ASPD from the DSM-III (APA, 1980) and the DSM-III-R (1987) in 57 female and 37 male methadone patients. They found that the diagnostic rates, reliability, and internal consistency were lower for women in all categories. Particularly with childhood criteria, many important gender differences were detected.

Gender differences in childhood criteria focused on age of onset and the nature of the acting out. For instance, women infrequently achieved the violent and aggressive childhood criteria in the DSM-III or DSM-III-R, such as fire setting or cruelty to animals (Rutherford et al., 1995). Adult women with ASPD typically had fewer violent and aggressive childhood symptoms (Salekin, Rogers, Ustad, & Sewell, 1998). Women more closely matched the previous emphasis on truancy, sexual promiscuity, and the like (Salekin et al., 1998).

Robins (1966) reported that women diagnosed as sociopathic while adults had a later onset of childhood behavioral problems (14 to 16 years), and were more frequently engaged in sexually deviant behavior than boys. In a related study, the rate of conduct disorder in children ages 4 to 11 was 6.5 percent for boys and 1.8 percent for girls; at ages 12 to 16 the rates were 10.4 percent and 4.1 percent, respectively (Offord, Adler, & Boyle, 1986; Offord, Boyle, & Rancine, 1991). These subsequent investigations confirm the previous findings reported by Robins (1966).

Pajer (1998) challenged the notion that antisocial behavior in adolescent girls was rare. In addition, Zoccolillo (1993) reported that conduct disorder (CD) was the second most common diagnosis given to adolescent girls. A related study found that 8 percent of 17-year-old girls in a sample met the criteria for CD (Kashani, Oraschel, Rosenberg, & Reid, 1989). Finally, a large epidemiological study of 15-year-old boys and girls found that 7.5 percent to 9.5 percent of the girls met the criteria for CD compared with 8.6 percent to 12.2 percent of the boys (Fergusson & Lynskey, cited in Pajer, 1998).

Silverthorn and Frick suggested that antisocial girls have a later age of onset for antisocial behavior and less aggression than their adolescent boy counterparts (cited in Salekin et al., 1997). They maintained that boys exhibited antisocial behavior with aggression, whereas girls engaged in antisocial acts such as stealing (Salekin et al., 1997). Rutherford et al. (1995) indicated that the diagnostic criteria for ASPD were validated on men and then applied to women. These researchers argued that although the same criteria are used to diagnose both males and females, studies have not established that the same consistency exists between childhood and adult antisocial behaviors for women (Rutherford et al., 1995). Moreover, these investigators suggested that the current criteria for conduct disorder and the various paths to ASPD were different for women as opposed to men. This finding was based on the clear observation of ASPD criteria in adulthood but with few of the specified childhood behaviors (Rutherford et al., 1995).

Gender-Role Stereotypes

The differences in the diagnosis of ASPD for women versus men have been attributed to various factors. One factor includes gender-role stereotypes. As previously mentioned, women are traditionally defined as passive and nurturing, compared with the more aggressive and destructive characteristics attributed to men. Historically, society has had a difficult time accepting the prospect that women can be violent criminal offenders (Smart, 1977). Indeed, the diagnostic labels of psychopath or antisocial personality disorder are said to represent more despicable subgroups of criminals (Leaff, 1978). Classifications such as these are even further removed from the typical stereotypes of woman, including those who kill.

The stigma attached to antisocial behavior and then assigned to female offenders contradicts the typical conceptualization of a woman. As Toch (1998, p. 151) explained: "Psychopathy is a wildly pejorative designation because individuals described with this designation are presumptively sleazy, unsavory, repugnant, and dangerous." Moreover, Arrigo & Shipley (2001) noted that the diagnosis of ASPD (psychopathy) evolved into a morally reprehensible category, especially when used to indicate an offender with a particular set of personality traits predisposing the person to long-term criminality.

Women's Characteristics and Symptomatology

Another factor postulated to affect the different prevalence rates between men and women is the dissimilar displays of their symptomatology (Mulder et al., 1994). Some investigators report that women are symptomatically similar to men; however, their absolute symptom rates are lower (Mulder et al., 1994). For example, when comparing women with and without ASPD with men with and without the diagnosis, the rate of deviance among male ASPD subjects was greater than that in their ASPD female counterparts (Mulder et al., 1994; Robins et al., 1991). Moreover, there was a sharper contrast in deviant behaviors or personality traits among women with ASPD than those without the diagnosis. Thus, whereas men were more likely to engage in deviant behaviors in general, those with ASPD were more likely to engage in adult criminal offenses.

Mulder et al. (1994) conducted a study in which 22 males and 22 females who met the criteria for ASPD were identified in a general population survey. Characteristics of the women with ASPD were compared with the diagnosable men, as well as with the rest of the community sample. The results were as follows: the overall lifetime prevalence rate for ASPD was 3.1 percent (males 4.2 percent, females 1.9 percent). Rates of ASPD declined with age: for those over 45 years of age, there was no one with ASPD; for those ages 25 to 44 years, 3.9 percent were diagnosed with this condition; for those ages 18 to 24, 5.7 percent were diagnosed with ASPD.

Mudler et al. (1994) also controlled for a number of social variables in their analysis. For example, those persons with ASPD who were married (especially women) were prone to higher rates of marital breakdown. In addition, women with ASPD were about 4 times as likely as individuals without ASPD to receive state checks. Also, these women were less likely to be educated and to have full-time employment. Then, too, women with ASPD were significantly more likely to live in rented housing than women without ASPD.

Both men and women with ASPD were substantially less likely than those without ASPD to have been raised by both parents until the age of 15. Rutter (1998) found that lack of contact with the father or poor health experienced by the parents increased the chances of antisocial behavior in boys, whereas early removal from the mother and the residential care setting of the child predisposed girls to antisocial behavior (Mulder et al., 1994). For women, relationship troubles were pervasive, followed by job problems, violence, and lying.

Comorbidity

When investigating the coexistence of other mental disorders, both men and women had much greater rates of lifetime drug and alcohol disorders (Mulder et al., 1994). However, for women with ASPD, the rate was almost 10 times greater than for those without ASPD. Men with this psychiatric condition were only 3 times more likely to abuse alcohol than their male non-ASPD counterparts. In addition, women with ASPD were significantly more likely to have met the diagnostic criteria for major depression than those women without the disorder. This was not the case for males with versus without ASPD. Women and men with ASPD were found to have increased rates of phobia (only significant for women). Mulder et al. (1994) explained that this finding contradicts the traditional view postulated by Cleckley (1950) that persons with ASPD are less likely to be anxious or fearful.

Mulder et al. (1994) noted that both genders had higher rates of suicidal ideation (thoughts of suicide) and suicide attempts. However, they pointed out that the suicidal ideation might stem from a comorbid disorder rather than from pure ASPD symptomatology. Women diagnosed with ASPD more frequently received psychiatric care both as inpatients and as outpatients, albeit for other psychiatric reasons not linked to ASPD symptomatology. Overall, women with ASPD were more likely to have been identified with comorbid psychiatric disorders for which they received mental health services.

Cloninger and Guze (1970b) found that out of 66 female felons, sociopathy or hysteria was found in 80 percent of the women. Sociopathy alone was found in 39 percent, hysteria alone in 15 percent, and both disorders were found in 26 percent of the women (Cloninger & Guze, 1970b). According to this study, 40 percent of the women with sociopathy also had comorbid hysteria. The investigators concluded that there was a significant relationship between sociopathy and hysteria. Today we recognize these conditions as ASPD and somatization/histrionic personality disorder, respectively.

The women in the Cloniger and Guze (1970b) study ranged from 17 to 54 years of age, with 75 percent of them between the ages of 20 and 35. The age range is significant because many researchers find that traits and behaviors of ASPD (psychopathy) diminish at middle age, usually around the midforties (APA, 1994; Serin, 1991). Family histories also provided information relevant to their diagnoses. Sixty-five percent of the women reported that at least one of their parents was absent from the household before they reached 18 years of age (Cloninger & Guze, 1970a). Moreover, parental antisocial behavior was common. On the basis of identified family history (drinking, work behavior, abuse, neglect, incarceration), the biological fathers of 55 percent of the women were given a suspected diagnosis of sociopathy or suspected alcoholism. Twenty-seven percent of the biological mothers received the same suspected diagnoses. Overall, more mothers (76 percent) than fathers (59 percent) for the female felons studied received some type of psychiatric diagnosis (Cloninger & Guze, 1970a).

School and work histories were also gathered through structured interviewing. On the basis of these data, Cloninger and Guze (1970a) found that low academic achievement was common, with 55 percent of the women having failed at least one or more subjects in school. In addition, the 66 women in the sample attended 271 primary and secondary schools. In assessing work history prior to incarceration, the researchers noted that 55 percent were unemployed and that 33 percent were on welfare. In addition, 47 percent of the women had been fired from a job at least once for poor performance (Cloninger & Guze, 1970a).

Many of the variables that were specifically found for the sociopathic women were either directly or indirectly related to the findings of the diagnoses (Cloninger & Guze, 1970b). For instance, 56 percent of those diagnosed were African American compared with 26 percent for other ethnicities combined. Seventy percent of sociopathic women versus 22 percent of other women had not lived with their parents the entire time while growing up. Although not indicative of antisocial behavior, 28 percent of the sociopathic women had a history of homosexual experiences compared with only 4 percent for all other women.

Substance abuse and delinquency were also found more frequently among the women in the Cloninger and Guze (1970b) sample. For instance, drinking problems were more common among sociopathic women (67 percent versus 22 percent). More specifically, drinking problems for Caucasian women (79 percent) were greater than for African American women (58 percent). In addition, the sociopathic women were more likely to have had problems in school and with the legal system, such as repeated fighting, juvenile and other arrest records, reform school, and prostitution.

Those women who had comorbid sociopathy and hysteria were more likely to report being raised in foster care or in an orphanage (Cloninger & Guze, 1970b). They also exhibited more histrionic personality traits. Histrionic personality disorder is characterized by "a pattern of excessive emotionality and attention seeking" (APA, 1994, p. 629). Fifty-three percent of these women reported the loss of both parents by the age of 18, compared with 18 percent for the other women. However, Cloninger and Guze (1970b) indicated that although female offenders with sociopathy and hysteria had similar backgrounds and lifestyles, the features for the diagnostic criteria for the 2 disorders were different. For instance, those with sociopathy had more extensive antisocial and criminal behaviors, whereas those with hysteria frequently reported recurrent symptoms in many of their bodily organs (Cloninger & Guze, 1970b).

Additional research has examined the relationship between ASPD and comorbidity. For example, Lilienfeld, Van Valkenburg, Larntz, and Akiskal (1986) conducted a study looking at the association between ASPD, somatization disorder, and histrionic personality disorder (HPD) in individuals and families among 250 psychiatric patients. These participants were interviewed in various inpatient, outpatient, and consultation settings. The relationship between ASPD and somatization disorder was significant for both men and women.

Indeed, individuals with somatization disorder were far more likely than those without it to have at least one first-degree relative with ASPD. A significant association was also found between ASPD and HPD within individuals. However, the relationship between HPD and the likelihood of having a first-degree relative with ASPD was not significant. In addition, ASPD and somatization disorder were only significantly associated in individuals without HPD.

Lilienfeld et al. (1986) suggested that individuals with HPD were likely to develop either ASPD or somatization disorder, depending primarily on the sex of the person. For instance, the investigators noted that men with HPD were more likely to develop ASPD and that women with HPD were more likely to develop somatization disorder. Thus, they concluded that considerable overlap existed between somatization disorder and HPD. However, the strongest association among the personality disorders occurred between ASPD and histrionic personality disorder (Lilienfeld et al., 1986).

More recently, Hamburger, Lilienfeld, and Hogben (1996) have indicated that ASPD and HPD coexist much more frequently than is expected by chance. Whereas ASPD consistently is found to be more common among males, HPD consistently is found to be more common among females (Hamburger et al., 1996).

It is interesting that some researchers suggest that the sex differences are attributable to gender biases in the criteria for diagnosis (Kaplan, 1983a). Other commentators (Warner, 1978) maintain that clinicians are biased in their application of the diagnostic criteria. Still other researchers contend that "ASPD and HPD represent caricatures of gender role stereotypes" (Hamburger et al., 1996, p. 42).

Gender Bias in Diagnosing

A number of social scientists allege that the relationship between HPD and ASPD in women is related to gender bias in the DSM-III-R (APA, 1987) and DSM-IV (APA, 1994) personality disorders (e.g., Hamilton, Rothbart, & Dawes, 1986). In brief, the debate stems from whether the diagnosis of the two psychiatric conditions is a result of actual base rates that reflect differences in men and women (Chodoff, 1982; Williams & Spitzer, 1983) or whether it is the product of gender bias in diagnosing (Kaplan, 1983a, 1983b). In this final subsection, we review several of the more relevant studies on the matter.

Warner (1978) examined the issue of sex bias in the DSM-II diagnoses for ASPD and hysteria. A hypothetical case history consisting of mixed features of both disorders was distributed to 175 mental health professionals. Eight diagnoses were given as choices, including ASPD and hysteria. When the patient was described as female, she received the hysterical diagnosis 76 percent of the time and the ASPD diagnosis 22 percent of the time. When the patient was described as male, he received the hysterical diagnosis 49 percent of the time and the ASPD diagnosis 41 percent of the time. As a result of these findings, Warner (1978, p. 842) concluded that a "tendency [existed] for therapists to perceive men as antisocial personalities and women as hysterical personalities even when the patients ha[d] identical features."

In responding to Kaplan's (1983a) critique of the DSM-III, Williams and Spitzer (1983) asserted that the differences in prevalence rates by gender were not necessarily influenced by sex bias. They further explained that social, cultural, biological, and genetic variables might be sex specific to some extent, causing disorders that involve extreme stereotypic feminine or masculine traits to occur more commonly in men or women (see also, Ford & Widiger, 1989). In addition, researchers thought that the DSM-III's diagnostic criteria were more direct and specific. However, they concluded that there was still a great deal of ambiguity in the diagnostic criteria for personality disorders (Ford & Widiger, 1989).

Kaplan (1983b) stated that histrionic personality disorder and dependent personality disorder are congruent with stereotypes of femininity. She further explained that criteria for these disorders, unlike those for ASPD, are perceived by some clinicians as the standard for women and even perhaps the goals for psychotherapy. Moreover, Kaplan (1983b, p. 802) provided additional observations on the DSM-III's diagnostic criteria for disorders as they relate to women, including vulnerability "to clinicians' (value-laced) intuition." As she concluded, "there is a connection between the fact that women's treatment rates for mental disorders are higher than men's and the fact that our diagnostic criteria reflect the male-centered culture in which they were created and used" (Kaplan, 1983a, p. 803).

Ford and Widiger (1989) conducted a study to assess the bias and base rate explanations in the differential prevalence of HPD and ASPD among men and women.

Randomly assigned male and female case histories varying in their ambiguity for the ASPD and HPD diagnoses were administered to 354 psychologists with different theoretical orientations (e.g., psychodynamic and cognitive-behavioral). The psychologists were either to diagnose the hypothetical patient as one of nine DSM-III disorders (including HPD and ASPD) or to rate the extent to which specific features taken from the case studies met 10 histrionic and antisocial diagnostic criteria.

Ford & Widiger (1989) found that there was a definite tendency for the psychologists to diagnose women with HPD and not with ASPD, even when the cases presented more antisocial than histrionic traits (Ford & Widiger, 1989). Although a tendency existed not to diagnose men with HPD, the researchers concluded that sex biases were more visibly evident for the female patients. In addition, they found that no sex biases were detectable for the other seven diagnoses (Ford & Widiger, 1989).

Mulder et al. (1994) indicated that both response bias in reporting symptomatology and treatment seeking by females were possible causes for the differing prevalence rates of ASPD in men versus women. In addition, some commentators contend that a confounding problem exists with past research on the issue of gender bias. In particular, it is onerous to differentiate between various types and sources of gender bias, including diagnostic, assessment, etiologic, or sampling practices (Widiger & Spitzer, 1991).

We note that although there are only a select number of studies on women with psychopathy, the research that does exist demonstrates distinct differences from what we know about psychopathic men (Mulder et al., 1994; Robins, 1966; Rutherford et al., 1995). This notwithstanding, the absence of any detailed and systematic analysis on women is still quite conspicuous and troubling. Moreover, as Mulder et al. (1994) indicate, no matter what the explanations are for the differences in diagnoses, women with ASPD are rarely discussed in the psychiatric literature.

CONCLUSIONS

This chapter explored the ASPD and psychopathy continuum. In particular, the emphasis on behavioral criteria for the ASPD diagnosis versus personality trait criteria determined by the PCL-R was examined. As the concept of psychopathy evolved into the more behaviorally oriented ASPD diagnosis by the DSM-III, DSM-III-R, and the DSM-IV, much of the focus on a narrower group of individuals with enduring personality characteristics was lost. Thus, as Toch (1998, p. 149) observed, "almost any offender in a correctional setting is hypothetically entitled to a diagnosis of antisocial personality disorder."

In addition, the chapter examined ASPD construct from a number of psychological perspectives. These theoretical orientations told us a great deal about how researchers understand the diagnosis of antisocial personality disorder and the construct of psychopathy. The chapter concluded by reviewing the literature on gender, including the problem of stereotypes when diagnosing ASPD (psychopathy) for men versus women. Several disturbing trends reappear, suggesting that mental health professionals are disinclined to recognize the appropriateness of assigning the ASPD label to women (including those who offend), notwithstanding evidence to the contrary. This practice is exacerbated by the dearth of empirical and related studies specifically focused on ASPD, women, and offender behavior.

Commenting on psychopathy, Cleckley (1982, p. 150) once stated that "the large group of maladjusted personalities whom I have personally studied and to whom this diagnosis has been consistently applied differs distinctly from a group of ordinary criminals." Accordingly, we note that not all psychopaths engage in criminal activity. However, for purposes of our inquiry, the discussion of ASPD (psychopathy) refers to those who do commit crimes, including predatory homicide. Our case study assessment focuses on those women (especially Aileen Wuornos) who meet the DSM-IV diagnosis of ASPD. The behavioral criteria for this diagnosis are largely met by the predatory homicides these women commit. The more in-depth personality characteristics of psychopathy are also applicable to our investigation. To date, the PCL-R has been validated only on men. In addition, its predescribed categories for both personality and behavioral features may not embody the experience of women. These comments aside, the next chapter endeavors to delineate what we do know about ASPD (psychopathy) and women who kill.

5

Understanding ASPD (Psychopathy) and Homicide

❖

INTRODUCTION

This chapter discusses the relationship between ASPD (psychopathy) and homicide for women. In particular, the chapter tentatively discusses several aspects of the ASPD-crime association, delineating the context within which the two phenomena appear to be inseparable. The chapter also explores Meloy's (1992) work on predatory violence and the psychopath. Relatedly, empirical studies documenting the relationship between psychopathic males and homicide are presented. Both sets of material provide a useful basis within which to assess the psychopathic female killer. Along these lines, the chapter includes a detailed review of Eronen's (1995) study, analyzing the link between mental disorders (ASPD) and homicide among women. The chapter concludes by speculatively suggesting what direction the research on female homicide offenders diagnosed with ASPD (psychopathy) must take, if the problems posed by these offenders are to be more adequately understood.

ASPD AND CRIME: ARE THE TWO INSEPARABLE?

The diagnosis of ASPD is unquestionably pejorative (Grinspoon & Bakalar, 1978). Indeed, those assigned this diagnosis are interpreted by many as the worst subclass of criminals (Arrigo & Shipley, 2001; Grinspoon & Bakalar, 1978). This designation is often fueled by the lack of remorse or empathy that these offenders display toward their victims, particularly when committing homicide. Unlike other mental disorders, ASPD is so closely connected with criminal behavior that "people who are first socially defined as criminals on account of their acts come to be psychiatrically diagnosed as antisocial on account of their personalities" (Grinspoon & Bakalar, 1978, p. 235). Thus, the association between crime and ASPD seems somewhat axiomatic.

Researchers contend that the nature or personality of those with ASPD makes the likelihood of violence much greater (Leaff, 1978; Rice & Harris, 1997). Moreover, some investigators suggest that an automatic connection exists between ASPD and crime (Leaff, 1978). To be sure, crime is one of the strongest indicators that antisocial personality is diagnosable, as it is heavily weighted on criminal behaviors (Shipley & Arrigo, 2001). The characteristics of ASPD (psychopathy); including, a lack of guilt or feelings of anxiety, the manipulation of others, and a focus only on oneself, enable those with this psychiatric condition to minimize the suffering of others (Arrigo & Shipley, 2001). In fact, Eissler maintained that when a psychopath is prevented from acting out, the individual becomes depressed and panicked (cited in Leaff, 1978). Commenting on this behavioral tendency in a young adult psychopath, Eissler stated that, "Sporadic or periodic destructiveness was an indispensable requirement for his maintaining a balanced feeling of well being and of being in contact with reality" (cited in Leaff, 1978, p. 85). Once again, we are drawn to the apparent propensity of ASPD (psychopathic) individuals to act violently and criminally.

Physical harm to others in the adult life of a psychopath can frequently be traced to patterns of cruelty to animals or others during childhood (Arrigo & Shipley, 2001; Leaff, 1978). In some instances, other adolescents or animals have been the targets of sadistic acts (Leaff, 1978). As children, psychopathic individuals are frequently belligerent and ready to fight (Forth & Mailloux, 2000). Addressing the phenomenon of psychopathy and violence, Hare and Hart (1993, p. 106) noted that "Given the characteristics of psychopathy listed in the PCL-R, it comes as no surprise that the disorder is implicated in the disproportionate amount of serious repetitive crime and violence."

Chapter 3 helped us understand the relationship between ASPD (psychopathy) and crime for women. Chapter 1 helped us understand gender differences in aggression, especially as a basis from which to explore female criminality. In particular, types of direct and indirect aggression were examined, and the connection between aggression and violence was made. However, we did not assess the association between affective and predatory aggression. Predatory aggression is relatively rare in men and women, since its primary purpose is to obtain food for other animals (Meloy, 1992). As we will see, discussing this form of aggression is important in comprehending predator homicide, including the murderous acts committed by women.

PREDATORY AGGRESSION

Meloy (1992) described predatory aggression and its relationship to psychopathy in his classic text, *The Psychopathic Mind*. Predatory aggression usually occurs between species, the exception occurring with humans. This phenomenon is based on "affective aggression," which is described as "an intense and patterned sympathetic activation of the autonomic nervous system due to external or internal threatening stimuli" (Meloy, 1992, p. 192). In other words, this type of aggression occurs when a person feels threatened or is frightened into action. In short, it is what underlies most human violence (Meloy, 1992). Predatory aggression and subsequent violence in humans can be marked by a number of characteristics. In what follows, we briefly describe these components.

Minimal or Absent Autonomic Arousal

In predatory aggression, there is an absence of sympathetic arousal for the autonomic nervous system. This system controls the "fight or flight" response. It is possible for an individual to go from predatory aggression to affective aggression once contact with the victim has been made. Meloy (1992) reported that this reaction is common among sexual psychopaths who are predatorily violent until they have actual physical contact with their victims. At this point, a psychological and physiological shift to a state of affective aggression and violence occurs, given sensory-perceptual triggers (e.g., touching or smelling the victim).

However, predatory aggression can also follow affective aggression (Meloy, 1992). For example, this happens when an explosively violent act is followed by a calmer, predatory mode. Meloy indicated that the shift could occur either as an attempt to satisfy more sadistic impulses in relation to the victim or to deceive forensic investigators in an attempt to conceal the motives for the affective violence. The shifting of aggressive modes is determined by interpersonal factors.

No Conscious Experience of Emotion

The person who engages in predatory violence will retrospectively report an absence of emotion for which he or she is consciously aware. Any emotion that is experienced is usually described as exhilaration, occurring prior to the actual violence, when the victim is stalked. For instance, Theodore Bundy, a convicted sexual psychopath, stated that "The fantasy that accompanies and generates the anticipation that precedes the crime is always more stimulating than the immediate aftermath of the crime itself" (cited in Meloy, 1992, p. 214). In contrast, individuals who commit an affectively violent act are overcome with emotion. Examples include rage, shame, fear, and the like.

Planned and Purposeful Violence

Predatory violence has a reason; it is planned and it is intentional. Planned and purposeful violence is not caused by a perceived threat from the victim. Meloy (1992) described the intentionality of the event by the attacker's control over when the violence occurred, against whom it was targeted, and what was the extent of harm. However, he also acknowledged that the violence may have had various unconscious or defensive purposes. For example, it might have been employed as a way to fulfill vengeful or retributive fantasies. Alternatively, it may have been experienced as a compulsion (necessary, repetitive behavior) in order to attain a sense of well-being (Meloy, 1992). Serial killers frequently exhibit a compulsion to kill in which they report feeling driven to commit murder for various reasons.

Another form of intent in predatory aggression is discernible in the need to obtain ultimate control over the victim through manipulation and deception. This type of control may also be used for personal or material gain, rather than for internal reasons. When predatory violence is employed for profit or as a means to an end, it is an exercise of intent by the perpetrator. Organized crime is a notorious illustration of this type of violence (Arrigo, 2004). Meloy (1992, p. 218) characterized these activities as "socially and environmentally stimulated homicides." Indeed, they are the most external and detached form of murder.

No or Minimally Perceived Threat

Meloy (1992) described this characteristic as the experience of being actively sought (stalked), rather than reactively attacked as a victim. Movement by the attacker is necessary to come into physical contact with the party harmed. The attacker in no way feels threatened by the victim.

Multidetermined and Variable Goals

Predatory violence is distinct from affective violence. The latter form of aggression has the sole objective of reducing perceived threat (Meloy, 1992). However, as we previously explained, predatory violence can have multiple conscious and unconscious purposes. It can fulfill vengeful fantasies, provide relief from compulsive drives, facilitate the exercise of control, and promote personal or monetary gain. The goals of predatory violence can also be influenced by environmental or other situational factors. Factors that can prompt and perpetuate this type of violence include, among others, religious beliefs, cultural values, media representations, criminal subcultures, aggressive families, and socioeconomic stressors (Meloy, 1992, p. 221).

Minimal or Absent Displacement of the Target of Aggression

In brief, this phenomenon refers to the fact that the target of predatory violence is not likely to be displaced or abandoned for an easier or more accessible victim. Indeed, despite the motivation of the aggressor, the injured party will be more tenaciously sought. This occurrence is the result of three factors (Meloy, 1992). First, the lack of autonomic or emotional arousal inhibits the individual from being fearful or relenting as a result of perceived consequences. Second, the goals of predatory violence are more object specific than those of affective violence. Third, the selective, sensory perception of those exhibiting predatory violence results in "tunnel" vision directed toward the selected victim (p. 224).

A Time-Unlimited Behavioral Sequence

The lack of autonomic arousal or affective arousal does not put the attack on a limited time basis. The physiological changes associated with autonomic arousal in affective violence do not factor into the predatory attack. The individual does not act out as a result of a strong emotional response that eventually subsides. Instead, the attack is restricted only by the attacker's capacity to inflict the violence.

Preceded or Followed by Private Ritual

To prepare for a predatory attack, some aggressors may select objects such as clothing, jewelry, unusual weapons, makeup, and the like. Psychostimulants are sometimes ingested prior to the violent attack. This practice is particularly common among psychopathic individuals (Meloy, 1992). The objects involved become associated with feelings of power and importance for the person. The object(s) used by the predator may become a fetish that "rekindles sexual fantasies that are then acted out during the predatory violence with the actual victim" (Meloy, 1992, p. 226; see also, Arrigo & Purcell, 2001; Hickey, 1997). For many of these attackers, the victim is also objectified as something to dominate and control. In some instances, a postmortem positioning of the victim's body represents a ritual that occurs after the predatory violence (Arrigo, 2004; Hickey, 1997).

A Primary Cognitive Dimension

This characteristic highlights the unique nature of human predatory violence. It includes rational thought, fantasy, and planned, goal-directed behavior (Meloy, 1992). In other words, unlike predatory violence found in other animals, there is a significant cognitive dimension to this type of violence when perpetrated by humans.

Heightened and Focused Sensory Awareness

Predatory aggressors are vigilant in their sensory awareness of their victim. The fixed, indistractability of an animal stalking its prey illustrates this phenomenon. Indeed, the aggressor is singularly focused on and mesmerized by her target. Typically, elements of sadism are found in human predatory violence (Meloy, 1992). Brenman found that "cruelty is maintained because omnipotence is felt to be superior to love, depression is defended against, and grievance and revenge are sanctified" (cited in Meloy, 1992, p. 231). In a letter written by serial killer David Berkowitz, the experience of focused sensory awareness is vividly depicted:

> While shooting these people, I actually became transfixed with the event. The report of the gun, the screams, the shattering of glass and windshields, the blaring horn, it all just possessed my mind so that I'd take no notice of anything else. (cited in Meloy, 1992, p. 231)

Self and Object Concept Dedifferentiation

During the predatory attack, the victim is frequently incorporated into the grandiose self-structure of the attacker, particularly with psychopathic and narcissistic individuals (Meloy, 1992). For example, this element occurs when an assailant selects victims according to a particular physical stereotype based on an internalized idea of someone who wronged the person. Despite a lack of attachment to the target, the individual will render the victim "a ragefully devalued, or enviously idealized, object" (Meloy, 1992, p. 232).

Unimpaired Reality Testing

In some cases of predatory violence, this element occurs when the aggressor cannot conceptualize the victim as a whole individual or human being, deserving of empathetic regard. Meloy (1992) argued that this characteristic is most likely in aggressively psychopathic individuals as a result of grandiose perceptions of self-importance. In addition, this is a common pattern of violent psychopathic behavior motivated by instrumental gain or revenge. Meloy (1992) further indicated that the reasonable person usually describes the level of violence as heinous.

Heightened Self-esteem

Humans who exhibit predatory violence are often associated with an inflated sense of self-worth. Factors such as narcissistic or psychopathic personality structures, fantasized violence, and goal attainment all add to the perceived sense of confidence and sadistic pleasure during the predatory attack (Meloy, 1992).These elements are consistent with a heightened sense of self-valuation.

Psychopathic Suitability for Predatory Violence

Meloy (1992) concluded that the preceding characteristics regarding predatory violence make it painfully clear that psychopathy is well-suited to predation. As he observed, "It is my hypothesis that the psychopathic process predisposes, precipitates, and perpetuates predatory violence by virtue of its structural and dynamic characteristic" (Meloy, 1992, p. 236). He further postulated that hyporeactivity of autonomic arousal experienced by psychopathic individuals could sustain the stalking of the victim. Fear and anxiety would not interfere with the predation. Moreover, while the psychopathic characteristic of splitting or warding off emotion might be an adaptive function in an abusive or a neglectful childhood, in adulthood it might represent an extremely maladaptive response. Meloy suggested that this ability allows the psychopath to be devoid of emotion during predatory violence and to experience exhilaration during the stalking phase of the violence.

The psychopath's perceived malice toward others sustains the planned, goal-directed, and instrumental quality of the assailant's predatory violence (Gacono, 2000; Meloy, 1992). Moreover, as Meloy (1992) explained, the sense of the other's evil and vile intentions directed toward the offender, fuels, rather than extinguishes, the killer's plan to commit a violent act. Predatory violence is not a product of an "alarm state," and the aggressor faces many factors that could moderate the desire to act out violently toward others (Meloy, 1992, p. 237).

Hypervigilant suspicion is also attributed to the psychopath who is unconsciously fearful of being the victim of the predation. Meloy (1992) suggested that this tendency is the result of the person's own continual processing of aggressive and sadistic thoughts and fantasies. For example, if the motivation for the violence is revenge or monetary gain, then the psychopath desires to render another person powerless, thereby feeling omnipotent.

Arguably, one of the most significant factors predisposing the psychopathic individual to predatory violence is the lack of attachment or affective bonding with another person (Meloy, 1992). This relationship is the result of several factors. First, the inability to empathize with the victim allows the individual harmed to be devalued. In addition, the lack of empathy makes sadistic gratification possible by way of the violent acts.

Second, the aggressive interactions of the psychopathic individual combined with the individual's profound detachment from the experience of others are likely predictors of recurrently cruel exchanges. Frequently, these interactions include little affection and a large potential for predation (Meloy, 1992). Third, the psychopath's ability to detach from other people increases the chances that he or she will treat the victim of predatory violence much like an object in a private ritual. Finally, the predatory violence, especially if it benefits from media attention, receives public fascination, and results in societal fear, will only serve to strengthen the psychopathic person's conceptualization that he or she is "larger than life" (Meloy, 1992, p. 240). In some instances, psychopathic individuals may believe that being mythologized in the media is their only opportunity to achieve notoriety.

In a related publication, Stone (1998) argued that ASPD and other personality pathology (including psychopathy) are important to comprehending some of society's most heinous murderers. After creating personality profiles from the biographies of 300 homicide offenders, he concluded that personality is a critical component in the motivation to kill (Stone, 1998). Based on Meloy's (1992) analysis, we fully agree with this assessment.

PSYCHOPATHIC MALES AND HOMICIDE

The strong association between psychopathy and predatory violence in males, particularly homicide, has been demonstrated by a number of researchers (Arrigo, 2004). For example, Yarvis (1995) compared the patterns of the DSM-III's Axis I and II psychopathology in 78 male homicide offenders, 92 rapists, and 10 males who raped and then killed their victims. In order to determine a diagnosis, Yarvis interviewed the subjects and their significant others, as well as read various archival data, including military, educational, medical, psychiatric, and police records. The highest rates of ASPD were found in rapist/murderers. All murders and two-thirds of the rapist/murderers showed some type of Axis II personality disorder.

In addition, Cote and Hodgins (1992) conducted a study evaluating the lifetime prevalence of major mental disorders among 87 male prisoners convicted for homicide compared with 373 prisoners who had never been convicted of murder. The Diagnostic Interview Schedule (DIS) was used to determine whether or not a major mental disorder existed. The rates of major mental disorders were higher in persons convicted of homicide, and the disorders typically existed prior to the actual murder (Cote & Hodgins, 1992). Moreover, the participants convicted of homicide exhibited more major depression and ASPD (Cote & Hodgins, 1992).

Geberth, Vernon, and Turco (1997) examined the crime scene behaviors and case histories of 68 male serial murderers to establish similarities in the psychological makeup and personal backgrounds of these individuals. In addition, characteristics that were congruent with the clinical criteria of ASPD, sexual sadism, and narcissism were identified. The sources of data consisted of crime scene photographs, police files, confidential police reports, and psychiatric/psychological reports. Through a case history evaluation method, the researchers found that the offenders exhibited aggressive and antisocial behaviors during childhood that evolved into elements of sexual sadism in adulthood. The pattern and manner of killing revealed domination, control, humiliation, and sadistic sexual violence (Geberth et al., 1997). In addition, the investigators concluded that the murders were carried out with little guilt or shame and with a total lack of remorse.

Firestone, Bradford, Greenberg, and Larose (1998) compared the psychological and diagnostic features of 48 homicidal sex offenders with a comparison group of incest offenders. Historical data, criminal histories, psychological inventories, and DSM diagnoses were obtained for both groups. With respect to ASPD (psychopathy), the PCL-R interviewers rated the homicidal sex offenders as significantly more psychopathic than the incest offenders on personality traits and antisocial behavior (Firestone et al., 1998). In addition, police records showed that the homicidal sex offenders had been charged with or convicted of other crimes both violent and nonviolent (Firestone et al., 1998).

Gacono, Meloy, Sheppard, and Speth (1995) studied the clinical characteristics and institutional behaviors of 18 successful insanity malingerers compared with 18 nonmalingering insanity acquittees in order to examine the relationship between psychopathy and malingering. The PCL-R was administered, and demographic and historical data were gathered for purposes of the study. The results indicated that insanity malingerers were more likely to have a history of murder or rape and to suffer from ASPD or sexual sadism. The PCL-R scores of insanity malingerers also suggested a greater presence of aggressive narcissism and antisocial lifestyle than in the nonmalingering insanity acquittees (Gacono et al., 1995). Moreover, the total PCL-R scores for the insanity malingerers were greater than for their nonmalingering counterparts (Gacono et al., 1995). Higher scores on the PCL-R suggest an increased degree of psychopathy. In a related study by Gacono (1992), serial killers experienced depression, conduct disorder as children, and problems with attachment. In addition, a need for power and control, a lack of empathy, a reliance on fantasy, and a tendency to engage in antisocial behaviors were all common among those in this homicide offender group.

Although far from exhaustive, the preceding studies demonstrate that a clear connection has been drawn in the relevant literature between predatory violence (particularly sexual homicide), ASPD (psychopathy), and men. Books, articles, and other forms of popular media have catapulted the male psychopathic killer into a mythological figure of tremendous fear and widespread curiosity. Of note, however, is that the construct of psychopathy only recently has been applied to women, especially during the past few years. The primary means of establishing psychopathy in an individual, the PCL-R, was validated on men (Arrigo & Shipley, 2001; Hare, 1991). Although the PCL-R has been used for limited research on women, it has yet to be validated on this population.

ASPD (PSYCHOPATHY) AND FEMALE-PERPETRATED HOMICIDE: REVIEWING THE LITERATURE

In Eronen's (1995, p. 1216) research addressing the phenomenon of female killers and antisocial personality disorder (psychopathy), he indicated that "female homicidal behavior has remained poorly studied." Small samples and the fact that murderous conduct is less common in women than in men are thought to contribute to this predicament. The purpose of Eronen's (1995) inquiry was to establish whether or not a definable connection existed between particular DSM-III-R disorders and female homicidal behavior. Eronen reviewed the forensic psychiatric evaluations of 127 female homicide offenders in Finland, over a 13-year period. From January 1, 1980, to December 31, 1992, the number of Finnish murders and manslaughters totaled 1,631. The Finnish police identified 97 percent of the offenders (1,579). Out of these identified offenders, 130 were female. However, in 3 cases the same individual committed more than one murder. Thus, Eronen investigated a total of 127 cases of female homicide.

Eronen (1995) reported that in Finland, an initial psychiatric evaluation is required for almost every homicide offender, in order to determine whether a more extensive evaluation is needed. On average, these examinations are initiated 5 months from the time that the offenders commit the crime for which they were arrested (i.e., the index offense). Approximately 3 percent of the individuals charged are later found not guilty (Eronen, 1995).

During the evaluation, the homicide offender undergoes an extensive psychiatric interview. In addition, the examinations include (a) standardized psychological tests such as the WAIS (test of intelligence), Rorschach (projective test of psychopathology), and the MMPI-2 (objective test of psychopathology); (b) laboratory tests to determine physical condition such as blood tests, EEG (electroencephalogram, which measures brain waves); and (c) observations of hospital staff for 4 to 8 weeks. If the diagnostic criteria are not met for a DSM-III-R diagnosis, the forensic psychiatrist is instructed not to make a diagnosis of a mental disorder (Eronen, 1995, p. 1216).

Results for this study were based on odds ratios calculated from 1-month prevalence estimates for DSM-III disorders obtained from the U.S. Epidemiological Catchment Area (ECA) study, previously mentioned in this chapter. Although Eronen's (1995) study was based on a Finnish population, he reported that the Finnish prevalence rates did not differ significantly from the figures obtained from the ECA research and other studies from the United States and Canada. To substantiate his position, Eronen cited examples such as the prevalence rates of alcohol abuse/dependence in a recent Finnish study, explaining that they were the same as those given in the ECA data. We note that this cross-validation has important implications for the applicability of the Finnish findings in relation to female homicide offenders in the United States.

The prevalence of DSM-III-R disorders among female homicide offenders ($N = 127$) was compared with the prevalence among the general population of Finnish women ($N = 2,100,000$). On the basis of detailed odds ratios and confidence intervals of 95 percent, female homicide offenders had about a 10-fold-higher odds ratio than did the general population for schizophrenia or for a personality disorder (Eronen, 1995). Moreover, female homicide offenders were 70 times more likely to have ASPD, alcohol abuse/dependence with personality disorder, and schizophrenia with alcohol abuse/dependence (Eronen, 1995).

The prevalence rates of ASPD for Finnish female homicide offenders were 12.6 percent compared with 0.2 percent in the general population of Finnish women. In addition, the female murderer had a 71.9 odds ratio of suffering from ASPD (Eronen, 1995). Thus, the likelihood of a female homicide offender's having ASPD was considerably greater than that of a woman in the Finnish community.

Eronen (1995) argued that because almost all homicide offenders in Finland were psychiatrically examined, the figures for the most severe mental disorders should be accurate. However, some offenders with milder symptomatology, including some personality disorders, might have been identified during the first psychiatric evaluation as not needing a follow-up evaluation. As a result, the prevalence rates for certain disorders such as alcoholism and some personality disorders could have been greater than what was initially found (Eronen, 1995).

One criticism of this study was the fact that the diagnoses of certain psychiatric conditions, particularly ASPD, were based on the index offense, making the relationship between the diagnosis and homicide somewhat "artifactual" (Eronen, 1995, p. 1217). However, as Eronen (1995) explained, the diagnoses were given only if all of the diagnostic criteria were met. Thus, while the index offense fulfills one of the criteria for ASPD, many other criteria need to be satisfied.

Overall, Eronen (1995) found that mental disorders seem to have a statistical relationship to female homicidal behavior in countries with low crime rates. However, he warned that the odds ratios could not be applied directly to the United States, given this country's high crime rate. Eronen concluded that although women only perpetrate a small fraction of all homicides, certain subgroups among women (e.g., those with ASPD) appear to have a considerably higher risk for murderous conduct.

CONCLUSIONS

The lack of research on female homicide offenders with ASPD in the United States is startling. This fact notwithstanding, Chapter 5 examined what we know about women who kill and who are diagnosed with ASPD or are suffering from psychopathy. In particular, the chapter focused on several dimensions of the ASPD-crime association, arguing that, in many important respects, the two phenomena are inseparable. In addition, the characteristics of Meloy's (1992) predatory violence construct were described. Relatedly, several facets common to this type of violence were matched with the characteristics of the psychopath. Meloy concluded that psychopaths were well-suited to this type of predatory, destructive behavior. The chapter also provided a brief description of several empirical studies examining the association between psychopathy in males and murder, highlighting sexual homicide. Finally, a detailed assessment of Eronen's (1995) study regarding mental disorders (particularly ASPD) in female homicide offenders was presented.

We contend that the relatively small numbers of women identified by the current diagnostic nomenclature, by research, and by clinicians do not tell the full story of homicidal women with *psychopathic* personality traits or those who commit predatory violence. We come to this conclusion on the basis of our assessment of the relevant literature canvassed in Chapters 1 through 5. In other words, when we examine the research on female criminality, ASPD and psychopathy, and women murderers with ASPD (psychopathy), we are led to conclude that the scientific community's knowledge about psychopathic female killers is incomplete.

It is notable that much of what we do know about female-perpetrated predatory homicide, especially for women with ASPD, has failed to investigate the quality of the relationships in the offender's life, especially during childhood and early adolescents. We contend that if our understanding of female killers is to improve, this matter must be given some systemic consideration. As such, Chapter 6 investigates this phenomenon from the psychological perspective of attachment theory. As we explain, the quality, frequency, and intensity of childhood bonds that do or do not form with parents or parental surrogates are extremely important to the formation of one's personality structure. Accordingly, the subsequent chapter reviews what attachment theory is, how it functions, and what its links are to psychopathololgy. We argue that pursuing this line of analysis is quite significant if the scientific community is to understand psychopathic female killers, including women like Aileen Wuornos.

6

Attachment Theory

❖

INTRODUCTION

This chapter focuses on attachment theory, beginning with the work of Bowlby. The theory is described and the categories of childhood attachment styles are developed through the seminal work of Ainsworth et al. (1978). In addition, studies exploring the continuity or discontinuity of attachment patterns over the life span are presented. This explanation is followed by a discussion of research specific to adult attachment. The differences between adult and childhood attachment are elucidated, and the categorization of adult attachment is delineated. Empirical and related literature demonstrating the relationship between adult attachment and psychopathology (personality disorders in particular) is examined. Next, the specific relationship between insecure attachment patterns (i.e., avoidant) and psychopathy is illustrated. In addition, the DSM-IV's reactive attachment disorder (RAD) and attachment disorder as defined by The Attachment Center in Evergreen, Colorado, are briefly explained. The Randolph Attachment Questionnaire and the Attachment Disorder Checklist are then discussed. The neurobiology of attachment, primarily highlighting the work of Schore, also is reviewed.

Although the diagnoses of RAD and attachment disorder are summarized, our inquiry utilizes the attachment patterns described through attachment theory, namely, the work developed by Ainsworth and Main. Even though the disorders are derived from the theory, they are not as descriptive as the theory or the attachment categories. More details regarding the focus on the theory rather than the diagnoses also are provided elsewhere in the subsection on RAD and attachment disorder.

BOWLBY'S ATTACHMENT THEORY

Attachment theory originated from the work of Bowlby, who was trained as a physician and as a psychoanalyst early in the twentieth century when object relations approaches to psychoanalysis were being formed (Levy & Blatt, 1999). In contrast to object relations theory, Bowlby's attachment theory focused on the affective bond formed in close interpersonal relationships (Levy & Blatt, 1999). He also introduced the concept of internal working models. "As a result of early attachment experiences, a child accumulates knowledge and develops a set of expectations (known as 'internal working models') about self, significant others, and the larger social world" (Rothbard & Shaver, 1994, p. 31). Bowlby's work focused on the observable interaction of infants and their primary caregivers (mothers in particular), and his work encouraged others to pursue future studies on the effects of early attachment patterns in relation to personality development (Levy & Blatt, 1999). Bowlby argued that these attachment relationships had a significant effect on the emotional, social, and personality development of an individual.

Attachment theory emerged from Bowlby's observations during World War II, following the deleterious effects that children suffered when temporarily separated from their primary caretakers, typically the mother (Bowlby, 1969). He noted that "the young child's hunger for his mother's love is as great as his hunger for food" and that without her the child experiences "a powerful sense of loss and anger" (Bowlby, 1969, xiii). He identified three distinct and predictable emotional reactions when an infant was separated from its primary caregiver: (a) protest, including crying, active searching, and resistance to the comforting of others; (b) despair, described as a state of passivity and blatant sadness; and (c) detachment, "which involves an active, seemingly defensive disregard for and avoidance of the mother if she returns" (Levy & Blatt, 1999, p. 545).

The central component of attachment theory is that humans maintain an evolutionarily adapted behavioral system, with the primary goal of keeping vulnerable infants in close proximity to their primary caregivers (Rothbard & Shaver, 1994). Infants engage in a variety of behaviors, particularly when they feel threatened, such as signaling, crying, and clinging to the caregiver, in order to elicit protection and closer proximity to this individual (Rothbard & Shaver, 1994). Bowlby (1969) asserted that a set goal for proximity between the infant and caregiver existed. When the child feels safe, the behavioral system is not activated, and the child is able to independently explore his or her environment. However, if the set goal for proximity is exceeded such that the child feels unsafe, this exploratory activity—considered critical for healthy cognitive, social, and emotional development—is dramatically reduced (Rothbard & Shaver, 1994).

The child's healthy development is contingent upon his or her trust in the caregiver's accessibility. When the child cannot rely on the sensitivity and reliability of the caregiver, the child will develop "secondary conditional strategies (e.g., anxious clinging and vigilance, or premature independence)" that become prominent (Rothbard & Shaver, 1994, p. 33). Although these strategies are adaptive in their neglectful caregiving environments, they may cause difficulties in later relationships and situations (Rothbard & Shaver, 1994).

Bowlby (1973) and Ainsworth (1969) postulated that infants develop internal working models that guide expectations about interpersonal relationships that are based on interactions with their attachment figures. These internal working models are the foundation of personality development. Indeed, their durability is based on the child's concept of self and others and on their expectations of interpersonal relationships (Levy & Blatt, 1999). For example, an infant whose needs are typically unmet may formulate a model of others as unreliable and insensitive and of the self as unlovable (Levy & Blatt, 1999).

AINSWORTH ET AL. (1978)/ATTACHMENT CATEGORIES

In accordance with Bowlby's attachment theory, Ainsworth et al. (1978) conducted a study known as the "Strange Situation." The research was designed to enact an infant's attachment behavioral system through several separations from an attachment figure and interactions with a stranger, while attempting to engage the child in exploratory behaviors by presenting many toys to capture the baby's interest (Ainsworth et al., 1978). Initially, the infant was presented with toys when the mother was present. Slowly, over time, a stranger was introduced into the setting, spoke with the mother, and invited the baby to play. Next, the mother left the infant with the stranger and then reunited with the child. The baby was then left alone. Thereafter, the stranger returned, and, at length, the mother returned for a final reunion (Ainsworth et al., 1978).

On the basis of observations of the infant's behaviors during separations and reunions, Ainsworth et al. (1978) established three core patterns of attachment, one secure (63 percent) and 2 insecure, namely, avoidant (21 percent) and anxious/ambivalent (16 percent). Those classified as "secure" were "distressed by separation, s[ought] comfort upon reunion, and explore[d] freely in their caregivers' presence" (Rothbard & Shaver, 1994, p. 34). Those classified as "avoidant" exhibited "little overt distress upon separation and d[id] not seek contact upon reunion. . . . they ke[pt] their attention directed toward toys or other objects, apparently to shift attention away from the wish to establish contact with their attachment figures" (Rothbard & Shaver, 1994, p. 34). Caregivers of avoidant infants tended to reject and ignore their children's attempts to create proximity, particularly close body contact. Finally, "anxious/ambivalent" infants "cr[ied] more often than others, [we]re distressed prior to separation, seem[ed] unable to be reassured or comforted, and [we]re so preoccupied with their caregivers' availability as to reduce or preclude exploration" (Rothbard & Shaver, 1994, p. 34). Their caregivers tended to respond inconsistently to their infants, vacillating between unresponsiveness and being overly affectionate. We note that many researchers representing a number of different cultures have replicated the findings presented by Ainsworth et al. (1978) (e.g., Main, Kaplan, & Cassidy, 1985; Sroufe & Fleeson, 1996; Waters, Wippman, & Sroufe, 1979).

Numerous studies have traced the impact of infant attachment patterns to later functioning in interpersonal relationships. Sroufe (1983) found that securely attached infants were cooperative, well-liked, resilient, and resourceful as preschoolers. Secure toddlers were more enthusiastic, persistent, compliant, and less aggressive (Matas, Arend, & Sroufe, 1978). At age 3.5, secure preschoolers were more likely to be leaders and to be sympathetic to the distress of their peers (Waters et al., 1979). Infants who were insecure avoidant were detached, hostile, and antisocial as preschoolers (Sroufe, 1983). At age 3.5, insecure preschoolers were more socially withdrawn and hesitant with other children (Waters et al., 1979). Finally, insecure anxious/ambivalent infants were identified as passive and helpless preschoolers (Waters et al., 1979).

A study examining the impact of children's attachment patterns at age 12 and 18 months in relation to elementary school aggression found that stressful life situations, inadequate or hostile parental care, and avoidant attachment were significantly related to aggressive behavior in boys (Renken, Egeland, Marvinney, Mangelsdorf, & Sroufe, 1989). Moreover, Erickson, Sroufe, and Egeland (1985) explored the impact of early attachment on subsequent social behavior at school. At the age of 4.5 and 5, avoidantly attached children were significantly more likely to act out, to be withdrawn, and to exhibit attention difficulties. The investigators discovered that the behavior of avoidantly attached children was the most different from securely attached children. In addition, teachers rated these children as more hostile, impulsive, lacking in determination, and withdrawn (Erickson et al., 1985).

THE CONTINUITY OF ATTACHMENT PATTERNS

Research findings support the stability of attachment patterns throughout the life span (Levy & Blatt, 1999). Two longitudinal studies (Elicker, Englund, & Sroufe, 1992; Grossman & Grossman, 1991, respectively) evaluated children over a 10-year period after their involvement with the Strange Situation study (Ainsworth et al. 1978) and found that core personality factors and social interactions were predictable over time. Secure attachments were predictive of more healthy relationships with teachers, parents, and peers. In a study by Waters, Merrick, Albersheim, and Treboux (1995), a 64 percent stability of attachment pattern was found in 50 individuals who were followed for 20 years. Moreover, a meta-analysis indicated that the avoidant/dismissing, secure/autonomous, and preoccupied (anxious/ambivalent) adult categories were stable, with 78 percent to 90 percent of subjects found to be in the same classification at different time periods (Main, 1995). Various factors contribute to the continuity or discontinuity of these patterns over time. Some of them include temperament, ongoing relationships with the same family members, negative life events, inflexible internal working models, and behavior patterns designed to elicit self-fulfilling prophecies (Levy & Blatt, 1999).

Elicker et al.(1992) conducted a study supporting the idea that early attachment patterns were important predictors for later social competence and interpersonal skills. Children classified in attachment patterns at age 12 and 18 months were evaluated again when they were between 10 and 11 years old. Children with secure attachments were more likely to be healthy, social, and competent, whereas children with insecure attachments were not as self-reliant. Moreover, children with avoidant styles demonstrated the poorest levels of interpersonal awareness and sensitivity (Elicker et al., 1992).

Other investigations have demonstrated that stressful life events or changes in family circumstances impact the continuity of the caregiving environment, thereby influencing the stability of a child's attachment patterns (Rothbard & Shaver, 1994). For instance, Erickson et al. (1985) found that a small number of children with secure attachment patterns later indicated insecure attachment patterns and that a small number of children with insecure patterns later demonstrated secure patterns. They examined this phenomenon from a sample of socioeconomically disadvantaged subjects, in which instability was common. Their findings revealed that changes in a caregiver's responsiveness and sensitivity impacted a child's attachment patterns, although not always resulting in an absolute change. For example, a child who developed an insecure attachment pattern might be quite vulnerable for some time, despite better treatment by a primary attachment figure. Additionally, a child with a secure attachment pattern might be more resilient during a period of inadequate caregiving. However, if this shift in caregiver sensitivity continued for a *prolonged* period of time, a shift in attachment patterns could be expected (Erickson et al.,

1995). Egeland and Farber (1984) also found that a mother's personality and emotional makeup influenced the stability of a child's security in an even greater way, as the child got older.

Finally, Lewis and Feiring (1991) demonstrated, particularly in male subjects, that the security of attachment, the environmental factors, and the vulnerability of a child impacted later psychopathology. Only 5 percent of secure males at age 6 showed symptoms of psychopathology as opposed to 40 percent of insecure males (Lewis & Feiring, 1991). As such, these investigators concluded that the combinatory effects of the factors they identified were linked to the presence and rate of psychopathology for adolescent boy respondents.

ADULT ATTACHMENT

Researchers began to focus on adult attachment as an expansion and elaboration of childhood attachment (Main et al., 1985; Sperling, Berman, & Fagen, 1992; Zelnick & Buchholz, 1990). Weiss (1982) stated that attachment in adulthood is different from attachment in childhood in three important ways:

> (a) instead of appearing only in relationships with caretakers, attachment in adulthood also occurs with peers; (b) attachment in adulthood is less pervasive in its potential deleterious effect on other behavioral systems than in infancy; and (c) attachment in adulthood is often directed toward a person with whom a sexual relationship exists. (cited in Sperling et al., 1992, p. 240)

Another meaningful difference between childhood and adult attachment is the role of the internal working models in the interaction with an attachment figure. In infant-adult attachment, the child has no previous experience that is impacting his or her behavior with the adult (Sperling et al., 1992). However, with adults, the presence of mental representations based on prior experience greatly impact how one acts with the potential attachment figure and how the person interprets that interaction (Sperling et al., 1992). Moreover, "the caregiver and careseeker attachment roles are interchangeable in adults, whereas in healthy adult-infant attachment they are fixed and stable" (p. 241).

Multiple attachments are expected in people across the life span (Hazan & Shaver, 1994). Infants become attached to their primary caregivers and have secondary attachments to other people with whom they interact. If multiple caregivers are accessible, infants demonstrate a clear preference, seeking and maintaining proximity to one of them (Ainsworth, 1982; Hazan & Shaver, 1994).

Investigators speculate that multiple attachments are hierarchically arranged (Hazan & Shaver, 1994). For an infant, the primary attachment figure is the "person who most consistently provides care and responds to their distress signals (p. 69)." According to Bowlby (1969), parental figures tend always to be members of the hierarchy; however, their positions change as the child ages and while other individuals are added or dropped from the hierarchy (Hazan & Shaver, 1994). Typically, as an adult, the individual forms a pair bond (usually a romantic relationship), and this partner is at the top of the hierarchy. Although most adults express a clear preference for one individual as their primary attachment figure, most will acknowledge multiple sources of support (Hazan & Shaver, 1994). In the adult pair bond, individuals need attention and reassurance from their partners, and most find distressing frequent, prolonged, or unexpected separations from their primary attachment figure (Hazan & Shaver, 1994; Vormbrock, 1993).

On the basis of Ainsworth's seminal work studying attachment patterns in children, Main et al. (1985) developed an interview schedule evaluating the internal working models of adults. The interview schedule was designed to compare the adult relationship of behaviors and the participants' degree of attachment to their parents. The interview makes a correlation between the quality of one's attachment relationship as a child and the impact of these attachment relationships on adult personality (Levy & Blatt, 1999). Ultimately, this research led to the creation of a new, but related, classification of adult attachment patterns or styles: secure/autonomous, insecure (avoidant/dismissing), insecure (dependent/preoccupied), and disorganized/controlling (Goldberg, 1991; Sperling et al., 1992).

This classification system describes each category somewhat differently because it relates to adults in particular (Goldberg, 1991; Sperling et al., 1992). In adults, an individual may be predominantly one style but may present differently in a particular situation. This difference is not necessarily maladaptive. Indeed, it is based on the recognition that the nature of adults' social context is much more complex than that of children. Researchers note that there can be a blend of patterns (Goldberg, 1991; Sperling et al., 1992). For example, "The potential for both security and insecurity is likely to be present in all of us" (Fonagy, 1999, p. 469).

Secure/autonomous individuals value attachments. If they had a positive relationship with their parents, they are able to talk realistically about their parents' imperfections (Goldberg, 1991). Those with a difficult childhood are able to acknowledge the pain they felt, to understand it, and to establish healthy relationships for themselves (Goldberg, 1991). Typically, secure adults "view others as trustworthy and dependable, the self as lovable and worthy, and relationships as a source of support and comfort" (Rothbard & Shaver, 1994, p. 61).

Avoidant/dismissing adults are likely to minimize the importance of intimate relationships, limiting the attachments they have (Goldberg, 1991). They might idealize their childhood experiences without being able to give any supporting details, or they might report negative experiences without any attention paid to the detrimental effects of those experiences (Goldberg, 1991). These adults tend to lack close social supports. Avoidant/dismissing adults generally do not view others as trustworthy and dependable, and they view "the self as either unlovable or (defensively) 'too good' for others, and relationships as either threatening to one's sense of control, not worth the effort, or both" (Rothbard & Shaver, 1994, p. 61). Avoidant individuals also have been found to be less likely to believe in the integrity of social agents, such as parents, authorities, or public figures (Collins & Read, 1990).

Dependent/preoccupied adults remain caught in old struggles with their parents, lack a sense of identity, and are unable to evaluate their role within relationships (Goldberg, 1991). They cannot move past details of early memories or those of present interactions with their primary attachment figures in order to have an objective overview of the relationship (Goldberg, 1991).

Anxious/ambivalent (preoccupied) adults are most likely "to view others as relationship partners but as largely unpredictable (sometimes available, sometimes not) and difficult to understand" (Rothbard & Shaver, 1994, p. 61). The self is commonly viewed as unlovable, and intimate relationships are viewed as the most important way to achieve a sense of security and identity (Rothbard & Shaver, 1994).

Finally, the disorganized/controlling pattern in adults is the most inconsistent of all the patterns. Adults with this style typically have unresolved mourning over an attachment figure (Goldberg, 1991). The loss could be concrete, such as the death of a loved one, or could be intangible, such as the loss of trust from abuse. Many individuals with this type of attachment pattern are maltreated as infants (Goldberg, 1991). These individuals show signs of ongoing cognitive disorganization when the attachment figure is discussed. For example, they may indicate prolonged disbelief about the loss of a parent and display persistent inappropriate guilt (Goldberg, 1991). "At all ages, disorganized individuals are also given an alternative or 'forced' classification of one of the other three alternatives: avoidant, secure, ambivalent" (Goldberg, 1991, p. 397). For purposes of our inquiry, the three primary attachment patterns are the focus of evaluation.

Rothbard and Shaver (1991) conducted a study using a 180-item adjective rating list, based on subjects' descriptions of their mothers and fathers, to assess disparities in attachment history between the different adult attachment groups. Secure individuals described their mothers as relaxed, easygoing, patient, and dependable. Insecure (avoidant or ambivalent) individuals described their mothers as nervous, depressed, frightened, worried, or confused, and reported feeling uncomfortable in their mother's presence (Rothbard & Shaver, 1991). Secure individuals typically had positive, healthy relationships with their fathers, whereas those with insecure attachment patterns felt alienated in their father's presence. Avoidant subjects were the most divergent from the other two with regard to "(1) lower levels of current parental communication and emotional support; [and] (2) lower levels of confidence in fathers' dependability and attentiveness during the subjects' childhoods" (Rothbard & Shaver, 1994, p. 55). Avoidant attachment patterns correlated with greater anger toward mothers and fathers. In addition, participants regarded parental figures as hostile, hurtful, mean, and hateful during the person's childhood (Rothbard & Shaver, 1994).

ATTACHMENT AND PSYCHOPATHOLOGY

Bowlby (1980) viewed aggression as an important result of separation and loss. As he stated, "the loss of a parent gives rise not only to separation anxiety and grief but to processes of mourning in which aggression, the function of which is to achieve reunion, plays a major part" (p. 37). However, he did not significantly use aggression or sexuality in his theorizing about mental difficulties (Main, 1995). Early security of attachment to both parents should provide a substantial buffer to problems related to expressing and controlling sexual and aggressive impulses (Main, 1995). According to Main (1995), direct physical or sexual abuse, as well as contact with a traumatized but not abusive parent who has suffered from physical or sexual abuse, is likely to negatively impact the development and control of aggression and sexuality.

Individuals with abusive caretaking histories are more likely to develop insecure attachments in adulthood (Cicchetti & Toth, 1995). Alexander (1993) found that insecure attachment was predictive of avoiding memories of abuse and personality disorders, including avoidant, dependent, and borderline. In a study that explored the relationship between child maltreatment and adolescent self-perceived insecure attachment style as predictors of offender and victim experiences, Wekerle and Wolfe (1998) found that avoidant attachment style was a significant predictor of female abusiveness and victimization.

Attachment patterns are theorized to play a critical role in personality development. The degree of differentiation or integration of the mental representations or internal working models of the various attachment categories have important implications for personality and psychopathology (Levy & Blatt, 1999). Numerous studies have found that borderline, histrionic, and dependent personality disorders are associated with a preoccupied attachment pattern (Alexander, 1993; Levy, 1993; Levy & Blatt, 1999). From a sample of 75 college students, Levy (1993) explored the relationship between attachment patterns, using a self-report instrument, and personality disorders, using the Millon Clinical Multiaxial Inventory. Preoccupied attachment was correlated with borderline, dependent, and passive-aggressive personality disorders. Dismissing avoidant attachment patterns were related to narcissistic, antisocial, and paranoid personality disorders. Finally, secure attached individuals reported fewer personality disorders of all types (Levy, 1993).

Rosenstein and Horowitz (1996) conducted a study with 60 hospitalized adolescents and found that an avoidant/dismissing attachment style was related to narcissistic and antisocial personality disorders, as well as self-reported narcissistic, antisocial, and paranoid personality traits on the Millon Clinical Multiaxial Inventory-II. In another study with 112 adult female incest survivors, investigators demonstrated that preoccupied attachment style was related to dependent, avoidant, self-defeating, and borderline personality disorder. Those with avoidant/dismissing patterns were identified as experiencing the least psychic distress, most likely as a result of their avoidance of negative affect (Alexander, 1993; Levy & Blatt, 1999).

In terms of attachment theory, Fonagy (1999, p. 471) argued that borderline personality disorder could be viewed as "a lack of integration of internal working models or, rather, the predominance of internal working models where self and object representations rapidly oscillate." He also postulated that some children abandon reflecting on their own mental representations or those of their caregivers as an extreme defensive response to traumatic situations. "They thus voluntarily abandon this crucial psychological capacity, with sometimes disastrous consequences" (p. 471).

The vast majority of traumatized, abused, and neglected children do not become "remorselessly violent" (Perry, 1997, p. 139). Perry contended that belief systems are the major factor in one's resort to violence. He spoke of a malignant combination of experiences—lack of early nurturance and attachment, chaotic environments, ongoing physical threats (O'Keefe, 1995), persistent fear, and identifying with the aggressor (Perry, 1997, p. 141). Indeed, as he explained,

> These violent offenders have been incubated in terror, waiting to be old enough to obtain "one of those guns," waiting to be the one who controls, the one who takes, the one who hits, the one who can "make the fear, not take the fear." (Perry, 1997 pp. 141–142)

ATTACHMENT AND PSYCHOPATHY

Bowlby (1969) identified three psychological states related to maladaptive or interrupted attachment patterns during a child's first 3 years. The first of these is the protest state, marked by intense emotionality. This is followed by the despair state, defined by withdrawal and hopelessness. Finally, after prolonged separation from the primary attachment figure, the third state of detachment manifests (Bowlby, 1969). Although detachment is an adaptive strategy to recover from the distress of protest and despair, there is no commencement of normal attachment behavior when the child is reunited with the attachment figure (Fonagy, Target, Steele, & Steele, 1997). The infant may be indifferent and fail to bond. In addition, there is an intensification of interest in physical objects and self-absorption, with only cursory sociability (Fonagy et el., 1997).

In 1946, Bowlby related affectionless psychopathy to the lack of a maternal object and to a biological predisposition (Fonagy et al., 1997). These researchers alleged that the attachment system was involved in both affective and predatory violence, whereas with the latter, the purpose of proximity-seeking was an intense defensive reaction of a violent nature. As they noted, "Violence and crime are . . . disorders of the attachment system. They are permitted by lack of concern for others (consequent on the inhibition of bonding) and motivated by distorted desires to engage the other in emotionally significant interchange" (Fonagy et al., 1997 p. 153).

A study by Huesmann, Eron, Lefkowitz, and Walder (1984) examined aggressiveness in 600 subjects over a 22-year period and demonstrated that aggressiveness consistently predicted antisocial behavior in a number of different situations (e.g., criminality, spousal abuse). There was a clear rise in antisocial behavior when individuals reached adolescence. Fonagy et al. (1997) asserted that parent-child attachment, which is pivotal during childhood, shifts during adolescence, putting more focus on social institutions and the adult figures that represent them (e.g., teachers, employers). The necessity of reconfiguring internal working models during this time renders adolescents at risk for acting out, particularly those whose early attachments and mental representations of relationships are distorted by maladaptive early experiences (Fonagy et al., 1997). The absence of a strong and healthy attachment to the parent may not be obvious in a child because of the adult's physical capacity to control the child. Indeed, as Fonagy et al. (1997, p. 159) observed, "the absence of parental control through emotional ties may not become fully manifest until the individual's behavior requires internal controls through morality, empathy, caring, and commitment."

Some research suggests that avoidant children potentially develop hostile, aggressive responses to their caregivers who are unavailable and rejecting (Sroufe, 1983). Moreover, Suess, (cited in Fonagy et al., 1997) found that avoidant infant attachment is a predictor of a pattern of attributing hostile intent in an ambiguous social situation. The child learns to expect hostility from early attachments, and his or her stable internal working models lead him or her to "preemptive aggression" in later situations (Fonagy et al., 1997, p. 162). These investigators noted that insecure attachment was a risk factor, along with biological and environmental components; however, they were not the direct cause of psychopathology.

Fonagy et al. (1997) indicated that the lack of meaningful attachment relationships leaves some individuals without the necessary mental capacities to organize their internal working models of relationships. This lack of reflection on their own and other's internal states could lead to criminal actions. In particular, these researchers reported that violence against another person might not be possible if it were not for the lack of mental representation of the *other* by the offender (Fonagy et al., 1997). Psychological conflicts cannot be resolved because of inadequate mental representation, and thus, violence is seen as a solution. The lack of internal representations of one's self and of others translates into the experience of ideas and feelings that are acted upon physically (Fonagy et al., 1997).

According to Fonagy et al. (1997, p. 165), "We assume that crimes against people are normally inhibited by the painful psychic consequences of identifying with the victim's mental state and the equally uncomfortable awareness of the beliefs and feelings of important others." As such, the relationship between attachment theory and crime can be viewed as a form of social control theory (Gottfredson & Hirschi, 1990; Hirschi, 1969). Without the capacity for empathy for or connectedness to others, sanctions by family, peers, neighbors, school, or employers would be futile (Fonagy et al., 1997). The ability to mentally construct social norms, then, is a necessary precursor to socialization and the ability to self-monitor. This ability to self-monitor is critical for the prevention of criminal acts.

Fonagy et al. (1997, p. 166) identified four ways that a failure of "mentalization" could lead to "moral disengagement." First, a person who is unable to contemplate the mental states of others would also have reduced self-awareness. Thus, this individual would have a diminished sense of personal responsibility for his or her actions. Second, these limitations on mentalizing might enable the person to disregard the psychological impact of an act upon another person. Third, devaluing or dehumanizing a victim would allow the victim to be treated as an object to be possessed or destroyed. Fourth, the inability to appreciate the "other" in such a person's internal working models would permit ideas and actions to be reconstructed and reinterpreted. In this way, "unacceptable conduct m[ight] be reconstrued as acceptable in a selective and self-serving manner" (Fonagy et al., 1997, p. 166).

In discussing the impact of early maladaptive patterns of attachment on the development of an individual capable of predatory violence, Fonagy et al. (1997, p. 167) concluded that

> Thus they were deprived of a relationship in which they could have felt sufficiently safe to explore the mind of the other, to find within it an image of themselves as thinking and feeling beings. Their limited and hostile internal working models are therefore overwhelmingly powerful, unchecked by the attenuating influence of a metacognitive capacity. Physical experience has a motivational immediacy because there is no insight into the merely representational basis of human interaction.

THE DSM-IV'S REACTIVE ATTACHMENT DISORDER

Reactive attachment disorder (RAD) is characterized as "markedly disturbed and developmentally inappropriate social relatedness in most contexts that [occurs] before the age of 5 years and is associated with grossly pathological care" (APA, 1994, p. 118). The inappropriate social relatedness is evidenced by either "a persistent failure to initiate or respond in a developmentally appropriate fashion . . . as manifest by excessively inhibited, hypervigilant, or highly ambivalent and contradictory responses . . . or diffuse attachments as manifest by indiscriminate sociability with marked inability to exhibit appropriate selective attachments" (p. 118). This disorder has been criticized for being too vague and for lacking behavioral descriptors often seen by those who work with attachment-disordered children (Randolph, 1997). According to Randolph, diagnosing a child with RAD and either conduct disorder or oppositional defiant disorder is a common practice used to compensate for the lack of behavioral description in the RAD diagnosis. For purposes of our overall inquiry, there is simply not enough information about Aileen Wuornos before the age of 5 to accurately diagnose her with RAD. Furthermore, the attachment categories are far more descriptive.

ATTACHMENT DISORDER

Randolph (1997) clearly stated that attachment disorder, as defined by the Attachment Center in Evergreen, The Attachment Disorder Symptom Checklist, and The Randolph Attachment Disorder Questionnaire (RADQ), is different from the DSM-IV diagnosis of RAD. As she explained,

> By contrast, the term "attachment disorder" refers to a syndrome of specific behavior problems that are seen in children who have a history of severe maltreatment, severe, chronic pain, or recurrent separations from the primary caregiver during the first two years of life. It is NOT synonymous with the diagnosis of Reactive Attachment Disorder, but subsumes this disorder as representing merely one aspect of attachment disorder. It is hoped that the present research [RADQ] may assist in the re-formulation of the attachment disorder diagnosis in subsequent editions of the DSM. (Randolph, 1997, p. 2)

According to Randolph and Myeroff (1998), attachment disorder is distinct from a diagnosis of RAD or conduct disorder. Randolph (1997) asserted that RAD is reflective of a lesser degree of psychopathology than is attachment disorder. She stated that children with attachment disorder must meet the diagnostic criteria of RAD and either oppositional defiant disorder or conduct disorder.

Attachment disorder is further defined by the inability to be genuinely affectionate with others and the failure to develop a conscience or the ability to trust others. The Attachment Center (2001) maintained that children who do not have healthy attachments have extreme control problems. They fail to develop a moral foundation, lack empathy, exhibit no remorse, are devoid of a conscience, and display no compassion toward others. Furthermore, these youth resist all efforts to be nurtured or guided; lack cause-and-effect thinking; act out negatively; lie, steal, cheat, manipulate; and are destructive, cruel, argumentative, and hostile. These adolescents lack self-control and, instead, are impulsive and superficially charming and engaging. The Attachment Center definition of attachment disorder also states that healthy attachments can be disrupted by the following: abuse, neglect, abandonment, multiple changes in caregivers, foster care, adoption, painful illness, fetal alcohol/drug exposure, and maternal depression.

THE ATTACHMENT DISORDER SYMPTOM CHECKLIST AND THE RADQ

Prior to the development of the RADQ, The Attachment Disorder Symptom Checklist, developed at Evergreen Consultants in Evergreen, Colorado, was the primary tool used to assess for attachment disorder (Randolph, 1997). This instrument was developed to describe the symptoms that treating clinicians had observed in children with attachment disorder. The checklist consists of 20 behaviors that the clinician determines are either absent, mild, moderate, or severe for a given child. The clinician then determines whether or not attachment disorder is present, according to the severity of the symptoms marked

(Randolph, 1997). Items on the checklist are stated in more general terms, lacking behavioral specificity. The checklist also relies on the clinician's judgment, rather than on objective measurement.

Randolph (1997) developed The Randolph Attachment Disorder Questionnaire (RADQ) to assess the presence of attachment disorder for individuals between the ages of 5 and 18. It was created from items on The Attachment Disorder Symptom Checklist, in order to provide a behaviorally specific and objectively scored tool to aid in the diagnosis of attachment disorder (Randolph, 1997). It is a 30-item questionnaire that is scored on a 5-point Likert scale. It can be used to determine whether behavioral problems in children are consistent with attachment disorder, what the severity of symptoms is, and which symptoms of attachment disorder the child is experiencing (Randolph, 1997).

The RADQ indicates attachment disorder if the score is above 65 and if pathogenic care (e.g., abuse, neglect, or several changes of primary caregiver) before the first year of life is noted. The severity of the disorder increases with escalating scores. Children with scores in the 65 to 75 range fall into the mild degree category of attachment disorder (15 percent of the RAD group) (Randolph, 1997). Without treatment, this group is thought to be at risk for developing borderline personality disorder during late adolescence. Children who score in the 76 to 90 range are likely to have a moderate degree of attachment disorder (55 percent of the RAD group). According to Randolph (1997, p. 12), "without intensive treatment, these individuals will most likely develop borderline or antisocial personality disorder in late adolescence, will have persistent difficulties in interpersonal and work situations as adults, and will be unable to appropriately care for their own children." Finally, children who score above 91 on the RADQ are probably severely attachment disordered (30 percent of the RAD group) and have many symptoms of conduct disorder (Randolph, 1997). According to Randolph (1997, p. 12),

> Children who score above 91 on the RADQ are quite severely disturbed and are likely to end up in the juvenile justice system if they do not receive intensive attachment therapy. . . . Their behavior problems usually make them dangerous to family members and school mates. Unless they receive extensive attachment therapy, it is highly likely that they will develop antisocial personality disorder or psychopathic personality style in late adolescence, and engage in persistent criminal behavior. They will be completely unable to parent their own children, and will be highly likely to seriously maltreat their own children. They represent a serious threat to society, as they are likely to kill or otherwise seriously harm others, and show no remorse for their actions.

Although the RADQ is far too behaviorally specific to apply to the case of Aileen Wuornos, the more generally described behaviors in The Attachment Disorder Symptom Checklist can be addressed more appropriately with archival data. As we analyze and interpret the data pertaining to Aileen Wuornos in Chapter 9, these behaviors are explored in relation to the psychopathic traits identified in the Psychopathy Checklist-Revised (PCL-R).

THE NEUROBIOLOGY OF ATTACHMENT

A detailed description and analysis of the neurobiological dimensions of attachment are beyond the scope of the present analysis. However, this growing area of attachment research should be mentioned, particularly including the work of Allan Schore. His neurobiological explanations of internal working models, self-modulation, moral development, affect regulation, and insecure attachments are summarized in this section. This area of research will undoubtedly grow and have important implications for understanding and treating attachment disordered children and adolescents in the future. In order to better comprehend attachment, the function and the chemistry of the brain are first briefly considered.

The brain is constructed from three parts, evolving at different times and for different functions (Levy, 1996). The reptilian brain or the brain stem was the first to evolve and regulates basic life functions (e.g., digestion, breathing, and reproduction). This part of the brain is necessary for primitive sexual and survival instincts. The next part of the brain that evolved was the limbic system, which was initially identified in mammals. It provides us with the ability to experience emotions and refines the capacity for learning and memory. The limbic system is the center of all relational bonds and regulates attachment behaviors. Finally, the neocortex (orbitofrontal) was the last part of the brain to evolve and is unique to humans. The neocortex or frontal lobe helps humans to reason and think, and inhibits emotional responses.

The brain stem and the limbic system together make the old brain, which controls maternal instinct, attachment behavior, and fight-or-flight responses (Levy, 1996). When an individual feels threatened, the amygdala releases stress hormones, including norepinephrine, increasing the brain's overall reactivity. Dopamine increases the heart rate and blood pressure, enabling the body to engage in a fight-or-flight reaction. Levy (1996) maintained that attachment disordered children typically have experienced abuse, neglect, and multiple disruptions that make trauma, fear, and anxiety imprinted on their old brains.

Internal Working Models

According to Schore (1994), by the end of the first year, a child becomes a social being with a complex psychobiological mechanism to process social and affective information. The child compares current social/emotional perceptual inputs with stored representations, also known as internal working models. Schore argued that internal working models that structure interpersonal relationships and regulate emotion are found in the orbitofrontal cortex of the right hemisphere of the brain. Affect regulation is maintained by the orbitofrontal control of the mesocortical dopamine system (Schore, 1994). "The frontolimbic system in the right cerebral cortex stores cognitive-affective schemas of styles of affect regulation, that is, inceptive internal working models" (Schore, 1994, p. 196).

Self-modulation of Aggressive Impulses

Schore offered a neurobiological explanation as to why some children learn to control narcissistic and aggressive impulses and why some do not. On the basis of life experiences or environmental conditions, the orbitofrontal cholinergic axons will forge a connection to the hypothalamus in order to modulate aggressive impulses. As Schore stated,

> The external regulation of the infant's age-appropriate narcissistic rage (separation protest) allows for the maturation of an internal mechanism that transforms unmodulated rage into healthy aggression and that psychobiologically supports states of autonomous functioning. The absence of such dyadic regulation, and an exposure to parental humiliation induced

shame and rage, can have long-term pathological consequences for the emerging personality. (Schore, 1994, p. 346)

Moral Development/Affect Regulation

Schore (1991) maintained that the right hemispheric prefrontal affect modulator, which develops by 18 months, was responsible for appraising situations and was comparable to what the psychoanalytic literature calls the superego. Central to the idea of moral development is shame. Shame is developed through the experience of being negatively judged by an individual, whose thoughts and feelings matter (Schore, 1994). Shame serves to interrupt any actions that violate one's moral code or society's mores (Lewis, 1992). Empathy is also critical for healthy moral development. Research indicates that orbitofrontal damage is associated with a poor ability for empathy (Martzke, Swan, & Varney, 1991). Investigators postulate that orbitofrontal dysfunction underlies psychopathic behavior (Schore, 1994). With respect to affect modulation and early moral development, Schore (1994, p. 353) indicated that

> At 18 months the child first exhibits moral prosocial altruistic behavior in the form of comforting—regulating the negative affect—of a distressed other. The caregiver influences the trajectory of the child's developing moral capacities by shaping the neurobiological structural system that mediates such functioning. . . . The orbitofrontal cortex is centrally involved in empathic and moral behaviors. Structural deficits in this system are associated with sociopathic pathologies.

Insecure Attachments

The development of a self-regulating capacity is contingent upon interacting with a regulating primary caregiver (Schore, 1994). "The ontogenetic attainment of an efficient internal system that can adaptively auto regulate catecholaminergic generated arousal, and thereby affect, cognition, and behavior, is absolutely dependent upon the emotional responsiveness of the mother" (Schore, 1994, p. 373). The comforting presence and healthy interaction with the mother enables the child to explore his or her environment. A lack of essential experiences at critical periods of development can significantly impair the development of attachment and self-regulatory systems (Greenspan, 1981; Schore, 1994). Joseph maintained that the relationship between a nonphysically affectionate mother and a child who is nonresponsive to physical contact creates "an atrophy of certain limbic nuclei in the infant's developing brain and a consequent social withdrawal and abnormal emotionality" (cited in Schore, 1994, p. 380). The insecure-avoidant infant has an impaired capacity to experience intense positive or negative emotions and tends to overregulate his or her emotional experiences (Schore, 1994).

CONCLUSIONS

This chapter explored attachment theory, beginning with the work of Bowlby, followed by the seminal study conducted by Ainsworth. Next, both research exploring the continuity or discontinuity of attachment patterns over the life span and research specific to adult attachment were presented. Adult and childhood attachment patterns were compared, and the categorization of adult attachment was described. The connection between adult attachment and psychopathology was illustrated. In addition, the relationship between insecure attachment patterns (i.e., avoidant) and psychopathy was demonstrated. The DSM-IV's reactive attachment disorder (RAD) and attachment disorder as defined by The Attachment Center in Evergreen, Colorado, were briefly described. The Randolph Attachment Questionnaire and the Attachment Disorder Checklist also were explained. Finally, the neurobiology of attachment, including moral development, self-regulation, and insecure attachment patterns, were summarized. Although the neurobiological dimensions of Aileen Wuornos's attachment patterns are not the focus of our investigation, canvassing this literature helps deepen our regard for the onset of attachment disorder, lived out in adolescence and adulthood.

The previous five chapters were instructive in that they provided a practical foundation from within which to understand female-perpetrated predatory homicide, especially when committed by women diagnosed with ASPD (psychopathy) and when issues of poor attachment clearly are evident. Indeed, our position is that this *is* the context out of which the life story of Aileen Wuornos must be presented, discussed, and critiqued. In Chapter 7 we explore a number of methodological questions germane to our investigation. These questions principally address the selection of participants (i.e., Wuornos) and justify our use of an instrumental case method.

7

Methodological Considerations

--- ❖ ---

INTRODUCTION

As we have argued, there is a paucity of research on female homicide offenders, especially with the diagnosis of ASPD (psychopathy). In addition, as we already explained, women are infrequently diagnosed with ASPD as compared with men. Indeed, according to existing research, psychopathy is primarily a male phenomenon defined by an instrument (the Psychopathy Checklist Revised, or PCL-R) validated on men for men (Hare, 1991). Although this type of personality disorder is disproportionately found in male offenders, a comparatively small number of men can be classified as psychopathic. According to the current diagnostic criteria, even fewer women are evaluated as such. Thus, the relatively small number of women offenders with ASPD makes empirical analysis of this population extremely difficult. Moreover, large-scale studies concerning these women are simply unrealistic.

We also note that women may not be accounted for by the current definition of psychopathy. In other words, the diagnostic nomenclature and clinical reporting ostensibly fail to adequately explain the behavioral and personality dimensions of women with this psychiatric condition. As such, in order to more accurately uncover the experience of ASPD (psychopathy) for women, an instrumental case study using detailed, in-depth, rich-in-context data collection is warranted. The typicality and uniqueness of the case study method provides the researcher with an opportunity to better understand how psychopathy in women emerges and how it fosters and contributes to their acts of predatory homicide. In this vein, we recognize that merely assuming the clinical and psychometric categories of the PCL-R presuppose the experience of women who kill serially, thereby restricting and, in the extreme, distorting the findings.

Another, more cogent consideration is that a great deal of debate exists regarding the diagnostic accuracy of the DSM-IV's ASPD diagnosis for women and the PCL-R classification of psychopathy for women (Salekin et al., 1997). While Aileen Wuornos's criminal history is sufficient for a diagnosis of ASPD, the PCL-R predetermines the personality and behavioral categories that otherwise would attempt to define her. The proposed case study method, then, provides multiple sources of information specific to her life story as a way to better articulate these experiences. In other words, we interpret Aileen Wuornos through her own life events and patterns of attachment rather than by solely relying on the diagnostic nomenclature developed by men for and about women.

In this chapter we explore several facets of our methodology germane to the story of Aileen Wuornos. In particular, some provisional commentary concerning the case study method and the instrumental approach are delineated. In addition, an evaluation of this method in relation to more empirically animated and other qualitative research designs is presented. A number of justifications outlining why Aileen Wuornos was selected as the agreed-upon case study for an investigation of female killers are presented. Several limits to our research method are discussed.

UNDERSTANDING THE INSTRUMENTAL CASE STUDY METHOD

A *case study* is "an exploration of a 'bounded system' or a case (or multiple cases) over time through detailed, in-depth data collection involving multiple sources of information rich in context" (Creswell, 1998, p. 62). An *instrumental case study* focuses on an issue (or issues), with the case used instrumentally to illustrate them (Stake, 1995). *Issues* are "matter for study regarding the specific case. Starting with a topical concern, researchers pose foreshadowed problems, concentrate on issue-related observations, interpret patterns of data that reform issues as assertions" (Stake, 1998, p. 92). Accordingly, in this book, the case of serial killer Aileen Wuornos is used to address the issues of attachment, psychopathy, and predatory homicide perpetrated by women.

Despite a lack of accessibility and availability of subjects, there is, perhaps, a more important reason for using the case study method. Little is known about this group of female homicide offenders. ASPD, psychopathy, and predatory homicide are all gendered constructs. Each of these is associated with and interpreted through a masculine lens. Thus, what is assumed to be true about women who murder and which persons meet the criteria for ASPD or psychopathy are based on masculine standards of reasoning and sense making.

Daly and Chesney-Lind (1988) examined this phenomenon in relation to female criminality. They noted that many "preferred modes of data collection are . . . gender-linked" (Daly and Chesney-Lind, 1988, p. 518). Moreover, they indicated that although both men and women rely heavily on statistics, women are more likely to use interviews and observations. Indeed, as they argued, "providing texture, social context, and case histories" is more important than categories or numbers in order to accurately understand how women become involved in crime (p. 518). Thus, as these investigators concluded, "This gender difference is not related to 'math anxiety' but rather to a felt need to comprehend women's crime on its own terms, just as criminologists of the past did for men's crime" (Daly and Chesney-Lind, 1988, p. 518). As such, we maintain that it is important to understand both ASPD (psychopathy) and homicide from a woman's perspective, contextualized in her life experiences. The proposed instrumental case study method represents a serviceable approach by which to accomplish this objective.

The research that is available (albeit primarily about men) is predominantly empirical in nature. The experience of homicide is complex and should not be limited to a category or to a hypothesis. Although these studies have some utility, the *human* experience is not explored. We maintain that qualitative studies are needed in order to investigate more fully the meaning and motivations embedded in female-perpetrated homicide.

Given the previous observations, we postulate that an instrumental case study method potentially deepens and enriches our understanding of women who commit serial murder, mindful of the connection among attachment, psychopathy, and predatory homicide. Although the relationship between psychopathy and homicide in males has been examined in the relevant literature, studies on the specific topic of ASPD (psychopathy) and females who engage in predatory murder is almost nonexistent. Thus, an instrumental case study approach providing nuanced and descriptive data on the life history and experiences of one woman (i.e., Aileen Wuornos) is well-suited to a detailed exploration of this phenomenon and its meaning.

INSTRUMENTAL CASE STUDY VERSUS EMPIRICAL METHODS

We recognize that other methodological approaches might be relevant to the expressed purpose of our inquiry. For example, empirical research designs are abundant in the literature on murder and mental illness. However, we contend that the instrumental case study method allows the investigator to consider, assess, and interpret the meaning of this relationship, thereby growing current knowledge about this phenomenon and returning the focus back to the individual's unique life experiences. As such, this study intends to add depth, complexity, and humanness to the primarily empirical research already in existence. Rather than limiting the findings to facts, categories, and numbers, the instrumental case study method adds detail, texture, and context to an appreciation of predatory homicide perpetrated by psychopathic women.

Along these lines, various sources of data are used to present the specifics of Aileen Wuornos's life, including her relationships with both family and community, as well as her descent into criminal (homicidal) behavior. The case study endeavors to encompass the subject's full experience through a detailed chronology of events that made her the person that she was and the killer that she became. Assorted published books and interviews with Aileen Wuornos provide insight into her thoughts and feelings concerning her life, her relationships, and her murders.

The case study approach allows the investigator to explore the subject's past and present life situations and the way that these events shaped the person's conduct. For our purposes, the life story of Aileen Wuornos is presented from childhood until her adult incarceration for the homicides she committed. Moreover, by applying attachment theory to relevant archival data, an interpretation of the way she perceived the people involved in these killings is described. In addition, her treatment as an infant and as a small child is examined in relation to her attachment style. Overall, the collection of data, the application of attachment theory, and what we as researchers perceive and process in relation to the information, coconstitute the assertions made and the lessons learned from the instrumental case study. We contend that this approach offers the reader a more holistic description of the person and phenomenon in question, rather than rendering both no more than isolated "parts" of the experience (e.g., motives). Moreover, the comprehensiveness of this approach enables the investigator to embrace the complexity of predatory homicide perpetrated by psychopathic women. In contrast, natural science methodologies typically limit themselves to linear consciousness or causality rather than to the multidimensional reality that affects human experience and behavior.

Frequently, the natural science approach applies criteria of science created for different phenomena to the human experience (Giorgi, 1994). By using this approach, the natural scientific approach often loses the individual's qualitative reality, focusing instead on measurement over meaning. The emphasis on measurement can lead to alienation and the loss of subjectivity, problems that potentially undermine any claims to the veracity of one's findings.

Given the vast lack of knowledge about the type of female homicide offender we are investigating, standard statistical measurements lack predictive and explanatory utility. Indeed, the small samples available make any results stemming from traditional empirical methods mostly unreliable. Moreover, researchers have yet to conclusively identify what they are attempting to measure (psychopathy in women). For instance, do women present with this personality disorder in precisely the same way as men? To what degree, if at all, does one's attachment style as an infant and a child correlate with a sense of detachment toward others while an adult? Of more importance for the present inquiry, can insecure attachment patterns lead to predatory homicide? These and related questions necessitate some response. Our instrumental case study approach uses case histories and theory as the primary method of descriptive analysis and as a systematic way to address these unanswered queries.

When a phenomenon is subject to experimental manipulation, it is taken out of its context and placed into the laboratory. In short, it is no longer explored in a human way, thereby losing its meaningfulness. When this outcome occurs, only the parts of human phenomena that conform to the scientific paradigm are studied (Giorgi, 1994). Conversely, the case study approach investigates "the particularity and complexity of a single case, coming to understand its activity within important circumstances. . . . [Thus], the qualitative researcher emphasizes episodes of nuance, the sequentiality of happenings in context, the wholeness of the individual" (Stake, 1995, pp. xi–xii). With this emphasis in mind, the story (and woman) elucidated in our subsequent analysis represents a complex, integrated system that cannot be reduced to a category or to a statistic. Although the "parts" may not appear to work well and although the purposes of the actor in question may be irrational at times, the human narrative nonetheless remains a coherent system (Stake, 1995).

Our task is to examine the impact of attachment patterns on ASPD (psychopathy), in relation to predatory homicide for Aileen Wuornos. Rather than accepting preexisting categories and diagnostic classifications as they are given, it is important first to present the story of the subject in question. Following a description of the case study materials and our careful reflection upon them, we make several assertions and interpretations with respect to the issues under consideration.

All research presupposes certain assumptions about the phenomenon studied, given investigator preconceptions and predilections (Ammen, 1990). Both quantitative and qualitative methodologies account for the impact of these biases in distinct ways. For example, the natural scientific approach controls for any "contaminating" investigator biases by calculating and restricting the research conditions. As a result, the subject is supposedly eliminated. The qualitative model addresses the presuppositions of the analyst by overtly attending to them prior to the commencement of the scholarly inquiry. This technique allows the researcher to be consciously aware of her perspectives in order to minimize their idiosyncratic influences on the direction and interpretation of the study (Ammen, 1990).

As such, we maintain that the focus of our investigation is on the meaning and complexity of the experience of committing criminal homicide as described through the life history of one woman with ASPD/psychopathy. In order to reach naturalistic generalizations, based on the data collected, our presuppositions (emphasis on meaning rather than measurement) are acknowledged and suspended as much as possible. Moreover, we note that there are no experimental conditions to be controlled.

Given the preceding observations, we submit that the instrumental case study method is better suited to answer the research question at hand. Moustakas (1994, p. 21) identified qualities of human science research that distinguish it from traditional quantitative methods. These same qualities are evident across case study research efforts and impact the appropriateness of our selection of a method over quantitative forms of inquiry. These qualities of human science research include the following six points:

1. Much of the subject matter or experiences investigated is not accessible through quantitative methodologies.
2. The focus is not on the parts of an experience but, rather, on the "wholeness" of the experience.
3. The goal of the method is to pursue the meanings and essence of the phenomenon rather than arbitrary categories and measurements.
4. Human experience is valued as critical for understanding human behavior and is considered important to the knowledge process of scientific research.
5. The research question reflects the personal commitment and involvement of the investigator.
6. Experience and behavior are coconstituted by the "inseparable relationship of subject and object and of parts and whole" (p. 21). In other words, the phenomenon cannot be separated from the subject who experiences it. In fact, the behavior and the experience are integrated into the phenomenon.

INSTRUMENTAL CASE STUDY VERSUS OTHER QUALITATIVE METHODOLOGIES

Other qualitative methods were not selected for our inquiry because they were not deemed appropriate strategies for the research question we investigate. Our decision to reject several of the more likely possibilities is briefly described. For example, the values, practices, or beliefs of a cultural group are not being explored in this investigation; thus, for our purposes, ethnography is not warranted. In addition, neither of us experiences antisocial personality traits nor have we been diagnosed with ASPD (psychopathy). We also have not been a party to any act of criminal homicide in relation to psychological research. Furthermore, neither experience over time, nor change, nor interpreting verbal interaction and dialogue is being examined in this study. As a result, grounded theory and discourse analysis are not relevant to the research question posed. Instead, we are interested in exploring the impact of early attachment on later predatory homicide, as examined through the life history of a female murderer with ASPD (psychopathy). As such, the case of Aileen Wuronos is of secondary (rather than of primary) interest, making an *intrinsic* case study inappropriate as the preferred method of investigation.

Finally, the phenomenological approach could not be used for this particular study. Although the narratives of female serial killers with early attachment difficulties diagnosed in adulthood with antisocial personality disorder (psychopathy) need to be acknowledged and researched by a means mindful of these women's voices, we were unable to gain access to this population. Thus, we could not conduct a phenomenological study within any reasonable amount of time. The problem we confronted principally was a function of the research backlog within the California Department of Corrections, the original data source we elected to pursue. Although a considerable degree of information could have been elicited about the experience of female-perpetrated predatory homicide for women with ASPD, this population of offenders was not reasonably or readily available, despite our concerted efforts.

We note that an instrumental case study analysis enables a more in-depth exploration of subjects at various stages of their lives. In other words, rather than our examining only a circumscribed period of time surrounding the homicide(s) committed by Aileen Wuornos, our method of inquiry provides a more inclusive look into the relationships and life events that shaped her personality and descent into criminal behavior. This methodology also permits us to use attachment theory as a basis from which to assess this phenomenon. Indeed, little is known about the group of women who kill for personal or material gain, wherein serial murder and psychopathy ostensibly figure prominently into their conduct. The case study approach allows the reader to chart and review the course of Aileen Wuronos's life events, fostering a deeper appreciation for those factors that may have led her to commit predatory homicide. For all the reasons just outlined, we conclude that the most appropriate methodology in relation to the research question posed is the qualitative approach of an instrumental case study.

SELECTION CRITERIA AND PARTICIPANTS

The case of Aileen Wuornos was selected from a population of cases of women with ASPD (psychopathy) who committed predatory homicide. The phenomenon observed in this case represents the phenomenon by and large. Although the story of Aileen Wuornos offers some typicality, especially through its uniqueness, it offers an opportunity to learn (Stake, 1998). It is important to keep in mind that case study research is not sampling research. Indeed, understanding the particular narrative is of singular importance (Stake, 1995).

The first criterion is to choose a case that maximizes what can be learned about the issues in question. Although the life experiences and crimes of Aileen Wuornos are unique, there is much that can be discovered about the role of attachment in predatory homicide from this specific instance. In addition, cases must be chosen on the basis of the likelihood that they lead to research understanding and assertions, and, sometimes, to the modification of generalizations (Stake, 1995). The story of Aileen Wuornos was chosen also because of the accessibility of materials relevant to the issues germane to our investigation. In short, the extremely controversial and high-profile nature of this case caused a flurry of media attention surrounding her life and her crimes. There are ample printed texts and audio/visual documents to construct a life history sufficient for purposes of this study. Overall, then, the rationale for using the case of Aillen Wuornos was based on the specific issues that constitute our inquiry, the potential to advance knowledge in the field, the available literature, the accessibility of appropriate materials, and the uniqueness of her life situation.

INSTRUMENTAL CASE STUDY METHOD

For purposes of our inquiry, the case or "bounded system" is one individual; namely, Aileen Wuornos. With respect to the data, multiple sources of information are utilized, including televised interviews, documents, books, and other audio-visual materials. The context for the case involves situating it within its appropriate setting. This setting encompasses the physical, familial, social, and economic dimensions of her story. With these elements in place, an instrumental case study is then conducted. Commenting on this methodological approach, Stake (1998, p. 88) offered the following observations:

> a particular case is examined to provide insight into an issue or refinement of theory. . . . the case is of secondary interest; it plays a supportive role, facilitating our understanding of something else. The case if often looked at in depth, its contexts scrutinized, its ordinary activities detailed, but because this helps us pursue the external interest.

Accordingly, the present analysis focuses on the impact of attachment in relation to ASPD (psychopathy) and predatory homicide perpetrated by one woman. The case of Aileen Wuornos is used instrumentally to illustrate this relationship and its attendant criminal justice and psychological implications.

Unlike the phenomenological approach, the case study method anticipates that a greater amount of interpretation or assertions will be made by the investigator, given the rich narrative data. The phenomenological method requires that theoretical speculation must be left behind. However, for purposes of our instrumental case study inquiry, assertions are made within the context of attachment theory. "For assertions, we draw from understandings deep within us, understandings whose derivation may be some hidden mix of personal experience, scholarship, assertions of other researchers" (Stake, 1995, p. 12).

In an attempt to clarify our own experiences with respect to the case of Aileen Wuornos and the relevant issues pertaining to her story, we identified our presuppositions earlier in this chapter (i.e., a preference for meaning rather than measurement). However, it is critical that we recognize and understand our suppositions and predilections in order to minimize the influence of personal bias. "Ultimately, the interpretations of the researcher are likely to be emphasized more than the interpretations of those people studied, but the qualitative researcher tries to preserve the multiple realities, the different and even contradictory views of what is happening" (Stake, 1995, p. 12). Thus, we note that presuppositions are not absent; rather, they are brought into conscious awareness through this self-reflective process. As the life experiences of Aileen Wuornos are recounted through our re-presentation of them, we will have an impact on the ideas shared with the reader, thus affecting how they are interpreted. In addition, through this more active engagement with the narrative and its meaning, the reader reconstructs "the knowledge in ways that leave it differently connected and more likely to be personally useful" (Stake, 1998, p. 95). Thus, both the reader and the writer coconstitute the generalizations and meanings derived from the case study analysis.

Drawing upon the insights of Stake (1995, p. 123), our method of inquiry incorporates a number of basic steps. Each of these is briefly summarized as follows:

1. The case begins with a vignette, allowing the reader to develop a feel for the time, place, and circumstances of the story. This treatment gives the reader a vicarious experience of "being there" (Stake, 1995, p. 63).

2. An extensive narrative description defining the case and its relevant contexts is presented. As we previously indicated, the data collected for our assessment of the story of Aileen Wuornos comes from books, taped interviews, television reports, and various other sources of print media. Relatively uncontested information is presented, including some interpretive observations about its relative importance and meaning (Stake, 1995). The narrative is a chronology of life events, lending itself to a better understanding of the pertinent issues (e.g., the role of attachment patterns in women who commit predatory homicide). Aileen's relationships with primary attachment figures are highlighted, starting as early as the data sources allow. Her attachment patterns as a child and as an adult also are elucidated. Although other criminal activities are briefly described, only one instance of predatory homicide is recounted in detail. The narrative extends from childhood until her incarceration for the identified predatory murder. In accordance with Stake's (1995) commentary, we also considered other theoretical structures to guide the data-gathering process. In compiling various sources of information, we identified possible multiple realities and gave attention to different viewpoints or conceptualizations when they occurred.

3. After the narrative is disclosed, the writer/researcher carefully develops a few key issues that relate to the broad general inquiry for which the study is undertaken. These issues demonstrate the complexity of the case. The issues are based on what the data indicate. In addition, for our specific purposes, we draw on attachment theory, related research, and our understanding of other similar cases in order to redefine the issues under consideration.

4. Triangulation of the information is the next step in the sequence. This triangulation occurs throughout the presentation of Aileen's life events. *Triangulation* entails "working to substantiate an interpretation or to clarify its different meanings" (Stake, 1995, p. 173). For our purposes, the convergence of various information sources, different theories, and the like "represent[s] the triangulation of ideas [that] help support the development of themes" (Creswell, 1998, p. 251). Triangulation is a process that validates the information given by using corroborating evidence from various sources to elucidate a theme or perspective (Creswell, 1998). For example, in our analysis of Aileen Wuornos's story, data critical to an assertion are carefully substantiated through multiple sources before making the assertion. In this way, we are mindful of circumstances that confirm or disconfirm the data (Stake, 1995).

5. At this juncture, assertions are presented and the analysis or interpretation about what is elicited or learned from the case is delineated. Prior to this stage, only relatively uninterpreted observations and narratives are offered (Stake, 1995). However, at this point, what is understood about the case and how generalizations pertaining to it can be conceptualized are summarized. Moreover, the reader takes the information presented and reconsiders his or her own comprehension of the case and any generalizations related to it (Stake, 1995).

   The data are analyzed by and interpreted through a variety of methods, including categorical aggregation and direct interpretation. In *categorical aggregation,* the "researcher seeks a collection of instances from the data, hoping that issue-relevant meanings will emerge" and, with *direct interpretation,* "the researcher looks at a single instance and draws meaning from it without looking for multiple instances" (Creswell, 1998, p. 154). These two means of analysis allow the investigator to examine the data and put them together in a meaningful, coherent way. The narrative is explored in a way that is mindful of the research question, assertions are processed, and the researcher establishes patterns. Next, *naturalistic generalizations* are developed and discussed. These are "generalizations that people can learn from the case either for themselves or by applying [them] to a population of cases" (Creswell, 1998, p. 154).

6. Finally, a closing vignette is presented. For our purposes, the vignette reminds the reader that the case presented signifies one woman's experience as a complex phenomenon. In addition, the vignette reminds the reader that the narrative is filtered through the writer/researcher.

LIMITATIONS OF THE INSTRUMENTAL CASE STUDY METHOD

There are a few limitations in using the case study method, and these shortcomings warrant some mention. First, the small sample can leave some question about the generalizability of the results. The data set is limited (N = 1). Consequently, despite the naturalistic generalizations that may be made, it is difficult to know whether the findings are applicable to a larger group of similarly situated women.

Second, the issue being explored in the present study, the limited time and financial resources of the investigators, and the inaccessibility of the subject precluded any direct observation of or interview with Aileen Wuornos. This type of immediate data collection would have provided an even greater source of information (and insight) into the phenomenon under consideration. Moreover, *member checking,* a form of validation by which the subject in question examines rough drafts or writing samples to help determine accuracy, clearly was not possible. However, a thorough analysis of viable secondary source material provides ample data with which to better understand attachment theory, psychopathy in women, and predatory homicide.

In general, qualitative research has many undeniable disadvantages. To summarize the words of Stake (1995), it is subjective, labor intensive, slow, and tendentious, and such research often raises more questions than answers. In addition, personal misunderstanding of material is common by both the investigator and the reader (Phillips, 1990). "The misunderstanding will occur because the researcher-interpreters are unaware of their own intellectual shortcomings and because of the weaknesses in methods that fail to purge misinterpretations" (Stake, 1995, p. 45). However, the instrumental case study method permits the social or behavioral scientist to describe the story of an individual contextualized within her own life experiences, rather than breaking the narrative down into disconnected, seemingly meaningless parts. Indeed, despite the challenges and limitations of our approach, it allows for a more in-depth understanding of the phenomenon through description and interpretation. "There are times when all researchers are going to be interpretive, holistic, naturalistic, and uninterested in cause, and then, by definition they will be qualitative inquirers" (Stake, 1995, p. 46). We concur with Stake's observations, particularly when examining predatory female killers predisposed to ASPD (psychopathy) when poor psychological attachment looms dangerously large in the women's lives.

CONCLUSIONS

This chapter reviewed a number of important methodological concerns relevant to our overall investigation. A brief review of the instrumental case study approach was delineated. An assessment of both empirical and other possible qualitative methodologies was presented. The decision to use Aileen Wuornos as the subject of our inquiry was discussed. A review of the specific components germane to our method was outlined. Several limitations to utilizing the instrumental case study method were identified.

The richness and importance of qualitative research is vastly undervalued and mostly underestimated. Human experience is a tremendous source of knowledge and insight that barely has been tapped. Case study research allows one to contemplate generalizations and patterns of meanings while continuing to appreciate the vast idiosyncrasies of genuinely human phenomena. We posit that the current research question can best be answered by using the instrumental case study approach. In the next chapter, we present the story of Aileen Wuornos. This narrative begins in infancy and culminates in adulthood when she committed and was convicted of the predatory murder of Richard Mallory.

8

Aileen Wuornos

A Case Study

❖

INTRODUCTION

In this chapter, the chronological development of the case of Aileen Wuornos is presented. As previously indicated, a variety of sources, including books, taped interviews, television programs, newspaper articles, and the like, are used to tell her story. From these sources, a variety of perspectives are offered. These include the description of events as recalled by Aileen Wuornos, as well as commentary from people who grew up with her, acquaintances throughout her life, two of her siblings, various romantic interests (particularly Tyria Moore), her biological mother, and friends and family members of her victims. In addition, statements from law enforcement officers, her defense attorney, the prosecuting attorney, two jury members, and a psychologist for the defense are provided.

It is widely accepted that Aileen Wuornos was not a reliable historian. Indeed, there are a multitude of instances when she stretched or misstated the truth, and there are other occasions when she clearly produced fabrications. We also note, though, that several individuals substantially corroborated some things that she professed or did. When differing points of view were detected on important issues, we endeavored to explain all sides of the controversy. Although we have presented the case of Aileen Wuornos in narrative format while being mindful of various perspectives, in some instances we interpreted events on the basis of the quality of the available information. Moreover, in the pages that follow, references and citations are kept to a minimum in order to prevent the interruption of the story's flow.

Even though many women have been convicted of murder and multiple homicides, some have called Aileen Wuornos the first *predatory* female serial killer. She hitchhiked and prostituted along the highways of Central Florida. She was convicted of killing seven men, using a .22 caliber handgun. She was executed by lethal injection at Broward Correctional Institution outside Fort Lauderdale, Florida. During an interview from prison, she angrily stated, "Nobody is looking at my life. Nobody's looking at my life and . . . what's my life about." This study takes seriously these chilling and desperate comments.

THE WUORNOS HOME

The Wuornos Home, an unprepossessing one-story ranch, its wood siding a sad, faded yellow, sat amidst a cluster of trees away from the roadside in suburban Troy, Michigan, just 16 miles north of Detroit. Benign-looking and otherwise unnoteworthy, it was nevertheless a house of secrets. . . . Near neighbors who over the years were never once invited to set foot inside even for casual pleasantries, recall the curtains always being drawn tightly across its small windows, excluding the outside world. . . . Aileen's home had a cyclone fence around the front and a huge back yard of close to two acres, planted with a weeping willow and an imposing maple tree. . . . Out back lived the children's menagerie—a changing cast of dogs, cats, pigeons, ducks, turtles, fish and birds. The subdivision was cliquish but—with the exception of the almost reclusive Wuornoses—most of the inhabitants got along reasonably well and even socialized. (Russell, 1992, pp. 11, 22)

Aileen Wuornos was born on February 29, 1956. Until the age of 11, Aileen and her brother Keith believed that Lauri and Britta Wuornos (the maternal grandparents) were their parents. There were five Wuornos children in total, or so Aileen believed. Diane (the daughter of Lauri and Britta) already had left the home as Aileen was growing up. Diane was rarely spoken of and was estranged from her parents. Barry (Lauri and Brita's son) was 12 years older than Aileen and was undoubtedly his father's favorite. He moved out of the house when Aileen was only a toddler. Lori (a second daughter of Lauri and Britta Wuornos) was only 2.5 years older than Aileen and was raised with Aileen and Keith. Lori was spared much of the abuse that Aileen and Keith suffered. Aileen and Keith were often mistaken as twins and were a mere 11 months apart. Both these children experienced severe bouts of victimization at the hands of Lauri Wuornos, their grandfather (Kennedy, 1992).

Lauri Wuornos was a strict disciplinarian. His son, Barry, would later say that Lauri was in no way tyrannical or abusive. Barry even claimed that the girls did not receive spankings at all. Yet, Barry was no longer living in the home by 1967, when Aileen was 11 and beginning her period of greatest conflict with Lauri.

Lauri Wuornos had dark skin and high cheekbones, looking almost Native American. He stood 5'9" tall. His stern demeanor always scared and intimidated Lori's friends. In the town of Troy, Michigan, he was considered opinionated, and he behaved as if he had a grudge against the world. A neighbor described Lauri as an "arrogant, pompous know-it-all" (Russell, 1992, p. 21). Other neighbors would attest to the fact that he could be heard screaming and yelling at his children from a half a block away. Indeed, one neighbor reported that "He didn't treat them like human beings. He treated them worse than anybody would treat an animal" (p. 24). Even Lori, who claimed that she was not physically abused, indicated that she was spanked until she would cry but found his verbal abuse much more painful. She described her father as having a frightening temper and a dogmatic presentation. He was a habitual drinker who often consumed two to three bottles of cheap wine in an evening.

Aileen described sadistic abuse at the hands of her grandfather. She described numerous beatings with a leather strap on her bare buttocks. On several occasions, she was required to lie face down, naked, and spread-eagled on the bed for her whippings (Russell, 1992). Aileen described being beaten on consecutive days while her skin was still raw from prior assaults. Her grandfather often told her she was "evil, wicked, worthless [and that she] should have never been born. She wasn't worthy of the air she breathed" (p. 11).

Aileen in no uncertain terms made it clear that she hated her "parents." Friends of Keith indicated that he stated the same, recounting that he and his sister were often locked in their bedrooms for hours at a time. In addition, other children in the neighborhood often observed Aileen and Keith with bruises, but they would not explain how they received them.

One particular experience called the *cat incident* left a horrible impression not only with Aileen and Keith but also with many of the other children in the neighborhood. Apparently, a family of wild kittens had been living in the attic of the Wuornos home. Lauri demanded that they all be taken to the pound but one. The remaining kitten had scratched young Aileen on the cheek. The next day he observed Aileen playing with the kitten, became enraged, ordered that she follow him into the sauna, and made her watch him hold the kitten under the water until it drowned. The Wuornoses kept a sauna as part of their Finnish heritage.

Britta, Aileen's grandmother, was complacent and did little to stop Lauri from abusing Aileen and Keith. Britta was an alcoholic, and her alcoholism would claim her life when Aileen was 15 years old. She was described as quiet and introverted but with a kind demeanor. Britta was a solid woman who wore her hair in buns and dressed in feminine, long skirts. She was distant with her neighbors but was often seen tending to her flowerbeds. She was characterized as emotionally frail and nervous, despite her sturdy physical appearance. Lori maintained that she and her mother did not have mother-daughter conversations (e.g., she started her period without knowing what it was). Aileen would later say that she idealized her mother (grandmother). Britta and Lauri had a distant, affectionless relationship. Except for their once-a-year family vacation, they did little with one another. They exhibited no physical affection toward one another or toward their (grand)children.

Other children in the neighborhood also described neglect. For example, referring to Aileen and Keith, a friend of the Wuornos children stated that "The Wuornoses were lucky if they got a bowl of breakfast cereal, let alone lunch money for school. Sometimes a teacher gave them a loan or other kids shared a sandwich with them. Generally, they took bag lunches because they couldn't afford hot lunches" (Russell, 1992, p. 28). Aileen recalled little support or kind treatment from the other children at school.

AILEEN'S BIOLOGICAL PARENTS AND INFANCY

Aileen and Keith were told at the age of 11 that Barry and Lori really were their uncle and aunt, not siblings. They were also told that the eldest child, Diane, was actually their mother. After Diane had abandoned them as babies, Lauri and Britta had adopted them. This news served to further alienate Aileen and her brother from their grandparents, and they were informed that their mother had remarried and had two other children. Lori would later claim that Aileen had an intense hatred for her grandfather that was readily apparent in their home.

Diane was quiet but friendly. She was physically petite, dark-eyed, and pretty. Lauri forbad her to date, so he was particularly incensed when she began a relationship with Leo Pittman, the local "hood." Leo Pittman was Aileen and Keith's biological father. He had red hair and freckles. Leo was 5'8", stocky, and athletic. He was raised by his grandparents and was known to be abusive to his grandmother. Leo was frequently truant from school, had poor grades, and engaged in petty criminal behavior. He was known to be moody and to have a violent, explosive temper. Aileen was later described in strikingly similar terms.

Although Diane and Leo seemed an odd match, friends speculated that he was her ticket to freedom from her father. At the age of 14, Diane eloped with Leo, who was then 17 years old. They married on June 3, 1954. Keith was born on March 14, 1955, with Aileen following 11 months later. Aileen was described as a fretful, unhappy baby who cried all the time.

After their marriage, Leo became extremely jealous, possessive, and abusive toward Diane. Following the birth of Keith, Leo made Diane stay at home with the shades drawn, even in the 90-degree heat. During the course of their time together, Diane reported that Leo beat her "probably about every other day." In addition to the beatings, he was described as hypersexual, having many affairs, and was an alcoholic. His criminal career also was accelerating, because he was committing a variety of petty crimes. In 1955, just a few months after Keith's birth, Leo joined the army to avoid jail time. The divorce between Aileen's parents, Leo and Diane, was finalized on November 14, 1955.

With the aid of an army allowance that she received, Diane rented the top floor of a duplex with a friend named Marge. Diane obtained a job as an operator with Michigan Bell. She reported a trouble-free pregnancy with Aileen, stating that she smoked less than a pack of cigarettes a day and claimed that she did not drink. Diane believed that she was brutally beaten by Leo when she was only about 1 to 2 weeks pregnant with Aileen. Diane had a breech birth. Aileen was characterized as a colicky, irritable baby. While pregnant with Aileen, Diane briefly lived with her parents on two separate occasions, both marked by arguments and stress. She questioned whether the stress of being a battered wife and fighting with her parents had any detrimental effect on her children.

Diane attempted to be a single mother for about 1 year. Friends described her during this time as a good mother. A man whom Diane briefly dated recalled going to see her around lunchtime on one occasion and heard loud, crying babies as he climbed the stairs. Entering her home, he saw her asleep on the couch. While she was in the same room as her children, she was unresponsive to the wailing of her babies. He woke her up, and she claimed to have been drunk and unable to hear them. Her downstairs neighbor later complained that Diane let her children cry all morning. Much to her friends' dismay, Diane left one day to go out for dinner and never returned. There was no phone call or explanation. The kids were left with her roommate Marge. Aileen was approximately 6 months old at the time. After Marge kept the kids for almost a week, she finally called Lauri and Britta to come and take the children with them. They took in their grandchildren and raised them as their own children for a number of years. Diane went to Texas, never clarifying why she left.

Aileen would later tell a slightly different, more dramatic version of her abandonment, stating that she was left in the attic at her grandparent's house where she was found covered with flies. Although this version is inaccurate, her perception of her abandonment is not. Leo Pittman never had any contact with Aileen. When Diane was 18 years old, she made a second attempt to reunite with her family. However, her presence made her mother (Britta) jealous, particularly when she gave Aileen and Keith any attention.

Diane believed that her mother turned hateful toward her when she experienced puberty. Although Diane denied that any significant sexual abuse occurred, she sensed that Britta felt that Lauri was sexually interested in her. Diane recalled that Lauri frequently touched her accidentally and that on one occasion kissed her passionately. Aileen later made claims that her grandfather sexually abused her also.

Once again, Diane abandoned her children. When Aileen was 2 and Keith was 3, she left them with the babysitter and did not return. Once again, her parents picked up the children. Diane was gone for good.

Although Leo Pittman led a separate life, his criminal history seems to foreshadow Aileen's descent into illicit conduct. He engaged in a variety of crimes, including breaking and entering and car theft. Ultimately, he was convicted of kidnapping and brutally raping a 7-year-old girl. He committed suicide while serving a life sentence for this crime.

CHILDHOOD, PEERS, AND PROSTITUTION

At the age of 11, Aileen was already described as being incorrigible and possessing a frightening temper. Her angry outbursts were often unpredictable and frequently unprovoked. As might be expected, she did not socialize well with her peers. Lori remarked that everyone viewed Aileen as a Jekyll and Hyde character. By the age of 8, she was already falling out with other kids. Lori vividly described Aileen's personality and anger. Indeed, as Russell (1992 p. 79) reports,

> It registered even then that her sister's mannerisms and smiles lacked authenticity; her mood and sociability seemed phony and forced. It was as if she knew she didn't fit and tried hard to tailor her personality to something she thought people would like and accept. But then, in a split second, her temper erupted and it was all over. No one wanted to be around her. Lori believed Aileen was troubled not by the way she was treated at home, but by something inside her. Something in her personality. And with her chemical abuse, the temper worsened.

As a young girl, Aileen was pretty and thin, possessing a broad facial structure, wide-set eyes, and blond hair. Although Aileen would later claim that she became a prostitute when she was 15 years old, many people who grew up with her confirm that she was only 11 when she did so. In 1967, there was a shallow ravine and a wooded pathway that connected the 2 small towns of Troy and Rochester, Michigan. Down in the ravine, there were a number of fortlike structures made from logs, pieces of plywood, and other scraps of material. One of these structures is where young Aileen performed sexual acts with boys for cigarettes or loose change. "This little girl had learned at a frighteningly early age to disassociate herself from her body; to blank off her emotions" (Russell, 1992, p. 13). As adults, numerous men who grew up with Aileen described being propositioned by her, beginning when she was 11 until the age of approximately 15, when she left town. A number of 12- to 15-year-old boys lost their virginity to Aileen. She would perform oral sex or have intercourse for cigarettes, change, or a couple of dollars. They also described castigating and denigrating her with names such as "Cigarette Pig." A friend of Aileen's brother Keith stated that "Everybody called her bitch, slut, whore, and an ugly bitch, before she even was. . . . She was ridiculed or whatever . . . abused" (p. 17). Aileen resigned herself to the role of social outcast:

> Aileen, who worked not just in the forts but in the backs of cars, or simply lay down in the dirt, stripping off her clothes without inhibition or emotion, sometimes taking on three boys at a time. Those boys are now men who today admit that she took no pleasure in it and there was little if any conversation. . . . Aileen's earnings went on cigarettes, beer, and, before long, on the drugs with which she became increasingly involved—mescaline, acid, and downers like pot and pills, were her preference. . . . At a shockingly young age, Aileen had become an object of ridicule, and no neighborhood boy would have willingly admitted to being involved with her. (pp. 14, 16)

On several occasions, Aileen made known her desire to have a boyfriend but was brutally rejected. Almost all agree that until high school, Aileen was without friends. She and her brother Keith had a strange bond in which they were protective of one another within their family but also would fight bitterly outside of it. Friends of Keith claim to have witnessed incest between the brother and the sister. Lori would always find it hard to believe that the two had sex, since they were always arguing and sometimes could be quite cruel to one another. Aileen told Mark Fearn, Keith's best friend, that she also had sex with her father (grandfather Lauri). Once again, Lauri's daughter (Lori) rejected the truth of this statement, finding it incredulous. Aileen also claimed that in plain view of Britta, Lauri grabbed Aileen and kissed her, forcing his tongue deep into her mouth. Although this event is unsubstantiated, Lauri's behavior toward Diane, Aileen's sexually explicit conduct, and the accounts of various individuals like Mark Fearn, make this assertion quite possible.

Aileen's disturbing behavior, rather than her artistic talent, drew attention at home and at school. As a child, she would dance around and pretend that she was singing into a microphone. Aileen wanted to be an actress or a performer when she grew up. She wished to have attention, to be admired, and to be rich. Those who knew Aileen indicated that she had always been preoccupied with money.

> Her "antisocial behavior," low grades and very poor relationships with classmates and teachers, did not go unnoticed at Smith Junior High. She'd also run away from home. . . . Aileen heartily disliked school and had always had problems there. Her poor hearing and slight vision impairment were noted by staff early on. (Russell, 1992, p. 41)

In April 1970, Carolyn Marcy, a school counselor and diagnostician, completed an evaluation on Aileen. As Russell (1992 p. 42) indicates, her report concluded that

> Aileen "loses interest quickly and can easily become a leader in discipline problems." Other tests found her to have a low verbal IQ (80) and an average performance IQ (106): "Everyday judgment based on experience tested average. Motivation for assimilation of facts, numerical concepts, word knowledge and social awareness were far below average." Tests also yielded the . . . conclusion that Aileen was not "comfortable" in the female role. . . . Barry

Wuornos had already made a layman's observation of Aileen as being "hard-headed" and "without conscience." . . . Marcy's report ended with the prophetically urgent words: "It is vital for this girl's welfare that she receive counseling immediately." The warning was not heeded. Aileen never did receive any counseling, either as an inpatient or outpatient.

TEENAGE YEARS, CRIME, AND PREGNANCY

Aileen began shoplifting in her early teens. She was caught on a number of occasions, including at the K-Mart where Britta was employed. Britta quit out of humiliation. In addition, Aileen was known to steal from the other kids in the neighborhood. Some would comment that it seemed that no one ever cared about Aileen. During Aileen's and Keith's teenage years, the situation with Lauri became much worse. Aileen became quite rebellious and would openly state her disdain for him. "Aileen did not have a single good, healthy, supportive or nurturing relationship with a man during her formative years" (Russell, 1992, p. 29). Aileen ran away frequently, would hitchhike, and was often brought home by the police. On one occasion, when Lauri knew in advance that she was going to run away, he insisted that she never come back. When he received a call from the police to pick her up, he refused. Consequently, she was sent to juvenile hall. Lori commented that Aileen's hate for Lauri Wuornos was epic and powerful.

Aileen's anger and aggression only grew in her teenage years. She was frequently thrown out of parties for being vulgar, being belligerent, and initiating fights. She had a short fuse and was easily provoked. In addition to using the drugs previously mentioned, Aileen began to drink vast quantities of alcohol, particularly beer.

Aileen became pregnant at the age of 14. She gave several different versions of how this event occurred, including that she was brutally raped at gunpoint and knifepoint for 6 hours by an Elvis Presley look-alike. She told many different "stories" over the years. For instance, Aileen claimed to have been raped nine times in her life. She reported that several of the rapes were the product of the men she eventually murdered. However, Aileen Wuornos told many different tales, some of which are firmly refuted by those who know her. Nonetheless, given her sexual promiscuity, it is likely that at some point she was raped, and possibly more than once.

With respect to her pregnancy, Aileen alleged on various occasions that the father alternately was Keith, Lauri, a neighbor boy, and an older man in the community. What we know for certain, however, is that Lauri and Britta sent her to the Michigan Children's Aid Society for help. The grandparents were ashamed of and angry with Aileen. Her caseworker noted that she was immature, impulsive, and had no conceptualization of the future.

Aileen had the baby just after her fifteenth birthday at the Florence Crittenton Unwed Mothers' Home in Detroit. She believed that her grandfather took pleasure at abandoning her there. She did receive letters from Britta. The baby was immediately given up for adoption. Moreover, despite Aileen's wishes to look at the baby, Lauri would not allow it. "Aileen's short life thus far had been one long series of rejections and losses" (Russell, 1992, p. 68). Aileen did not make friends with the other girls at the institution. Her pregnancy was never discussed within her family, and her extended family was unaware that it had occurred. Lauri begrudgingly allowed Aileen to return home. At this point, her hatred for her grandfather had reached its peak, and she felt thoroughly abandoned and rejected by her grandmother.

Aileen reenrolled at Troy High School but dropped out after a few months. She finally made a friend in the tenth grade, a girl named Dawn Nieman (now Botkins). Dawn was also frequently in trouble in school and was expelled for fighting with others when Aileen dropped out. According to Dawn, Aileen never talked about the baby and never mentioned being raped. Dawn noted that Aileen seemed to be protective of Keith and Lori and that she would often give them money she made from prostitution. In an interview with Court TV (1999), Dawn Botkins stated, "I always knew that something was going to happen to Aileen. Either something was going to happen to Aileen or Aileen was going to hurt someone else because this was the life she was in and nobody would give her a break."

Dawn also recalled the way in which Aileen's peers treated her.

> {They] treated her like shit. . . . One time Aileen was coming out of a store and these guys hit her with their car . . . not enough to hurt her, but they just knocked her. Aileen was emotional, but she never sat there and cried to have people feel sorry for her. She'd get pissed off. . . . They hated her even more for getting mad. (Russell, 1992, p. 82)

After Aileen dropped out of school, she then spent some time at Adrian's Girl's Home. After the passage of several months, she returned to her grandparents' house, only to run away again. This time, Lauri kicked her out for good. At the age of 15, Aileen was sleeping in wooded areas and abandoned cars in freezing weather, as well as hitchhiking on the highway (Aherns, 2001). She occasionally stayed with Dawn's family. Neighbors knew that she was homeless and heard the rumors that she was a prostitute. No one offered to help her.

At this time, Keith was living with friends, and Lauri took Britta on vacation for a few days to help calm her down. When they returned, their daughter Lori noted that Britta was drinking openly. Lori suspected that the drinking was because of Aileen and Keith, but her mother never told her for sure. Her mother was soon bedridden, suffering from delirium tremens, and she deteriorated into convulsions. She was never taken to the hospital, and on July 7, 1971, Britta died. Lori later commented that on several occasions her father failed to call an ambulance for Britta and that he let her die. The autopsy revealed that she died from cirrhosis of the liver from drinking. Apparently, Diane, Barry, and Lauri knew of Britta's alcoholism; however, Lori, Aileen, and Keith were kept in the dark. Doctors had warned Britta that the poor condition of her liver would certainly kill her if she ever drank again.

Aileen's behavior at Britta's funeral was abhorrent. As Russell (1992, p. 73) explains,

> Aileen showed up at the funeral home, viewed Britta's casket, then frivolously switched the nameplates on the men's and ladies' restrooms. She then had to be thrown out for lighting up a cigarette and defiantly puffing smoke in Britta's face, saying, "If I want to blow smoke in the old slob's face, I will!" . . . Behind her rampant idealizing lay Aileen's anger at Britta for deserting her and not saving her from Lauri.

Blaming Aileen and Keith for Britta's death, Lauri told Diane that if she did not take them both away, he would kill them. Diane initially intended to take them back with her to Houston, stating, "You haven't gotten love here and I made a mistake" (p. 75). According to Diane, their criminal records precluded her from being able to take them to Houston.

Aileen than began a cross-country journey that took her to Florida. "I was 15 just going on 16. . . . it was January 2nd when I hit the road . . . and I was on the road ever since all throughout my life off and on everywhere, except for Daytona. I settled down there in my twenties." (Aileen Wuornos, Court TV, 1999)

ADULTHOOD, LOSSES, AND RELATIONSHIPS

Within 5 years of Britta's death, Aileen would lose both Lauri and Keith. On March 12, 1976, Lauri committed suicide by means of carbon monoxide poisoning in his son Barry's garage. Aileen did not attend the funeral. In 2 years Keith battled the throat cancer that spread to his brain, lungs, and bones. On July 17, 1976, Keith passed away at the age of 21. No one remembers Aileen's visiting her dying brother, despite her claims of visiting him often. Diane came from Texas to attend his wake. She noted that Aileen was uncharacteristically vulnerable, following her around for attention.

Aileen married a wealthy man 50 years her senior approximately 2 months after Lauri committed suicide. Lewis Gratz Fell was 69 years old, and Aileen was just 20. They met when he picked her up hitchhiking. Aileen was interested in money, and he was interested in having a young blond on his arm. Despite his financial assets and their wedding vows, Aileen continued to drink heavily, stayed out all night, and spent a lot of money. The marriage lasted only 1 month. Lewis filed for a divorce and a restraining order against Aileen for beating him with his own cane. Aileen later told Lori that she beat him for reprimanding her for one of the many shopping sprees she went on.

Aileen continued to frequent bars, carouse, philander, and play pool. On July 13, 1976, she was arrested for assault and battery after hurling a cue ball at a bar manager so hard that it was lodged in the wall. She was angry because he closed her pool table after she became rowdy and threatening to other patrons. Aileen only paid a fine for this incident. However, her criminal behavior continued to escalate. Under the alias of Sandra B. Kretsch (from a license she stole), she was arrested for Disorderly Conduct. In 1977, she received two Driving Under the Influence (DUI) convictions and two arrests for weapons offenses. Aileen had a variety of criminal charges under a variety of pseudonyms.

As an adult, Aileen moved around routinely, and sometimes she lived with Lori and her husband. She did not have any regular employment and never helped with household chores. She continued to be argumentative and threatening, particularly to men (e.g., Lori's husband). She bragged openly about how she survived on the road. For example, she convinced a minister and his family who resided in a different town to take her in and help her. She stayed for a few days and then left after burglarizing their residence. She also would boast about all of the truck drivers that would pick her up for sex.

Shortly after Keith's death, Aileen arrived in Texas, unannounced, to stay with Diane for 2 weeks. Diane reported, "I could see the violence in her, and she frightened me to death. . . . There's something that's in her that frightens me" (Russell, 1992, p. 92). Diane claimed that she went to bed each night fearing that Aileen would kill her in her sleep or at least steal her car. Diane gave her bus fare and asked her to leave. Aileen reported that she hated her mother and wanted to leave.

In 1981, at the age of 25, Aileen had a brief relationship with a 52-year-old man named Jay Watts. It was primarily a sexual relationship. Jay described the relationship as a casual, 2-month affair. For Aileen, it was the closest thing to having a boyfriend that she had ever experienced. Watts characterized her as sexual and affectionate. He would later claim that she was moody but never violent. On May 20, 1981, Aileen held up a convenience store with a .22 caliber pistol for $35 and 2 packs of cigarettes. She was charged with robbery with a deadly weapon. Aileen was sentenced to 3 years imprisonment in the Correctional Institute in Lowell, Florida. Commenting on this crime, Aileen maintained that she had purchased a gun at a pawnshop after having a fight with Watts. Aileen stated that she did not think about the consequences of her conduct. Instead, she was focused on whether her boyfriend would stand by her side if she were caught robbing a store. She wanted Watts to prove that he loved her and, if necessary, would rescue her. Although Watts did not love Aileen, he helped her out as much as possible and maintained contact with her during the beginning of her prison term. At this time, she vehemently professed her disgust for lesbians. However, this attitude would soon change.

A psychiatric evaluation of Aileen was conducted while she was in prison. She was characterized as

> an unstable individual who, besides claiming to have been repeatedly sexually abused, had suffered a lot of emotional upheavals in her life. . . . Clinically, she is judged to be of average intelligence. . . . There is no indication of a thought disorder and specifically no loosening of associations or delusions. (Russell, 1992, p. 101)

After prison, Aileen hitchhiked to Washington, D.C., to meet a man named Ed whom she made contact with through the personal ads in a biker magazine. Upon their initial contact, Aileen expressly indicated that she was a lesbian and that there would be no sexual contact. Ed reported that she looked older than 27, was still slender, but was puffy around the eyes. All together, she spent about 4 weeks under his roof. He described her as being moody and a heavy drinker. She was always talking about religion or violence. She frequently had fits of rage and, on a few occasions, threatened to kill Ed. Once he took her to a local medical center because she wanted to obtain tranquilizers. A female counselor pulled him aside and told him to take her threats quite seriously and to remove her from his life as soon as possible. When she vacated premises and left people, Aileen consistently stole from those who had given her a place to stay.

In 1984, Aileen had her first homosexual love interest; however, it was a short-lived experience. When Aileen spoke to her sister Lori, she would talk of men, always focusing on violence or on being used. Around this time, her criminal behavior was also escalating. She was arrested for forging two bad checks, totaling $5,595. She never showed up for her court hearing. In 1985, she was stopped in a stolen vehicle. According to Aileen, she was prostituting herself sometimes 25 to 30 times a day.

Aileen was basically alone in the world until she met Tyria (Ty) Moore. Their relationship last 4.5 years, spanning the time during which Aileen committed murder almost until she was arrested. Aileen's defense attorney, Tricia Jenkins, characterized the affair in the following way: "It was the only relationship that I could ever find that was close. . . . It was constant and that lasted over any period of time. . . . And she [Ty] was the first person that had ever given her [Aileen] a relationship." (Court TV, 1999)

Ty and Aileen met in a gay bar in Daytona, Florida, and shortly thereafter were living in a series of apartments, trailers, and cheap motels. Prior to her involvement with Aileen, Ty was described as fun, easygoing, and friendly. She made friends effortlessly and was close to her family, although they lived in Ohio and she resided in Florida.

Ty Moore had no criminal record except for a breaking-and-entering charge for retrieving her belongings from an ex-lover's home. She also regularly attended church.

Ty was a short, stocky redhead who was often mistaken for a man. Ty lived with one of her best friends, Cammie Greene, who was married with two young sons. Aileen would later steal Cammie's driver's license and use her name as an alias.

Cammie reported that despite Ty's more masculine appearance, Aileen took on the male role. She also noticed that Aileen would order Ty around. The proprietors of a recreational vehicle (RV) park that Ty and Aileen later frequented, witnessed Aileen "beat the hell" out of her lover (Russell, 1992, p. 141). Cammie readily spoke about Aileen's ferocious temper and ability to tell tall tales. For example, Aileen claimed that she was a special agent in another state and, on another occasion, reported that she shot a bear that came crashing through her cabin in Colorado. Aileen continued to have a fascination with fame and often said that someday there would be a book written about her. She told Cammie not only that she and Ty were going to be like Bonnie and Clyde but also that they would be doing society a favor.

Aileen was painfully jealous of Ty's relationship with Cammie, as well as Ty's close relationship with her family. Aileen was particularly hateful toward Cammie's husband. Although Ty regularly was employed, typically as a chambermaid at hotels, Aileen strongly encouraged her to stay home so that she could take care of Aileen. It made Aileen jealous to think of Ty's interacting with others. She was fearful of Ty's leaving her. Conversely, Ty hated Aileen's prostituting but never attempted to stop her. According to Aileen, she made between $150 and $300 a day. They both drank excessively, and Ty's work performance and general attitude began to decline. Now in her thirties, Aileen was losing her looks. According to her defense attorney, Tricia Jenkins, "She was extremely overweight. She was very, very haggard. She was not able to attract the same type of man and that was very demoralizing for her" (Court TV, 1999).

Aileen would later claim that Ty was financially dependent on her and threatened to leave her if Aileen could not provide the lifestyle Ty wanted. Many individuals have refuted this claim, including people whom they lived with and the owners of several hotels where they stayed. Aileen and Ty rented rooms for weeks at a time and typically became quite friendly with the staff. Ty's stepsister, who stayed with them for part of a summer, was frightened of Aileen. With the exception of Aileen, there was a consensus that she called the shots in her relationship with Ty. Moreover, Aileen implied that Ty was partially responsible for the crimes she committed, stating that "You can't be that powerfully in love in a world that is so screwed up. It might wind up making you commit crimes . . . lead you into criminal behavior if you are too powerfully in love" (Court TV, 1000).

RICHARD MALLORY: AILEEN'S FIRST VICTIM

Richard Mallory, a 51-year-old man from Clearwater, Florida, owned his own electronics repair shop. He had gray hair and a mustache, and stood 5'11" tall. Mallory was slender, weighing approximately 170 pounds. He had been divorced for many years and, admittedly, loved spending time in gentlemen's clubs and procuring the services of prostitutes in his free time. In the years prior to his initial meeting with Aileen, Mallory had encountered scores of prostitutes, many of whom knew him by name. No one reported being sexually assaulted by Mallory. However, in 1958, he was convicted of assault with attempt to rape and spent 9 years in a Maryland prison. This conviction was never brought out in Aileen's trial; however, he had no other criminal complaints. In addition, Mallory had no history of attacking the many women he encountered during the near 20-year period prior to his murder. Aileen alleged that he had raped her. However, this allegation was thoroughly inconsistent with all the forensic evidence from his crime scene and body. Aileen made the exact same claim for each of the other six victims she killed, all of whom had a more unblemished record and a more lackluster personal life than Mallory. With Mallory as the first victim, the predatory homicide that ended his life is the focus of our analysis.

Aileen gave several versions of how the murder took place. Some of them are briefly presented here. On the basis of one of Aileen's reports and the available forensic evidence, Russell (1992, pp. 147–159) described the first of these versions as follows:

> By early evening a handful of northbound rides from Fort Myers had deposited her outside Tampa on I-4. . . . She was lingering there when Richard Mallory stopped to pick her up. . . . They had a common destination in Daytona so he invited her to hop in. They whiled away a pleasant drive across the state, chatting companionably and drinking. Richard smoked a little pot, but she wouldn't join him. . . . He stirred her a vodka and orange.
>
> Somewhere along the highway they made a pit stop and he bought her a six-pack. . . . She was tired . . . but as they hit the fringes of Daytona close to midnight, Richard asked, "Do you mind if we stop somewhere and talk some more?" She suggested a spot near Bunnell, where they parked again, talking and drinking. . . . She admitted to being a professional call girl. "Do you want to help me make some money, cause [sic] I need some money for rent and everything?" . . . They talked prices and moved to a more deserted spot in the woods. . . . She peeled off her clothes before he did. . . . They hugged and kissed a little. . . . "Why don't you take off your clothes? It will hurt if you don't," she said finally. . . . What if this guy took back the money he'd given her, or rolled her? What if he was going to rape her?
>
> He was still sitting in a non-threatening position behind his steering wheel when she made her move. She had been standing just outside the open passenger door when suddenly she reached in, making a grab for her small blue bag containing her spare clothes, which lay on the car floor. . . . He smelled danger and lunged across to try to stop her getting the bag. . . . She yanked out her gun and aimed it towards her companion. "You sonofabitch! I knew you were going to rape me!" "No I wasn't! No I wasn't!" he protested. . . . She leaned into the car and fired quickly, pumping a bullet that first hit his right arm, then traveled lethally onward, striking him in the right side . . . crawling out of the driver's door, slamming it behind him, trying desperately to put something between him and his attacker. . . . She ran around the front of the car to where he stood, disabled. "If you don't stop, man, right now, I'll keep shooting!" . . . firing a second bullet, which hit him in the torso, knocking him back up and making him fall to the ground. Then a third. Then a fourth. He did not die immediately. But the bullet that struck the left lung, . . . coming to rest in the chest cavity. . . . It caused a massive and fatal hemorrhage. . . . He struggled for ten, maybe twenty . . . minutes. She watched him die.
>
> She then . . . moved him enough to get at his pockets, taking his identification and money. . . . She spied cardboard and a discarded piece of red carpeting and she dragged those over to where he lay. . . . First she put the cardboard over his body, then she stretched out the carpeting on top to hide as much of him as it would. Still naked, she found the ignition keys and moved the Cadillac to Quail Run, another isolated spot nearby, where she hastily dressed. She drank her last beer while pondering her next move. She considered putting the car through a car wash before going home to shower, then thought better of it. . . . She was

forced to stop and get gas. She threw some of the . . . man's clothing into the woods, far from his body. Later, she would throw the rest into trash dumpsters.

During a Court TV interview (1999), Aileen stated, "it took me 17 years to finally kill somebody . . . to have the heart to do it . . . a rapist or anybody. But I finally got really stone cold and said you know, enough is enough." When Aileen returned home after murdering Richard Mallory, Ty commented that she was able to smell alcohol on Aileen but that she was perfectly coherent and acting normal. Aileen had driven Mallory's car home, and she and Ty used it the next day to move from their hotel room into an apartment. Ty reported that Aileen was in good spirits. Next, by herself, Aileen took the car to a deserted trail near the beach, buried the body, and took everything out of the car. She then wiped away all of her fingerprints with a red towel. She left Richard Mallory's automobile and threw his keys in the bushes of someone's yard along the way. On December 6, using Cammie Greene's stolen license, Aileen pawned Richard Mallory's camera and radar detector at a local pawnshop.

During their first night in their new apartment, Aileen told Ty, "I killed a guy today" (A & E, 1998; Court TV, 1992, 1999; Russell, 1992, p. 152). Ty testified in court that it shocked her when Aileen said this without emotion, almost nonchalantly. Aileen told her that she shot the man and put his body in the woods, covered it up, and dumped the car. Ty later told police and testified that Aileen never said that Richard Mallory abused or raped her. Aileen had no bruises and showed no signs of having been attacked. Under oath, Ty testified that "No, I saw no sign of injury, no" (Court TV, 1999). Ty reported, "I wanted to get out of the relationship then . . . but I just . . . I was scared" (Russell, 1992, p. 153). Ty never went to the police; however, much later, they went to her.

FORENSIC EVIDENCE

The car was found first, and it had been stripped of all identification and wiped clean of fingerprints. On December 13, 1989, Richard Mallory's body was discovered across the river from his car, approximately 5 miles away. His body had begun to decay. He was discovered lying face down, with his legs crossed at the ankles. "He was fully clothed in a short-sleeved white shirt, blue jeans, 2 pairs of socks and brown loafers. . . . His jeans were fastened and fully zipped and his brown belt was buckled, though the buckle was twisted four inches or so off-center. His front pockets were pulled slightly inside-out as if they had been emptied" (Russell, 1992, p. 155). An autopsy revealed that he suffered 4 gunshot wounds to the chest. The bullets, which were copper-coated and hollow-point, were fired from a .22 caliber handgun. At least one bullet entered his body while he was still in the vehicle. His blood alcohol level was .05, which is in the lower limits of intoxication.

AILEEN'S CONFESSION

After being taken into police custody, Aileen confessed to the murder on January 16, 1991. The confession lasted 3 hours and 20 minutes. During her confession, she presented different versions of the events that transpired. First, Aileen indicated that she was angry because Richard Mallory would not take his pants off to have sex. She indicated that they fought about it, and then he became abusive (Court TV, taped police confession, 1999):

> So I jumped out of the car with my bag. I grabbed the gun and I said, "Get off me." And he
> said, "what's going on?" And I said, "you son of a bitch, I knew you were going to rape me."
> And he said, "No I wasn't, no I wasn't." I said, "Oh yes you were, you know you were going
> to try to rape me, man." So anyway, I told him to step away from the car.

She then told a slightly different version of what happened (Court TV, taped police
confession, 1999):

> We started fighting and everything else. . . . So I jumped out, and he grabbed my bag and I
> grabbed my bag, and the arm busted. And I got the bag again and I pulled it out of his hand.
> And that's when I grabbed the pistol out. And when I grabbed the pistol out, I just shot him
> in the front seat.

Commenting on Aileen's confession, the prosecuting attorney for the Richard Mallory
case, John Tanner, stated that

> At that point she could have just driven away or got out the other door and left, run, whatever
> she wanted to do. . . . But she just described getting out of the automobile, walking out the
> front of the car. . . . Mr. Mallory was back on his feet, she shot him again, he fell on the
> ground and then she walked over and shot him twice more. (Court TV, 1999)

CONCLUSIONS

This chapter reviewed the tragic family and life circumstances of Aileen Wuornos. The
product of neglect, violence, mistreatment, and abandonment, she found herself in the
maelstrom of drug and alcohol abuse, possible incest, prostitution, failed relationships,
and criminal conduct, including murder. To be sure, Aileen's story was fraught with mis-
ery, pain, and suffering; she became anesthetized by sexual promiscuity; she experienced
the allure of illegal substances; she engaged in delinquency and crime; and she was the
object of victimization and exploitation.

Nonetheless, she was found guilty of murder and was executed. For our purposes,
the question is, How can we make sense of her vile and despicable conduct as a female
serial killer? To address this matter, the subsequent chapter returns us to attachment theory, personality development as linked to ASPD (psychopathy), and predatory homicide.
In short, we consider what connections can be made between Aileen's very troubled adolescence and her disturbing adult behavior. Accordingly, given what we know about
Aileen Wournos's life story, Chapter 9 endeavors to interpret and analyze these data and
their meanings.

9

In Search of Meaning

Analyzing and Interpreting the Data

❖

INTRODUCTION

In this chapter, several issues pertaining to the case of Aileen Wuornos are explored. These issues are directly related to the life events presented in the previous chapter and are understood to signify Aileen's unique, personal story and our interpretation of it. Overall, the chapter examines the relationship among female-perpetrated predatory homicide, failed parental attachments in early childhood, and antisocial personality disorder in adulthood. More specifically, however, the following questions are systematically reviewed: (a) Can childhood interactions with primary attachment figures be an important early marker of adulthood behavior and personality development, particularly the onset of ASPD or psychopathic traits? (b) Can the inhibition of early bonding or attachments and abandonment, as well as emotional, sexual, and physical abuse, lead to detachment, apathy, and lack of empathy for others? (c) Can hostility and aggression that becomes part of an individual's internal working model result in preemptive aggression and predatory murder?

In order to address these important matters, the behavioral, cognitive, and affective states exhibited by Aileen Wuornos are noted, as are her personality traits and motivational forces that confirm or disconfirm the link among attachment patterns, personality, and the potential for serial killing in women. To accomplish these tasks, Aileen is rated informally on The Attachment Disorder Symptoms Checklist. In addition, using the items for the Psychopathy Checklist Revised (PCL-R), a description of her psychopathic traits is delineated. Moreover, the murder of Richard Mallory is compared with the hallmarks of predatory aggression, as described by Meloy (1992). A summary description of the connection found among insecure attachment, psychopathy, and predatory violence also is provided. Finally, naturalistic generalizations are presented.

ATTACHMENT PATTERNS IN CHILDHOOD:
AVOIDANT/DISMISSING STYLE

Aileen experienced inconsistent care, as well as emotional, physical, and possible sexual abuse at the hands of one on her primary attachment figures. She subsequently demonstrated an avoidant/dismissing style, characterized by detachment, hostility, social withdrawal, impulsive behavior, and poor interpersonal sensitivity and awareness. Various examples of her primary attachment pattern as avoidant/dismissing are demonstrated throughout this chapter.

Aileen's story is filled with abandonment, abuse, and neglect. Bowlby (1969) asserted that the inability to bond or form attachments and, therefore, to develop empathy for others is often a result of inconsistent or nonexistent caring, especially during the person's childhood. Aileen's mother, Diane, unequivocally abandoned her daughter when she was a baby. Descriptions from Diane's friends indicated that she was inconsistent in her accessibility to Aileen and erratic with the nurturance she gave her child. Diane was a single mother, and Aileen was generally described as an irritable, a colicky, and a difficult baby. Sometimes the child's cries were met with comfort; at other times, they were completely ignored for hours. In addition to the inconsistent care-giving, Diane deserted her children when Aileen was approximately 9 months old. She did not say goodbye to Aileen and Keith, failing to see them again until approximately a year later when she briefly entered their lives.

According to attachment theory, it is critical for the child to develop trust and security from the primary caregivers. Without this development, the child begins to form an internal working model of others as unreliable, untrustworthy, and unresponsive to the infant's needs. When Aileen was an infant, her proximity-seeking behaviors (e.g., crying, screaming) were intermittently reinforced, and, consequently, they occurred more frequently (initially resembling an anxious/ambivalent pattern). These very behaviors were quite aversive to Diane, who responded to them less and less, until she ultimately forsook her children. Thus, we see the manifestation of a vicious cycle. Indeed, had Aileen been more secure in her mother's accessibility and consistency with respect to sensitive caring, her proximity-seeking behaviors might not have been triggered so easily and frequently. However, it appears that Aileen developed secondary conditional strategies, such as hypervigilance and detachment, to cope with her exposure to abuse and the failure to have her needs met.

Aileen had no direct contact with her biological father, Leo Pittman. However, his criminal behavior and psychopathic traits are demonstrated consistently in the available literature. Although the primary focus is on the environmental aspects of personality development (e.g., attachment patterns), the biological component of temperament and of psychopathy cannot be ignored. Aileen's fits of rage mirror those of her biological father. Many other aspects of her criminal behavior, including her predatory nature and lack of empathy for other human beings, are also strikingly similar to that of her biological father. However, there are many confounding environmental variables that prevent a linear biological link.

Perhaps the most damaging relationship that Aileen had was with her grandfather, Lauri Wuornos. From a young age, she experienced brutal physical and emotional abuse from the man she believed was her father. There was also unconfirmed sexual victimization by him, although it appears quite likely that it occurred. His emotional abuse extended from repeatedly calling her degrading names to drowning her kitten in front of her. From an attachment theory perspective, this is what Aileen was learning: (a) I am evil, wicked, worthless, and hated by those who are supposed to love and protect me; (b) those who are supposed to love me hurt me; (c) life is filled with terror, rejection, and pain; (d) others cannot be trusted, and so I must be hypervigilant, in order to protect myself from others.

Her internal working models consisted of a view of *self* as unlovable and wicked and of a view of *others* as hostile and rejecting. In order to cope with debilitating abuse, she shut down her ability to feel and became detached from her own feelings and those of friends and intimates. A grandiose self-view seemed to develop to protect Aileen from the unbearably painful truth of her rejection by others. She made comments to many that one day she would be famous and that she would be the subject of books and movies. Aileen also created elaborate embellishments about her life experiences to impress those she encountered as an adult.

Let us consider for a moment Bowlby's (1969) three reaction states to separation from a primary attachment figure: protest, despair, and detachment. Aileen's abandonment from her biological mother was a real separation. However, her extreme abuse from her grandfather, the passive compliance of her grandmother, and their lack of verbal and physical affection toward Aileen, resulted de facto in separation and loss. According to Bowlby (1969), this loss results in powerful anger. Although detachment is an adaptive strategy in the face of such abuse and neglect, most children (including Aileen) cannot bounce back, and their ability to bond with others in a healthy way is inhibited.

Britta, Aileen's grandmother, stood by complacently while her granddaughter was abused. Reports indicated that Britta was an alcoholic who suffered from anxiety. Although Aileen did have some positive interactions with her grandmother, she could not turn to her for protection or emotional support. Britta did not have significant emotional exchanges or conversations with her (grand)children. She seemed to be affectionless, consumed by her own unhappiness. Caregivers of avoidant children tend to be rejecting and to ignore their children's attempt to create proximity. Britta and Lauri were rejecting in their own ways. Lauri was overtly violent and emotionally abusive, whereas Britta was overtly oblivious and emotionally unavailable.

Research indicates that adults with avoidant attachment patterns have low levels of parental communication and emotional support, and poor relationships with their fathers during childhood (Rothbard & Shaver, 1994). In addition, research suggests that mothers of avoidant/dismissing or anxious/ambivalent individuals are nervous, depressed, frightened, worried, or confused (Rothbard & Shaver, 1991). Clearly, these latter descriptors fit Britta, and they informed the interactions she had with her granddaughter. Finally, avoidant attachment patterns correlate with the individual's increased anger toward his or her mother and father, and with parental figures being hurtful, mean, and hateful during the person's childhood (Rothbard & Shaver, 1994). Aileen made no secret about her rage toward her grandfather. Moreover, Lauri did not conceal his disdain for his granddaughter. Their disgust toward one another was verbalized frequently in the Wuornos household. In addition, Aileen verbalized to Keith's friends her hatred of her grandfather. Finally, Aileen's decision to blow smoke into the face of Britta's corpse at her funeral, referring to her grandmother as an "old slob," made palpable her resentfully inspired final act of defiance.

Aileen felt like an outsider or a "black sheep" in her own family. Neither her primary attachment figures nor her peers wanted her. Intense feelings of abandonment and isolation traumatize an individual and create a negative anticipatory effect (Schurman-Kauflin, 2000). Children learn that there is no one there when the bad things happen (e.g., fights at school or a skinned knee). Children with insecure attachments come to believe that there will be no one there to help them when stressful situations arise (Fonagy et al., 1997). According to Meloy (1988), psychopathic individuals typically turn their feelings of social isolation to feelings of withdrawal, aggression, and hostility. This appears to have been the case with Aileen Wuornos. Perhaps what is most psychologically damaging is when the worst life experiences occurring at home are coupled with rejection by and isolation from peers. As investigators report, attachment with parents has a stronger impact on an individual's ability to interact with others than any other relationship. Clearly, then, Aileen was in trouble from the start.

Attachment to Siblings

Undoubtedly, Aileen was closer to Keith than to Lori, even when she believed that Lori was her sister and not her aunt. This attachment to Keith could be viewed as a function of their proximity in age or because of their relationship as brother and sister. However, their attachment was most closely related to the abuse they suffered. Keith's friends reported that despite their constant fighting, they could be quite protective of one another. Aileen and Keith both suffered extreme victimization at the hands of Lauri, and both felt unwanted. They gave one another a sense of protection, no matter how fragile. According to Schurman-Kauflin (2000), the sibling bond is derived from the comfort that they provide to one another during abusive periods. In the same study, the author noted that despite verbalizations of great love for one another, these same siblings could be remorselessly violent toward one another. These observations are consistent with the exchanges between Aileen and Keith. They bitterly fought both physically and verbally. In addition, according to some of Keith's friends, they engaged in consensual incest.

Although their bond was unhealthy in many ways, Aileen felt a tremendous loss when Keith died of cancer at the age of 21. Although she professed to be close to her brother, many claim that she never went to see him in the hospital over a 2-year period. In many ways, the relationship between Aileen and Keith seemed incongruent and incredible. However, Aileen was oblivious to the inconsistencies of her words and actions. She felt especially alone in the world after her brother's death. Conversely, Aileen's relationship with Lori was mired in jealously and fear. Aileen was jealous because Lori escaped the abuse at home, instead receiving preferential treatment. Lori was fearful of Aileen's temper and physical threats (e.g., Aileen's chasing her with a knife).

Prostitution: Aileen's Early Detachment from Mind and Body

It is difficult to imagine how Aileen Wuornos could start selling her body at such a young age. Nonetheless, she had been taught that she was an object to be abused. Accordingly, young Aileen used her body as a means to an end (e.g., money and cigarettes). Many of those who solicited or accepted her sexual services commented that Aileen had a tough attitude and was indifferent to the sexual contact. She was dehumanized and demoralized repeatedly through the humiliation following physical objectification and verbal assaults.

Indeed, nicknames such as "Cigarette Pig," "slut," and "whore" served only to further break her spirit, lending credence to the vicious and vile names that her grandfather called her time and time again.

Some individuals who have insecure attachment patterns in infancy and early childhood are able to develop more secure, healthy attachment patterns with improved caregiving or are able to develop many positive and nurturing secondary attachments. However, the insensitive and scornful treatment showered upon Aileen Wuornos by others was incessant, brutal, and intense both in the home and by her peers throughout her childhood and teenage years. This early abuse and rejection planted the seeds of hatred and rage.

By puberty, Aileen was already demonstrating hatred for herself and for others. She did not see people, particularly males, as a source of comfort, companionship, or warmth. On the rare occasion that Aileen reached out to establish romantic adolescent companionship, she was flatly rejected. The only emotion she readily expressed was anger, which functioned to further alienate her from others. However, anger was safer than feeling hurt or sad. After all, what good would these sentiments do her, except to make her more weak and vulnerable? Her internal working model was so firm that she did not trust or express her own feelings, choosing instead to view others with hostile intent and without compassion. She had learned not to value human interaction because doing so would only cause her pain. People are good for what they can give you materially or physically; there is no intrinsic worth in a human being: this is the lens through which Aileen viewed herself. Although she was unlovable, her physical self could provide her with the things she really needed like cigarettes, money, alcohol, and rides.

ATTACHMENT PATTERNS AS A TEENAGER

Aileen's feelings of being alone and abandoned were exacerbated when she learned that Lauri and Britta were really her grandparents rather than her parents. By this time, Aileen was openly defiant toward her grandfather and patently clear about her hatred of him. However, as a child, she was so physically intimidated by her grandfather that her lack of attachment to him was not so readily apparent. Without being socialized to care about the opinion of her grandparents or others in authority, Aileen regularly acted out in school and engaged in delinquent and criminal conduct. She learned not to care about what others thought of her or how her actions made them feel. After all, no one had ever taken her feelings into consideration. Indeed, she had always been treated as a nothing, so what did she care what everyone else thought? In addition, Aileen believed she knew better anyway.

Aileen was convinced that she had to look out for herself. In her quest for stimulation and self-fulfillment, she was frequently truant from school, stole, and used drugs and alcohol. Her escapist behaviors also extended to running away. Separating herself from her emotions was no longer enough; she needed to be physically away from her grandfather, Lauri.

Aileen was incredibly impulsive and would fly off into seemingly unprovoked fits of rage, which would only increase during her adult years. Aileen's sense of self-worth was so fragile and so defended against, that even the most trivial remark could send her into a blind rage. For her, the trivial became an extreme insult (Schurman-Kauflin, 2000). Aileen's inability to mentalize self and others in a rational way led her to act out physically what she was unable to process psychologically.

Individuals with psychopathic traits hold a narcissistic self-concept that is usually an extreme defense for a veiled and diminished sense of self-worth (Schurman-Kauflin, 2000). The view of self, which begins as unlovable, in extreme cases can shift to one of omnipotence as the individual defensively sees himself or herself as "too good for others, and relationships as threatening to [one's] sense of control, not worth the effort or both" (Rothbard & Shaver, 1994, p. 61). Aileen ostensibly made this shift.

Her internal working model of others was so negative and rigid that she consistently interpreted aggressive, hostile intent, when none was present. Her belief that others were a source of ridicule and pain was repeatedly reinforced during her formative years. This experience was based in reality to a point; however, Aileen created a self-fulfilling prophecy in other but benign situations. She encountered situations and people with a chip on her shoulder, believing that the world owed her something because of the way she had been treated. Indeed, she distanced herself from making attachments with those who could have directed or influenced her life positively.

Aileen had a brief friendship with Dawn Botkins in the tenth grade. This friendship was short-lived and their common ground was that of being *outsiders*. Dawn said that she was intrigued by Aileen's tough veneer and her behavior as a prostitute. What this view confirms, however, is that Aileen was an oddity to be examined. Eventually, Dawn got married, and, once again, Aileen felt abandoned. Shortly thereafter, Aileen hitchhiked to Florida. Another tie to normalcy, belonging to and acceptance by someone, anyone, had been severed.

When a child is raised in a chaotic, unforgiving home, the attachments that the child establishes with friends can make a tremendous difference. There was no one, except her brother Keith, who validated Aileen's pain, no one who made her believe that she was undeserving of the abuse she endured. Even Keith did not protect Aileen from the torment she received from other children. Aileen's lack of interpersonal ability and inhibited bonding to others seems to separate her path from that of Keith, who also suffered abandonment and alienation from his family. Despite Keith's family relationships, he had a best friend throughout his childhood. He had a number of acquaintances, many of whom paid to have sex with Aileen but who failed to acknowledge her in public. As they entered their teenage years, Keith had girlfriends, but Aileen had no one.

Aileen was connected neither to anyone nor to anything, nor was she bound by relationships or expectations. She reacted moment to moment with the only feelings that were safe to experience—rage, fear, hatred. The only expectation anyone ever had of Aileen was that she was bad and evil, someone who would amount to nothing. The people she should have been able to trust the most had broken every taboo. Human behavior is learned from and molded by those who are entrusted with tending to the needs of helpless children. For Aileen, this trust had been violated repeatedly and cruelly.

We note that many children experience abhorrent abuse but do not murder or otherwise victimize others. Indeed, in some healthy way, many bond to society, to its institutions, and to groups or individuals. Aileen knew right from wrong. However, she just did not care. But why should she? No one gave a second thought to harming her. For some who experience debilitating abuse, their distrust turns to resentment and then to intense levels of anger (Schurman-Kauflin, 2000). Aileen slipped beneath the radar in all the possible ways she could have made attachments. Thus, she did not develop an internal working model that included empathy. She was not connected to family, friends, teachers, or employers. She could never hold down a real job. Until Tyria Moore, Aileen had no significant romantic attachments.

At the age of 15, Aileen experienced three devastating losses. First, she had a baby and placed it up for adoption, without even holding the infant as she had wanted to hold it. Second, Lauri threw Aileen and Keith out of the house. Whereas Keith was able to stay with friends, Aileen was reduced to sleeping in the woods. Third, just a few short months later, her grandmother, Britta, passed away. Her grandfather made it clear that if she came around the house, he would kill her. Aileen was finally and completely abandoned by any semblance of family in her life.

Aileen had not been adequately prepared by her family to interact with the world in a healthy, adaptive way. Her personality development was crude and her defense mechanisms primitive. Aileen was wearing an emotional suit of armor, constantly ready for battle and typically taking the offensive. Although this suit of armor could protect her from emotional pain, it also prevented her from making healthy attachments. Aileen would hurt others before they did so to her. She used aggression to defend against what she perceived to be threats to her sense of well-being. She never learned how to engage others such that her emotional needs could be met in a meaningful and nondestructive way. Aileen's internal working model created expectations of herself, of significant others, and of the larger social world, regarding the latter two as hostile, unpredictable, and unreliable. She was predisposed to a life of violence without provocation. Her own beliefs and outlooks left her in a constant state of fear and arousal.

Aileen frequently was a victim as a child and typically was the abuser as an adult. Her profound sense of distrust in others and her hypervigilance constantly made her fearful of abandonment, betrayal, or abuse. At a young age, Aileen learned that the physical aggressor held the power. With each instance of victimization, Aileen defiantly might have thought that one day no one would be able to touch or harm her: she would be in control; she would never be helpless again. This is the way that her hate grew.

AILEEN'S ASSESSMENT: THE ATTACHMENT DISORDER SYMPTOM CHECKLIST

Technically, this checklist was not administered by a treating clinician prior to Aileen's turning 18 years of age. However, archival material about her life indicates that she fell in the severe range on the majority of the attachment disorder symptoms as defined by Evergreen Consultants (Randolph, 1997). Randolph (1997) found that children who are severely attachment-disordered have a strong likelihood of developing ASPD or psychopathy if they go untreated. Moreover, these individuals are far more likely to kill or cause serious injury to someone else (Randolph, 1997). Aileen's history demonstrates the same relationship.

For purposes of the present inquiry, the RADQ is not utilized, since the items are far too behaviorally specific to score with archival data. In addition, the use of the Attachment Disorder Checklist is also not valid; however, it acts as a tool to further examine the connection between insecure attachment through childhood and adolescence, and the development of psychopathic traits in adulthood. Furthermore, examples given are almost exclusively from childhood and adolescence. Additional descriptions of many similar characteristics are provided in the section on Aileen's Psychopathic Traits. Many of the behaviors and traits identified by the Attachment Disorder Symptom Checklist are consistent with those included in the PCL-R.

Superficially Engaging and Charming (Moderate)

Lori, Aileen's aunt, described how when they were growing up, Aileen's friendliness or expression of pleasant emotions always appeared insincere, as if she were playacting. Further description is provided in a later section.

Lack of Eye Contact on Parental Terms (Not Ratable)

Indiscriminately Affectionate with Strangers (Severe)

By the age of 11, Aileen was already approaching strangers and neighborhood boys to engage in sexual activities for money or cigarettes. Whereas she could not establish healthy adaptive attachments, she would engage in this type of highly maladaptive and physical contact with strangers.

Not Affectionate on Parents' Terms (Moderate)

This trait was scored only as moderate, since Aileen's parents would rarely initiate affectionate behavior. One Wuornos ritual required that the children kiss their parents good night before they went to bed. Aileen loathed having to do this and was deeply resentful as a result.

Destructive to Self, Others, and Material Things (Severe)

Aileen engaged in behaviors that were self-destructive, including prostitution, drinking, smoking, and drug use, throughout her prepubescent and adolescent years. She put herself in situations in which she may have been raped. She seemed to have no regard for her body and, as a result, was abused. Aileen also engaged in physical altercations with her peers, commencing from a young age.

Cruelty to Animals (Absent)

Aileen was noted to have owned and to like animals. Her grandfather, Lauri, however, made Aileen watch as he drowned her kitten.

Stealing (Severe)

Aileen began shoplifting at an early age. This included theft from the store where her grandmother, Britta, worked.

Lying About the Obvious (Severe)

Aileen was well-known for pathological lying. Various individuals who grew up with her would attest to the fact that she seemed to lie even when it served no real purpose and when her statement was obviously untrue. Although Aileen may have been raped at least once, she made up a melodramatic tale of being raped at knifepoint and gunpoint for 6 hours by an Elvis impersonator, when she became pregnant with her child.

No Impulse Controls (Severe)

Aileen is described as hyperactive and impulsive from a young age. The teachers, family members, and neighborhood children in her life all noted this trait. She was short-tempered and would lash out violently without provocation and with little consideration for the consequences.

Learning Lags (Severe)

Aileen had poor grades and poor relationships with classmates and teachers. She was described as having difficulty with inattention and was identified as a leader in discipline problems. Aileen did not like school, and she fell behind her classmates with regard to grades and behavior. She was evaluated in the school to help determine what was contributing to her social and academic deficits. Her verbal IQ was below average. Furthermore, her knowledge of numerical concepts, vocabulary, and social awareness were far below average.

Lack of Cause-and-Effect Thinking (Severe)

Aileen repeatedly failed to consider the consequences of her actions. A caseworker assigned to her as a teenager stated that she was immature and completely lacked forward or future thinking. Aileen seemed to only feel as if the world did things to her. She seemed incapable of considering how her actions might have negative repercussions.

Lack of Conscience (Severe)

Aileen engaged in a variety of criminal and destructive behaviors as a child and adolescent (e.g., prostitution, theft, assault, drug use) that caused her little, if any, distress. Her only affective response to any of her behaviors was linked to getting caught or being punished. When they were teenagers, Lori feared for her life after Aileen chased her with a knife around the home, where she was baby-sitting. Lori was quite certain that Aileen would have had no qualms about cutting her with the knife. This trait became much more apparent in Aileen's adulthood.

Poor Peer Relationships (Severe)

By the age of 8, Aileen was already known for her explosive temper and was without friends. Lori sometimes tried to include Aileen along with her playmates but soon regretted her attempt when Aileen became controlling and threatening. As a teenager, Aileen was thrown out of numerous parties for becoming belligerent. Throughout her entire scholastic career, she had only one friend, shortly before she dropped out of school for good. Aileen was ostracized from a young age as a result of her inappropriate conduct and bad attitude. Her frightening temper and inability to connect with others made her a loner.

Preoccupation with Fire (Mild)

While not described in the preceding narrative, Aileen and her brother set a fire in their prepubescent years that actually burned Aileen herself. In later interviews, Aileen claimed that her burns exacerbated the teasing she received from her peers. Although she engaged in a variety of other illegal activities, the one incident of fire setting was noted in the available materials.

Persistent Nonsense Questions and Incessant Chatter (Moderate)

Aileen's aunt, Lori, noted this quality when Aileen was an adult. She specifically indicated that Aileen often rambled on about religious issues or things having to do with violence. Lori described her conversations with Aileen as crazy at times. Although there is little specific information available regarding this symptom prior to the age of 18, this item was rated on the basis of the strength of its quality as exhibited by Aileen while an adult. In this context, we used past behavior as a predictor of future conduct. In addition, Aileen's hyperactivity and inattention during her early school years suggest that this trait was most likely present. Given our reliance on mostly adult conduct, this behavior was rated moderate rather than severe.

Inappropriately Demanding and Clingy (Mild)

As an adult, Aileen demonstrated this quality with her biological mother, at her brother Keith's funeral, and in her relationship with Ty. However, the available material about Aileen as a child and teenager consistently describes her as a loner who did not need to be consoled, even after the harshest of treatment by peers.

Abnormal Speech Patterns (Not Ratable)

History of Severe Maltreatment in the First 2 Years of Life (Severe)

During Aileen's first 2 years of life, she experienced several changes in her primary caretakers. Her biological mother, Diane, abandoned her when she was less than 1 years old. For a period of time before she left, Diane provided inconsistent care, sometimes responding to Aileen's needs and sometimes not at all. After briefly returning a year later, Diane left again. The extreme physical abuse for Aileen began as a child, but after the age of 2.

Parents Seem Exceedingly Angry Toward the Child (Severe)

Aileen and her brother Keith were singled out and suffered physical abuse at the hands of Lauri, their grandfather. However, the animosity between Aileen and Lauri was unparalleled. As a young child, she experienced his physical abuse with little resistance. Yet, as a teenager, she would verbally lash out at Lauri, telling him how much she hated him. He had been telling Aileen that she was evil and worthless for years. Lori noted that Aileen suffered the worst of her grandfather's scorn. Aileen ran away on several occasions, and Lauri finally refused to let her return home, making her sleep in the woods. After Britta's death, Lauri told Diane that if Aileen came around, he would kill her. Lauri's hatred for Aileen seems to be the first catalyst for her hatred of all men.

Out of 20 symptoms, Aileen was rated as experiencing 11 of them in the severe range, 3 as moderate, 2 as mild, 3 as not ratable (because of lack of information), and 1 as absent. Only 1 of 20 was definitely absent, and more than half of the items were rated as severe. It appears that Aileen would have met the criteria for severe attachment disorder as defined by the Attachment Center in Evergreen. Although sufficient behavioral information was not available to complete the RADQ, it is predicted that she would have fallen in the above 91 range, that is, the severely attachment disordered range. According to Randolph (1997), severely attachment-disordered children, if not extensively treated, will most likely develop antisocial personality disorder or psychopathic personality. Furthermore, she indicated that these individuals represent "a serious threat to society, as they are likely to kill or otherwise seriously harm others, and show no remorse for their actions" (Randolph, 1997, p. 13). Unfortunately, Aileen never received treatment, and her maltreatment by family and peers continued unabated.

OPPORTUNITIES LOST

At the age of 14, a school psychologist evaluated Aileen. Her rage and behavior problems did not go unnoticed at school. At the end of the report, an emphatic warning was given, "It is vital for this girl's welfare that she receive counseling immediately" (Russell, 1992, p. 42). As previously noted, Aileen never received any counseling as an inpatient or outpatient, either as a child or as an adolescent.

While in prison for armed robbery in 1981, another psychiatric evaluation was performed on Aileen. It was determined that she was quite unstable, although not psychotic. Despite her obvious instability, she did not receive psychological services. While living with Ed after her release from prison, he took her to a medical center to obtain tranquilizers at her request. A female counselor noted in no uncertain terms that her threats of violence should be taken seriously. A few weeks later, she was committed to an inpatient treatment facility, given that she drank herself into a stupor. Her anger and violence were not addressed. Those individuals who evaluated Aileen at trial would represent her next contact with mental health professionals.

ADULT ATTACHMENT PATTERNS

Aileen continued to demonstrate an avoidant/dismissing style of attachment in adulthood. There had been no positive change in her relationship with her parents. Now they were simply deceased, having failed repeatedly to make her feel loved or wanted. She also had lost her brother Keith. No significant friendships or other types of intimate associations emerged to neutralize her detachment and lack of ability to relate to or care about others. At this stage in her life, we question how much of a difference such an attachment could even have made. Her internal working model regarding herself, others, and the world was rigidly in place. This style served to protect her from painful emotions and abuse as a child. Subsequent attachment experiences confirmed her childhood internal working model. Her hostile and negative beliefs about others persisted into adulthood, especially as she continued to lack felt security. Nothing mitigated what she had learned as a child in her grandparent's home. The world was a hostile place.

As an adult, Aileen was virtually without family. She would occasionally stay with Lori, but they fought bitterly. Aileen showed up unannounced to stay with Diane in Texas. Aileen was so emotionally detached and angry by this time that Diane stated that she feared for her life with Aileen under her roof. After several weeks, she asked Aileen to leave. Once again, Aileen felt unwanted by her mother. Aileen had failed to develop the personality traits that would act as a buffer, staving off negative and destructive impulses. She had not learned to incorporate the feelings of others into her decision-making. The worth of others was minimized to improve her self-concept. She had to believe that everyone else was beneath her or she had to accept the opinion of others that she was a whore, slut, bitch, or pig. Although her personality development was adaptive in an abusive home, she was not prepared to function adaptively in society.

The incessant abuse that Aileen endured with little nurturance prepared her to always expect the worst. She believed that those who were kind had ulterior motives and could not be trusted. She did not experience anxiety associated with the negative appraisal by others that the average person encounters. Aileen was perpetually self-focused and lived for the moment. She gave little thought to the impact of her actions on herself or others.

Aileen had a brief sexual relationship with Jay Watts and did appear to enjoy the relationship. Until Ty Moore, Aileen's brief relationships were parasitic in nature. She was homeless when she began seeing Jay and needed a place in which to live. When she left, she stole checks and clothes. After leaving prison for the armed robbery conviction, her relationship with Ed was, with the exception of one incident, nonsexual. She needed a place to live. Although she resided in his house for only 1 month, on many occasions she would fly into a rage and threaten Ed's life. It appeared as if Aileen had no ties to social convention. Her opinion of men was increasingly hostile, as evidenced by numerous conversations with Lori and her interactions with Ed. Once again, she stole from Ed after he asked her to leave. Aileen had another brief homosexual relationship. She was not bound by the need for approval from family, friends, or lovers, until Ty Moore entered her life.

Aileen's Anxious/Ambivalent Style with Ty

Aileen wanted to be cared about, to be part of something, but she learned early on that that wish was not to be fulfilled. When she finally had her first experience of belonging, albeit in her late twenties, she clung to it jealously and furiously like a valued possession that others might try to steal. The relationship with Ty began as a sexual one but grew into a 4-year association that lasted throughout the murders. Aileen demanded to be the center of attention and was painfully resentful of Ty's connections to family and friends. Aileen wanted Ty to have no one else in her life, just as Aileen was without other companionship or friends. Aileen had to be convinced that she was the most important person in Ty's life and sometimes resorted to physical violence to quell her rage at feeling slighted or ignored.

During this time period, Aileen almost frantically clung to the relationship as a source of identity and security. She demonstrated an anxious/ambivalent style in this one relationship. Aileen viewed Ty as unpredictable and had difficulty understanding and evaluating her romantic and interpersonal association with Ty, given this context. Despite

Aileen's tough, narcissistic public persona, she most likely felt unloved and worthless inside.

Aileen desperately wanted the love that Ty seemed to give but was insecure and unable to trust in the relationship. She was particularly jealous when Ty's stepsister came to stay with Ty and Aileen for the summer. Their sense of family made her feel insecure and even more alone. Aileen was unable to appreciate Ty's need for family and other friends, since her ability to empathize with others was severely inhibited. She focused on the anger and resentment she felt, and reacted according to those sentiments. Aileen so intimidated and frightened Ty's stepsister that she went home early. Once again, we note that Aileen never felt completely loved or accepted by her family; thus, she learned to devalue the importance of these connections.

When Aileen was a child, her relationship with her primary attachment figures taught her that it was not possible to count on other people. She had never been in a relationship, and she wanted to be loved. Yet, this experience also frightened her, because she had no mental representations of how to love someone and to be loved in a healthy, adaptive way. Frequently those persons with an anxious/ambivalent style, correlated with borderline personality disorder in the research, will direct both care-seeking and angry, aggressive behavior toward their attachment figure (West & Keller, 1994). This interpretation is applicable to Aileen's and Ty's relationship. On some occasions, Aileen was desperate for attention from Ty. On other occasions, she physically attacked her. Aileen was unaccustomed to reflecting on her emotional states and certainly those of others.

According to West and Keller (1994), an individual with an anxious/ambivalent attachment style is always on the brink of feelings, including incredible possessiveness, aggressiveness, or despair, because of one's lack of felt security. This pattern becomes a self-fulfilling prophecy when the attachment figure responds to such behavior in a rejecting manner reminiscent of the person's past attachment relationships (West & Keller, 1994). As such, one's negative internal working models are then reinforced.

Ultimately, Aileen's sense of identity was determined by her ability to dominate and control. The attachment she felt toward Ty was far too little and far too late. Aileen dominated this relationship through physical abuse and emotional manipulation. This behavior is consistent with the work of Wekerle and Wolfe (1998), who demonstrated that the avoidant attachment style was a significant predictor of female abusiveness and victimization.

Aileen's fits of rage and jealousy made her adult primary attachment figure (Ty) eventually leave her. Once again, she was abandoned. One of the few instances of selflessness that Aileen demonstrated was her confession to the police. She made this confession in order to prevent Ty from being charged for crimes that she did not commit. With this one intimate relationship, Aileen had moved from being detached and dismissive to being enmeshed. Both styles of insecure attachment are defensive reactions to the loss of the attachment figure and the attachment relationship (West & Keller, 1994).

AILEEN'S PSYCHOPATHIC TRAITS

Although a PCL-R was not technically administered to Aileen, archival material about her life indicates that she falls in the definite (yes) range on the majority of the psychopathic traits as defined by Hare (1991). Research demonstrates a correlation between avoidant/dismissing attachment patterns and the development of ASPD (psychopathy)

(Levy, 1993; Rosenstein & Horowitz, 1996). Aileen's history substantiates this relationship.

PCL-R TRAITS EXAMINED

Grandiose Sense of Self-worth

As previously mentioned, this sense of narcissism seemed to have developed as a protective function for Aileen. Indeed, she believed that the world owed her something. On many occasions, she stole from and manipulated others. Those who briefly lived with Aileen or had the audacity to challenge her noted her sense of entitlement. Even the slightest challenge to her judgment or wishes resulted in an uncontrollable rage and a barrage of insults. Ostensibly, Aileen created a world in her own mind where she was someone quite important and untouchable by others. She bragged to many people about how she would become famous and have books written about her. She made up tall tales that fabricated her importance and accomplishments. Her sense of self overshadowed any consideration of other people. She had long been isolated from others, and her sense of self-focus was overwhelming. Her immediate gratification was paramount to the needs or consequences of anyone else. She reigned as queen in a world of her own making.

Proneness to Boredom/Need for Stimulation

From the age of 11, Aileen's lifestyle was one of dangerous, thrill-seeking behaviors. She engaged in promiscuous sexual activities and sought a drug-induced high from smoking and drinking. As a teenager, her risk-taking behaviors continued as she misused and abused a multitude of drugs. Aileen stole and committed a variety of other crimes. Many persons reported that she started fights for no apparent reason. She enjoyed hitchhiking and being on the move. Despite her detachment from sexual activity as a child and teenage prostitute, as an adult, Aileen was described as having a voracious sexual appetite.

Pathological Lying

Multiple sources from a young age agree that Aileen lied, even when the lie seemed to serve no apparent purpose. She fabricated events, despite their transparency, making her look ridiculous to others. Aileen claimed that she held important positions, such as an FBI agent, and that she killed a bear in Colorado. Although it is likely that Aileen was raped at least once, she made up a melodramatic tale of being raped at knifepoint and at gunpoint for 6 hours by an Elvis impersonator, when she became pregnant with her child. There were many other stories that Aileen told regarding her pregnancy. The forensic evidence does not support Aileen's story of sadistic rape and torture by Richard Mallory. At times, Aileen's lying was done for the sake of it, distorting the truth for the satisfaction of conning someone.

Conning/Manipulative

If someone lent a helping hand to Aileen, she remorselessly stole from that person. For instance, she devised a scam in which she lived with a preacher and his family and then burglarized their home before her departure. In addition, Aileen stole the identities of many women who took her in, including Lori, her aunt, using their aliases to commit a number of crimes.

Lack of Remorse or Guilt

Aileen saw herself as the victim. She murdered seven men who were unarmed and ultimately defenseless, and she felt that she was justified. She believed that everyone in the world was out to hurt her. Her victims were objictified into the role of the enemy, the rapist. She hurt them before they hurt her. Her inability to empathize with the emotional experience of others allowed her to minimize the impact of her actions upon them. In an interview with Court TV (1999), Aileen stated that she regretted killing her victims. However, she blamed the police for allowing her to kill and went on to further state that if they had stopped her from killing, she would have been acquitted for Richard Mallory's murder. Aileen demonstrated through her words that her sense of remorse was linked only to her own consequences. She regretted being caught and being placed on death row. On one hand, she verbalized remorse for her situation. On the other hand, she rationalized that people were going to rape her and therefore deserved what they got. Aileen consistently indicated that her sentence was unjust, and she blamed the victims, society, and the circumstances in which she found herself for the death of the seven men.

Shallow Affect

Aileen did not show the normal range and depth of emotion of most people. From a young age, she learned to inhibit her emotions. Those who grew up with her would talk about her ability to be detached during a sexual encounter. Lori, Aileen's aunt, described how when they were growing up, Aileen's friendliness or expression of pleasant emotions always appeared insincere as if she was playacting. This is not to say that Aileen did not have strong emotions; however, like most other individuals with psychopathic traits, she was not able to describe and experience the subtleties of various affective states (Hare, 1991). Aileen's primary emotional response was anger.

Another example of Aileen's shallow affect can be traced to statements that she loved her brother, Keith, and her grandmother, Britta, very much. However, by all accounts except her own, Aileen did not visit Keith in the hospital over a 2-year period while he was dying of cancer. Moreover, at Britta's funeral, Aileen was disrespectful, blew smoke in her dead grandmother's face, and called her a disparaging name.

Callous/Lack of Empathy

Aileen viewed others as objects to be manipulated and used for what they could give her. Despite her difficulties growing up, as an adult she encountered some individuals who tried to help her by giving her a place to stay or by giving her money. Emotionality and generosity were signs of weakness for her to exploit. She stole from the homes of the people who tried to help her, including family (Lori), acquaintances, ministers, and others. She took clothes, jewelry, driver's licenses, and other valuables with a feeling of entitlement.

During her confession to the police and later during interviews with programs like Court TV and A & E, Aileen recounted nonchalantly how she murdered and why the victims deserved it. The only time she described a murder with emotion or appeared shaken was when she was on trial for the killing of Richard Mallory. Admittedly, the secondary gain for her when expressing such sentiment was immense as her life hung in the balance. In addition, Aileen was known to physically abuse Ty. Although all who witnessed this abuse identified Aileen as the primary physical aggressor, Ty also fought back.

Parasitic Lifestyle

Aileen almost completely avoided steady, gainful employment. She briefly held a job cleaning in a hotel but quickly quit because she did not like others' telling her what to do. Aileen would use as variety of demeanors to obtain what she wanted. She either would present herself as helpless and in need of help (e.g., the ministers' families who took her in) or would demand what she wanted through threats and coercion. Aileen was briefly married to a wealthy man almost 50 years her senior, in order to feel important and live off his money.

Poor Behavioral Controls

Hare (1991, p. 37) used the following words to describe this trait: "short-tempered, responds to frustration, failure, discipline, and criticism with violent behavior or verbal abuse . . . takes offense easily . . . becomes angry and aggressive over trivialities." Aileen unquestionably met this description. There are many more examples of such behavior than could have been reasonably included in this case study narrative. Even when she stood to lose from reacting in this fashion, Aileen would explode in anger at peers, sexual partners, acquaintances, and strangers. Throwing the cue ball at the head of a bar manager is one such instance. Another example not included in the narrative was when she attacked a city bus driver. Lori cited numerous illustrations of Aileen's acting out of control and being verbally and physically violent toward her and her friends. Aileen was thrown out of many parties for being belligerent.

She frequently read hostile intent into a benign situation. Although this trait can be understood within the context of how she was raised, this trait had deadly consequences for Aileen's victims. For example, in her confession to police, Aileen described how Richard Mallory did not completely remove his jeans, and she therefore believed that Mallory was going to rape her and steal her money. Aileen's irrational appraisal of trivialities, as well as her lack of empathy, contributed to her use of preemptive aggression. Hare (1991) also noted that this trait and the inability to control one's behavior are further weakened by alcohol, making unprovoked violence common.

Promiscuous Sexual Relationships

Aileen engaged in promiscuous sexual behaviors since her prepubescent years. Those who had more casual relationships with Aileen described her as hypersexual and aggressive. Her relationship with Ty began as a sexual one. Aileen was involved in prostitution from the age of 11 until her arrest. Clearly, her sexual relationships could be described as impersonal and casual. According to reports, Aileen consensually committed incest with her brother, Keith, and may have been forced to have a sexual relationship with her grandfather, Lauri. In addition to Aileen's claims of sexual abuse, her precocious erotic behavior at such a young age, along with her affective detachment, are quite common in children who have been sexually abused.

Early Behavioral Problems

By the age of 11, Aileen was already prostituting herself, was often truant from school, frequently lied, and was drinking alcohol and smoking cigarettes. She was already described as incorrigible, with a violent temper. She was disruptive in the classroom and hated school. Her behavior problems exceeded those of other children, and she was considered the black sheep of her family.

Lack of Realistic Long-Term Goals

Aileen seemed unable or unwilling to plan for the future. She lived a nomadic existence, hitchhiking from one place to the next, without regular employment. Prior to her murders, she boasted about her future fame. Her aspirations were inconsistent with her talents and abilities. Sadly, eerily, and ironically, this goal was achieved through murder. As a teenager, one of Aileen's caseworkers during the time she was pregnant commented that she was impulsive and immature and that she had no conceptualization of the future.

Impulsivity

As previously noted, Aileen was described as impulsive from childhood forward by most who knew her. She acted as she felt at the moment with little thought about or concern for the consequences of her actions. At the age of 14, a psychological evaluation by the school determined that Aileen had problems with inattention and was a leader in discipline problems. Aileen would react impetuously. She was opportunistic, particularly with regard to the seven murders. If someone had something she wanted or if she felt slighted or threatened in any way, Aileen's responses far exceeded what would have been appropriate given the situation. She also displayed no regard for the consequences of her conduct in relation to her victims.

Irresponsibility

Generally, Aileen had no sense of duty or loyalty to friends or family. Those who tried to help her often fell victim to verbal and physical threats as well as to theft. Aileen stole her Aunt Lori's driver's license and used her identity when she was arrested for various crimes. Her behavior put others at risk. One clear exception to her lack of loyalty was when she agreed to confess to the police to clear Ty from any involvement with the murders. Ty was the one and only relationship in Aileen's life when she demonstrated this type of loyalty. However, Aileen's behavior did put Ty at serious risk for arrest and prosecution as an accessory to murder. Aileen consistently failed to honor financial obligations, in addition to her many thefts. Aileen and Ty left many motel rooms without paying their bills.

Failure to Accept Responsibility for One's Own Actions

Aileen always had an excuse for her behavior. With respect to her murders, she consistently blamed the victims, claiming that they attacked or raped her, in the face of contradicting forensic evidence. In addition, she blamed the police for *allowing* her to keep killing so that they could make money from her future book and movie deals. She rationalized the behavior of her victims, describing them as threatening, and she maintained that they deserved to be murdered. When she became pregnant as a teenager, she produced a variety of wild stories to deflect responsibility away from her promiscuous sexual conduct.

Juvenile Delinquency

By the time she turned 17, Aileen had been arrested for shoplifting and for running away from home. She spent time in both juvenile hall and a girl's group home for her incorrigible behavior.

Criminal Versatility

Aileen committed offenses in 10 out of the 12 criminal categories in The Hare Psychopathy Checklist–Revised Manual (Hare, 1991). Her crimes included theft, possession of stolen property, shoplifting, auto theft, armed robbery, possession of narcotics, assault, first-degree murder, possession of a weapon, prostitution, driving while intoxicated, reckless endangerment, forgery, fraud, failure to appear, and the like.

PREDATORY HOMICIDE: RICHARD MALLORY'S MURDER

The development of Aileen's personality and her expectations of self and others were forever scarred by her relationship with her primary caretakers, Lauri, Britta, and Diane. She failed to bond with others or make meaningful attachments to society. Her attachments to her primary attachment figures were either dysfunctional or simply nonexistent. Aileen's parenting did not train her to be a functional, interpersonally aware individual. She learned to be suspicious, guarded, angry, distrustful, and aggressive. There was no one in her life to instill in her a positive sense of self or others.

The incessant abuse that Aileen suffered at the hands of her grandfather, as well as the emotional and sexual abuse that she experienced from her peers and neighborhood boys, planted within her the seeds of hatred and distrust toward men. Aileen claimed that she was raped on a number of occasions. Although some of those allegations appear false, it is quite likely that she was raped at least once. Undoubtedly, this experience validated her perception of others (particularly men) as threatening and as objects to be loathed. During these early encounters with victimization, Aileen lacked power and control. She engaged in acts of preemptive aggression, including murder, to restore her sense of well-being and of experiencing control (Schurman-Kauflin, 2000). Rather than waiting to be abused, she took the offensive against the object she hated or otherwise scorned.

Aileen bragged to Cammie Greene that she and Ty would be like Bonnie and Clyde and that they would be doing society a favor. It seems as if Aileen felt so wronged in her life that she established a sense of entitlement when lashing out at those who had so viciously and cruelly wronged her. According to Schurman-Kauflin (2000), victims are compartmentalized into stereotypes in order for the offender to minimize the crime he or she is about to commit and the harm he or she is about to inflict. Aileen viewed Richard Mallory as a rapist and as an object to be destroyed. He had material possessions that she wanted, and Aileen's perception of him allowed her to conclude that he deserved to be killed.

According to Aileen's confession, Richard Mallory refused to fully remove his clothing prior to any sexual intimacy, triggering within her the belief that he had hostile intent toward her and that she needed to attack him before he harmed her. Aileen's assault seems to have been motivated by anger, believing that Mallory might try to rob or rape her. Thus, it appears that Aileen did not act out of fear or in defense of her life. However, on the basis of forensic evidence and Aileen's first confession to the police, it appears that Mallory took no direct aggressive or threatening actions toward her. As such, Aileen's expectation of aggression and violence from others, coupled with her impulsive behavior and intense anger, resulted in her committing acts of murder. This behavior enabled her to maintain control and to acquire the victim's material possessions. For example, Aileen kept many items from Mallory's car and used the vehicle the following day to relocate.

Psychopathic individuals need to feel that they are in a superior position. They engender a narcissistic self-concept, with little belief in the worth of other individuals (Schurman-Kauflin, 2000). Psychopaths are intolerant when made to feel humiliated or when placed in a submissive position (Schurman-Kauflin, 2000). In her interview with Court TV (1999), Aileen described how it took her 17 years to prepare for murdering a person. As she stated, "But I finally got stone cold and said, you know, enough is enough." At this point in her life, Aileen was the aggressor, refusing to accept an inferior status. Indeed, trivialities were deemed insults in need of retaliation in order to preserve her facade of grand importance and entitlement. Psychopathic individuals can sustain anger from past insults. Eventually, this anger grows exponentially, functioning as a catalyst for revenge against either the person involved or someone else in a vulnerable position (Meloy, 1988).

Aileen harbored an incredible amount of anger and resentment toward the many people who had placed her in the role of victim throughout her life. Her violence and criminal activity had been escalating since her prepubescent years. There was little doubt that Richard Mallory would have welcomed Aileen's services as a prostitute. However, despite his previous conviction, during the 20 or so years of cavorting with women in the sex trade industry, Mallory did not attack a woman. Moreover, the evidence did not support Aileen's later claim that she had been sadistically raped. Richard Mallory was transformed into an object that needed to be destroyed. He was stereotyped into the role of the enemy, a person who wrongfully had harmed her. Killing him made Aileen feel secure and in control.

In addition, the psychopathic individual is unable to accept her or his own faults or vulnerabilities and, thus, transfers them onto the victim (Meloy, 1988). In other words, the offender projects her or his own negative traits onto the person harmed, who is defined as someone who deserves to be destroyed. In addition, the psychopath's inability or unwillingness to consider the consequences of the violence enacted against the victim enables the offender to commit the act without reflection, that is, instantaneously and impulsively. Aileen's bonding with others was inhibited, particularly with respect to men.

Her victims were objectified, viewed as rapists or abusers; they were not perceived as a father, brother, minister, husband, partner, and the like. Aileen's actions toward her victims precluded any remorse for her own conduct (Holmes & Holmes, 1994). In short, the psychopathic individual perceives the victim as a bad person who deserves his or her fate (Schurman-Kauflin, 2000).

Psychopaths who commit murder do experience high levels of anxiety, but it is not related to remorse for their actions (Schurman-Kauflin, 2000). Their anxiety stems from an inability to cope effectively with life stressors (e.g., holding down a regular job). Despite their grandiose self-view, reality constantly reaffirms that psychopaths are inadequate, resulting in their anger and frustration (Schurman-Kauflin, 2000). The anger and anxiety builds and is reduced to the criminal event (i.e., homicide) (Cronin, 1996). Hurting another person can be viewed as a means to an end, or it can provide, in and of itself, a sense of relief. The psychopath is indifferent to the use of violence in order to feel better (Blackburn, 1969; Schurman-Kauflin, 2000). For instance, Ty described Aileen's demeanor as calm and normal following the murder of Richard Mallory. She was not frantic, nor was she in a fight-or-flight state. When she finally told Ty about the murder, Aileen stated that she killed a man, not that she was raped or that she feared for her life.

The affective detachment that Aileen developed at a young age was evident in her ability to remain apathetic about the crime she committed. She had grown to view violence and hatred as normal and acceptable. Commenting on this phenomenon, Schurman-Kauflin (2000, pp. 74–75) indicates that

> The multiple murderers fail to bond with family or make attachments to society, so there is no parameter of empathy to constrain the individual from committing atrocious acts. . . . The killer refuses to get emotionally bonded with anyone. . . . a sense of right and wrong (morality) is not programmed into these individuals.

Research by Schurman-Kauflin (2000) found that patterns of abandonment and horrific abuse characterize the childhoods of women who grow up to be serial killers. They externalize the pain to something or someone outside themselves. This personality characteristic also was evident in Aileen Wuornos.

Indeed, throughout much of her life, Aileen had been at the mercy of men with whom she had sex for money, cigarettes, drugs, or a place to live. She wanted the ultimate control over life and death. She already controlled the money, the situation, and what she would and would not do. For years she had felt powerless in the face of the sexual and aggressive impulses of the men around her; however, her attitude shifted once she began to kill. Indeed, after killing Richard Mallory, her thoughts did not include remorse or guilt. Instead, she considered how to avoid detection and how much money she had taken from him. He was not a man to be mourned; he was a body to be discarded.

Aileen learned that those with the power also wielded and regulated violence and intimidation. Although repeatedly suffering anxiety and fear, she developed virtually no adaptive coping strategies. She was socialized to modulate her own emotions through detachment and to control her environment through aggression and violence. In spite of the abuse she endured, Aileen learned to identify with the aggressor. The world was made up of two kinds of people: victims and offenders. She chose the latter category. Her rigid internal working model of herself and the world she inhabited did not allow for anything in between. She no longer would be the victim.

With respect to female serial killers, Schurman-Kauflin (2000, p. 118) noted the following:

> Within their lives, they [feel] powerless against a parade of horrible events, and in order for them to restore a sense of balance (at least in their minds), they use the murders of other people like many people use a cigarette. . . . They [seek] a calm in their lives that they will never have, and deep down, they truly know it will never "fix" their lives.

A cycle of escapist activities from substance abuse to petty crimes that originated in early childhood culminated for Aileen into something much darker. No one was there to heed the warning signs. In her extreme and tragic case, she spiraled downward into predatory homicide.

Aileen's relationship with her primary attachment figures set the stage, firmly building for her a foundation of detachment and anger. Her biological predisposition to criminal behavior and psychopathy stemming from her biological father also could not be ignored. Most likely, not only was Aileen biologically vulnerable, but also her emotionally neglectful and physically abusive environment fostered psychopathic traits that contributed to predatory violence. Aileen never experienced a warm, nurturing environment, a setting that otherwise would have enabled her to safely explore and reflect upon the emotional experiences of herself or others. Aileen's dysfunctional interactions and her lack of felt security in all of her associations, intimate or not, served to reinforce her negative expectations and to exacerbate her fury and emotional separation from others. She was, quite simply, alone.

Meloy (1992) cautioned that despite emotional detachment from others, psychopathic individuals aggressively engage with objects. Psychopathic individuals are skillful at rationalization, minimization, and the projection of blame (Hickey, 1997). Up until her execution, Aileen continued to blame the victims for provoking the murders and to blame the police for allowing them to continue unabated.

THE HALLMARKS OF PREDATORY AGGRESSION/HOMICIDE (MELOY, 1992)

Minimal or Absent Autonomic Arousal

Aileen's actions during and after Richard Mallory's murder did not suggest that she was reacting from a fight-or-flight response. Pamela Mills, the jury forewoman in her case, commented that Aileen did not behave like someone who was in fear for her life. Aileen described how she shot Richard Mallory, then methodically walked around the vehicle and shot him three more times. Then she hid the body, stole the car, and took all of his possessions. Finally, she used his car the next day to help relocate and then disposed of the car. Meloy (1992) explained that predatory aggression sometimes follows affective aggression in a psychopathic individual. For example, an explosively violent act can then precipitate a more calm, predatory mode. These shifting affective states can help the psychopathic individual to conceal evidence and the like.

No Conscience Experience of Emotion

Aileen consistently felt and expressed no remorse for the murder of Richard Mallory. Shortly after committing the crime, she returned home and stated to her girlfriend, Ty, "I killed a guy today" (Court TV, 1992, 1999). Ty testified that it shocked her to witness how apathetic Aileen was, expressing no emotion about this incident. Aileen had so objectified and devalued her victim that the killing was methodical. Aileen's description of it mirrored her lack of emotional response to the criminal event.

Planned and Purposeful Violence

To the extent that Aileen exerted control over her victim and determined the amount of violence to be inflicted upon him, this crime was purposeful. It appears that her attacks on Richard Mallory and her subsequent victims were intended to act out vengeful or retributive fantasies, as well as to achieve monetary gain. Aileen began carrying a pistol and a bottle of Windex in her bag to assist her when cleaning fingerprints from a vehicle. Her main focus was to obtain the ultimate control over her victim. She also profited by stealing her subjects' material possessions. Aileen's murder of Richard Mallory (and the other victims) was an exercise of planned intent and not the reaction of someone who feared for her life.

No or Minimal Perceived Threat

Despite Aileen's claim that Richard Mallory attacked her, she initiated the contact with him and was armed with a handgun. The forensic evidence and Ty's observations did not support Aileen's claim that she had been attacked in any way. Her irrational hypervigilance, sentiments that made Aileen believe everyone was out to hurt her, resulted in a constant fear of predation. She chose to strike first and to be the hunter rather than the hunted.

Multidetermined and Variable Goals

The killing of Richard Mallory was not solely to remove or displace a perceived threat. As previously mentioned, the motives and goals for this crime were multifaceted, including the potential to fulfill vengeful fantasies, to have feelings of power and control, and to acquire monetary gain.

Minimal or Absent Displacement of the Target of Aggression

Once Aileen decided that she would kill Richard Mallory or the next man who picked her up, there was no changing the course of events. According to Meloy (1992), the lack of autonomic or emotional arousal precludes the individual from becoming fearful or relenting because of perceived consequences. Aileen's flagrant use of her victim's vehicle demonstrated a lack of fear about the possible consequences of her own actions (e.g., arrest, death penalty). Richard Mallory represented the hostile object. She sensed negative and hostile intent from her victim. These feelings allowed her to carry out her plan without any distress.

A Time-Unlimited Behavioral Sequence

Aileen's attacks were not limited to a short-lived emotional response. Law enforcement investigators estimated that she spent several hours with Richard Mallory. She could have decided to abort her plan of murder at any moment; however, she did not do this. Aileen's lack of autonomic arousal permitted her to spend considerable time with the victim, as well as to take her time with hiding the evidence.

Preceded or Followed by Private Ritual

Prior to each murder, Aileen is thought to have drunk alcohol. In addition, she always took a variety of items from her victims, including tools, clothing, money, jewelry, and so on. However, it is unclear whether all of these items were taken for their material value or whether any of them represented a trophy or a reminder of her omnipotence and control over her victims.

A Primary Cognitive-Conative Dimension

This indicator implies that the crime was a product of rational, goal-directed behavior. Aileen was in touch with reality. She was fully cognizant of her actions at the time of the crime.

Heightened and Focused Sensory Awareness

This indicator relates to the singular focus on the target and the fixation on sensory experiences during the homicide. Clearly, Aileen did not deviate from her intent to kill Richard Mallory. Indeed, she went around the car to fire more bullets into him after initially shooting him in the car. However, her observations concerning the murder were not descriptive enough in relation to her sensory experience. Thus, we do not have a clear sense of whether her sensory awareness was heightened.

Self and Object Concept Dedifferentiation

During the predatory attack, the victim is often incorporated into the narcissistic self-structure of the offender (Meloy, 1992). For example, this condition happens when the attacker chooses her victims, on the basis of an internalized idea of someone who has wronged her. All throughout her life, it appears that Aileen suffered years of abuse at the hands of men. She was demoralized, working as a prostitute from age 11. Although the victim may be a stranger to whom the assailant is not attached, the attacker will make the victim "a ragefully devalued . . . object" (Meloy, 1992, p. 232). The victims who introduced themselves to Aileen for sex (e.g., Mallory) met all of the specifications of those who had wronged her.

Unimpaired Reality Testing

Although the victim may not be considered a whole person, worthy of regard or empathic reflection, the offender is not out of touch with reality. Indeed, even though the offender's crimes and lack of human compassion may seem "crazy," the assailant does not suffer from perceptual disturbances in the traditional sense. Aileen seemed to experience an emotional disconnection and a violent rage. This rage toward men in particular went unchecked as a result of her moral disengagement.

Heightened Self-esteem

As previously mentioned, Aileen developed a narcissistic self-view to defend against deep feelings of loss, rejection, and self-loathing. The control over life and death served only to enhance and reinforce her sense of omnipotence. Moreover, Aileen always believed that she would become the subject of books and movies. The media coverage of her crimes allowed this goal to be realized. She achieved notoriety through her transgressions.

FROM INSECURE ATTACHMENT TO PSYCHOPATHY/PREDATORY HOMICIDE : A SUMMARY

It is likely that Aileen began with a biological predisposition for psychopathy (Schore, 1994). However, what is known for certain is that she experienced pathogenic care from her primary caregivers from the time she was born until her teenage years. She had multiple, inconsistent caregivers as an infant and suffered severe physical, emotional, and verbal abuse from her grandfather throughout her formative years. Aileen also may have endured sexual abuse. Her grandmother was not emotionally available. Aileen most likely developed an avoidant/dismissing attachment pattern that resulted in inhibited bonding and prohibited interpersonal awareness.

Admittedly, many children who are brutally victimized fail to develop psychopathy or to commit predatory homicide. Thus, we are led to ponder what happens to children like Aileen Wuornos, such that they descend into an abyss of moral disengagement and predatory violence. In part, the answer is linked to biological vulnerability. However, more fundamentally, the answer appears to be based on an individual's development of self and others and on one's ability to establish healthy attachments to fellow human beings. In addition to demonstrating insecure attachment patterns, we submit that Aileen easily would have met the behavioral criteria for attachment disorder, as well as the diagnostic criteria for RAD. Regrettably, the warning that Aileen needed psychological help was not heeded, and her destructive view of herself and others grew to malignant proportions.

The ability to reflect upon the emotional states of others and to appreciate them as whole human beings rather than as hostile objects, inhibits most individuals from remorselessly killing or physically harming people. The fabric of civility is held together by the idea that we treat others as we would like to be treated. If the other person is not conceptualized as an equal or is not viewed as having value or feelings worthy of consideration, acting in one's self-interest, at any cost, becomes the norm.

The value of bonding and security between primary caregivers and children is immeasurable. Aileen's development of self was permeated by the sense that she was evil, worthless, and unlovable. The world and others were viewed as violent and hostile. Individuals who experience victimization may be removed from an abusive situation or may have secondary attachment figures that provide love, security, and the opportunity to attach. Many children who grow up in chaotic homes find solace in the environs of their friends or from a trusted teacher, religious leader, coach, or counselor. Aileen had no one. Her ongoing abuse resulted in detachment from her own and others' emotions as an adaptive strategy. She learned not to feel for herself and especially not for anyone else. Aileen's ability to separate herself from negative affect in her abusive home was quite adaptive; however, it led to destructive consequences in adulthood.

Aileen failed to develop self-evaluating emotions that are necessary for self-regulation (Schore, 1994). Empathy and moral development were halted at a brutally young age, by the lack of sensitive caregiving that she was afforded. Aileen's socialization of mainstream values and morals was devastated by the severity of her pathogenic care. Whereas others sometimes recover as a result of the strength of caring family and friends or a strong sense of identity, Aileen failed to develop a positive sense of self, and there were no relationships to mitigate the damage done in the Wuornos household. Rather than living by the ethic of treating others as she wanted to be treated and rather than believing that people are basically good, Aileen lived by a dark moral code of harming others before they hurt her. She positioned people in the world into two categories: predators and prey. Quite possibly, Aileen's own aggressive thoughts and impulses reinforced her belief that others were hostile and menacing (Meloy, 1992).

Aileen developed a sense of narcissism and omnipotence to overcome her feelings of worthlessness. Even though she devalued and disdained the men to whom she sold herself, Aileen repeatedly engaged in this behavior because she could not support herself or her drinking habit with steady, gainful employment. The profound and unrelenting contrast lodged within these notions (i.e., to be superior and omnipotent versus to be degraded and demoralized) threatened Aileen's fragile sense of self. She slipped deep into her feelings of rage and harshly objectified the men who, for so many years, objectified her. The sharp contrast between her constructed view of self and the one imposed upon her by the devaluing other became too much for Aileen to bear. Her inability to reflect on her own emotional state or to resolve her cognitive dissonance in a healthy way led to violence and, finally, to murder.

Aileen, who was impulsive by nature, was not restrained by the fear of judgment from anyone. When these rageful feelings and thoughts enveloped her, empathy for other people or concern for personal consequences did not inhibit or impede her behavior. By destroying the hated object, she restored a sense of omnipotence, satisfying vengeful fantasies and monetary needs. If an individual cannot or does not reflect on the pain and suffering of the victim and/or the victim's family and if an individual cannot or does not consider the consequences of his or her illicit conduct, then the immediate gratification of the murder is undeniable. Indeed, the psychic scales are tipped in favor of restoring one's sense of self, eliminating a threatening and hated object, and acquiring material possessions. Arguably, Aileen's narcissism led her to believe that she was above the law. She used the vehicles of her many victims, in addition to pawning some of their belongings, with little fear about her capture.

Aileen's inability to experience attachment or bonding to others enabled her to so devalue Richard Mallory that she killed and destroyed him, in a cold, calculated, and remorseless way. Her early victimization and lack of healthy attachments inhibited the formation of empathy and self-regulating thoughts, while promoting moral disengagement, aggressiveness, hypervigilance, and impulsivity. Indeed, from our assessment of Aileen Wuornos's life story and its meaning, it appears that her enduring lack of attachments and her subsequent psychopathic personality organization were essential features motivating her predatory homicidal behavior.

NATURALISTIC GENERALIZATIONS

In this final section, we summarize the themes already presented elsewhere in the chapter. Although our data included a single case and source information germane to it, thereby limiting the generalizability of our findings to a population of similar cases, our naturalistic comments are based on the interpretation of material through experience. Accordingly, broad interpretations learned through the instrumental case study of Aileen Wuornos, attachment theory, and psychological research include the following:

1. An individual's attachment to primary attachment figures in infancy and childhood impacts personality development and the person's capacity for interpersonal relationships well into adulthood.

2. Abandonment, abuse, and nonresponsive caregiving can lead to insecure attachment patterns, severely impacting the internal working model of self and other. In extreme cases, bonding is inhibited, and the child may never recover. The individual cannot reflect easily on the emotions of the self or others.

3. Those with a biological predisposition for criminality and psychopathic traits are particularly vulnerable to poor attachments to primary caregivers.

4. Healthy, secure attachment patterns can act as a buffer for violent and aggressive impulses. Avoidant/dismissing attachment patterns can foster an antisocial or psychopathic personality devoid of empathy and awareness of the other.

5. An internal working model that views the self as unlovable and others as hostile will increase the likelihood that preemptive aggression will occur.

6. A person without attachment to family, friends, or society will experience little psychic distress when committing predatory homicide or other acts that blatantly violate social mores.

7. In certain female offenders, violence and aggression are used to restore a sense of personal well-being. These behaviors facilitate a feeling of power and control that was absent during their childhoods.

8. Most individuals do not commit predatory homicide because they can identify with the feelings of and consequences to another human being. In addition, most people have multiple attachments to individuals and institutions whose appraisal of them is valued. Those women who did not bond with their primary attachment figures and who use detachment as a defensive strategy have few or no attachments to others. This situation produces moral disengagement.

9. Although it is typical for all psychopathic individuals to blame the victim, it is easier for the female homicide offender to engage in this behavior. Gender-role stereotypes typically place the woman in the role of victim. The idea of a victim-precipitated homicide is more readily accepted when the woman is the offender.

10. It is quite natural for a person to bond and attach with primary attachment figures. Humans, and certainly women, are social animals with an innate desire to belong and to be loved by other people. When a child consistently is denied this bonding and when other significant relationships are not established, a basic human need is thwarted, potentially with disastrous consequences. The person who is treated as less than human can learn to dehumanize, objectify,

and devalue others and those who otherwise represent important attachment relationships.

CONCLUSIONS

In this chapter we analyzed and interpreted the data representing the life narrative of Aileen Wuornos, mindful of locating the story's meaning. In particular, we examined one woman's experience in relation to a complex and underinvestigated phenomenon, namely, the relationship between avoidant/dismissing attachment patterns and the development of ASPD/psychopathic traits leading to predatory homicide. This case was filtered through our own sensibilities as investigators and then interpreted on the basis of theory and research, as well as on Aileen's life experiences and understanding of her unique story. In addition, we note that the reader coconstituted what was learned and the meanings that emerged from the case, on the basis of the readers' lived experiences. Although we cannot quantify or generalize to the population of female serial killers as a whole, the circumstances and events embodied and endured by one woman can lead to the vicarious comprehension of other similar cases. These include instances of female-perpetrated predatory homicide in which ASPD (psychopathy) and attachment patterns are significantly and directly called into question.

The next chapter reflects on the case of Aileen Wuornos and examines future strategies. In the final analysis, it is not enough to identify problems at the crossroads of criminal justice and mental health. It is important to assess what can be done in the face of them. Female killers are a very real phenomenon, and several suggestions for meaningful intervention are needed. Accordingly, Chapter 10 reviews the domains of forensic correctional psychology, law and public policy, and criminal justice administration and management. At issue is how these arenas can respond to the problems posed by women who commit predatory homicide in which poor attachment in childhood and psychopathy in adulthood figure prominently into the analysis.

10

Implications, Future Research, and Conclusions

❖

INTRODUCTION

In this chapter we focus on the implications of our analysis, mindful of Aileen's Wuronos's troubling case and life story and that of other similarly situated female serial killers. In particular, our commentary includes an assessment of three areas germane to female-perpetrated predatory homicide. These practice domains consist of forensic/correctional psychology, law and public policy, and criminal justice administration and management. Admittedly, the observations that follow are somewhat speculative and provisional. However, we recognize that practical, workable strategies addressing female criminality are needed, especially in the instance of murder as we have explored it. We conclude the chapter by summarizing our overall investigation, highlighting what each of the previous chapters endeavored to accomplish.

IMPLICATIONS FOR FORENSIC/CORRECTIONAL PSYCHOLOGISTS

Prevention in Infancy, Childhood, and Adolescence

Perhaps the most important implication of our study is the importance given to quality parenting. This is caregiving that is genuinely sensitive and consistently responsive to the physical and emotional needs of the child. No other relationships influence a child's life as significantly as those with the primary caregivers, particularly during infancy. Although this notion is a somewhat antiquated and sometimes unpopular belief, nonetheless, healthy, adaptive children with a positive sense of self and others are shaped by parents who attend to them regularly and lovingly. Indeed, by the time a child reaches school age, the critical development of empathy, self-regulation, affect-modulation, a conscience, and the like, already have occurred (Schore, 1994). Even though teachers, counselors, day-care workers, and others need to establish positive and engaged roles with children, the most meaningful and impactful relationships that they will ever have are with their primary caregivers.

As a society, we must be mindful of the link between juvenile delinquency and adult criminality. Along these lines, it is important to teach parents or their surrogates how to provide better, healthier caregiving and how to be vigilant about and ready to intervene on behalf of infants and children who receive pathogenic care in the home. Clearly, our inquiry illustrated the need for early intervention, especially with children at risk for involvement in the criminal justice system who suffer from the unmet needs of severe attachment. As pathogenic care becomes more commonplace, so too will the most violent of crimes, including predatory homicide. Society can continue to build prisons in which it warehouses a growing delinquent and criminal population, or it can take pro-active steps to more effectively respond to the interconnected problem of youth violence and adult criminality.

As such, our analysis demonstrated that better parenting was one of the strongest factors in preventing or curtailing the development of psychopathy. Children's initial internal working models are formed at a young age by their primary caregivers. Significant change can be effected best by sensitive and consistent caregiving in infancy and early childhood. Mental health professionals and school personnel should be educated regarding the interpersonal, behavioral, and emotional manifestations of insecure attachment in children. In addition, the potential consequences for failing to address attachment issues should be elucidated. The screening of children who exhibit symptoms of attachment disorder or of insecure attachment patterns could help with identifying those youth in need of mental health services before a controllable problem escalates into violence or some other form of criminal behavior. Indeed, whereas some of the available research supports success outcomes when treating attachment disordered children, success outcomes for treating psychopathy mostly are nonexistent.

One facility dedicated to the treatment of attachment disordered children is the Attachment Center in Evergreen, Colorado. The Center treatment is built around an intensive, 14-day holding therapy program; however, additional studies are essential if practitioners are to identify the most effective ways to address attachment needs in children. In addition, continued research into the neurobiology of attachment and emotions are necessary. These investigations will help us understand the origins of attachment, giving clinicians some additional insight into the treatment of this phenomenon.

We also note that psychopathic individuals typically are created, not born. Accordingly, it is important for psychologists to look at the various critical junctures in a person's life where the professional can intervene, endeavoring to break the cycle that leads to psychopathy and predatory homicide. Indeed, prevention and intervention on behalf of insecurely attached children are crucial to establishing meaningful personal change. Regrettably, Aileen Wuornos slipped through the cracks as a child. School personnel identified her need for treatment, and no one attended to those needs. Unfortunately, children with detached, neglectful, or abusive parents cannot count on their mothers or fathers to pursue or follow up on the provision of services. Therefore, mental health specialists (with the aid of teachers and school counselors) conscientiously must pursue programs that can benefit these children.

Mentoring programs give children another opportunity to form healthy attachments to a sensitive and responsive adult. Other prevention programs include parenting classes for high-risk adults expecting a child. In addition, education programs regarding the development of healthy attachments and the implications for children need to be provided in correctional and mental health settings.

A stronger focus on infant mental health should be pursued, particularly with high-risk cohorts (e.g., low socioeconomic status, single-parent families, substance using/abusing mothers and fathers, and parents with mental health issues or regular contact with the criminal justice system). For example, mother-and-baby groups could be implemented more widely in settings that assist at-risk parents. These groups would allow the mothers or parents to attend counseling sessions with their infant. In addition to receiving support from the mental health professional and from other parents, the therapist could intervene on an immediate level. For instance, the mother could be instructed on how to hold and look at her baby. In addition, the parent's reaction to the infant's proximity-seeking behaviors could be observed directly, and constructive feedback could be provided routinely.

Early diagnosis or identification of behaviors consistent with insecure attachment is critical for successful early intervention. Psychologists could act as consultants in the community for individuals most likely to provide services to children. Moreover, persons who make placement decisions for youth need to be educated about the connection between attachment patterns and psychopathy. Also, forensic psychologists who evaluate juveniles for presentence, treatment, and placement recommendations need to be familiar with the impact of severe pathogenic care on children. Then, too, those individuals who conduct custody evaluations would do well to be cognizant of potential (or likely) attachment issues and the implications they hold for the child. In these situations, the court has the authority to determine placement, therapy, or psychoeducation for the youth and the youth's family. Forensic psychologists have an important responsibility to inform the court about the child's likely risk for future violence. Knowing the risk factors associated with developing attachment disorder and, in the extreme, the manifestation of psychopathy supports a strategy of prevention.

Treatment for Women with ASPD (Psychopathy)

Whereas Battered Women's Syndrome has received considerable media scrutiny and public attention, forensic psychologists must become more skilled at detecting those female offenders who kill for their own gain, with little regard for human life. Victim precipitation is involved in the majority of homicides committed by women (Flowers, 1994). However, some women murder in a predatory fashion and do so from the position of the aggressor. Thus, those women who kill in cold blood should not stand to benefit from the victimization of battered women. Indeed, our assessment does not intend to minimize the plight of battered women. Rather, we seek to draw a strong distinction between those who murder because of a perceived threat (i.e., battered women) and those who kill for money, revenge, sport, sexual gratification, boredom, and the like (female-perpetrated predatory murder).

Arguably, the implications for clinicians are the most cogent. Forensic psychologists who work with the courts by conducting evaluations and providing testimony, as well as those mental health specialists who assist correctional institutions, have the most contact and direct influence on the lives of female homicide offenders. Included in this category are clinicians who perform competency to stand trial evaluations, mental state at the time of the offense (insanity pleas), and risk assessments. Each of these types of evaluations could be relevant to a woman who commits predatory homicide.

Closely linked to the identified psychological assessment practices is the forensic and correctional psychologist's ability to recognize the complexity of female homicide offenders. For many years, criminological theories, psychological research, and public perception have all defined women in gender-role stereotypes. If a woman committed a crime as heinous as predatory murder, she was deemed mentally ill. Indeed, this conduct was believed to be so far removed from what was expected of a woman that it was thought that she had lost touch with reality. In addition, understanding that the development of psychopathy often begins with pathogenic care implicates theories describing the evolution of criminality in women.

We note that it is possible to make sense of a woman's killing someone whom she perceives to be a threat to her life, particularly if the woman senses that the party in question will harm her children. On some level, this action is congruent with the offender's role as a mother. Indeed, this type of self-protection is understandable, and we recognize that mothers of various types will fight to the death to protect their offspring. However, it is much more troubling to hear about a case in which a woman kills her children, a stranger, or even a husband when the victim has not engaged in any harmful acts. Admittedly, compared with male offenders, these cases are few; however, from our perspective, this fact does not mean that these cases should therefore be ignored or dismissed. On the contrary, we argue that it is crucial for these more thorny, difficult, and contentious cases to be addressed systematically. To this extent, then, understanding how a psychopathic woman develops a malignant and dysfunctional perception of self and others enables the clinician to better comprehend these murders and the way that they can be performed without any semblance of remorse.

It is regrettable that far too many feminists virtually have ignored these types of cases, believing that acknowledging psychopathic female serial killers would somehow diminish or otherwise compromise the rights gained for women who killed their abusers (Bell & Fox, 1996). However, our inquiry demonstrates that not all women use homicide in a defensive mode. Moreover, to advocate (rightly) for equality with men in a number of instances seems disingenuous, especially if old stereotypes are used to contravene the responsibility of women in other instances. In other words, it seems at least illogical to suggest that women are capable of the same range of pro-social behaviors as men, yet argue that they are limited in their ability to destroy, by nature of gender. Indeed, women who receive pathological treatment as infants and children can also be shaped to view the world as hostile. In short, they can act out with preemptive predatory aggression.

Predatory homicide is an extremely difficult crime to accept no matter who the culprit is. However, good clinicians should be aware of the variety of thoughts, emotions, and behaviors utilized by female homicide offenders. Not every woman perceives her world in the same way. Both understanding how the experience of empathy and of bond-ing with others is initiated and recognizing when a maladaptive view of self and other emerges, need to be explained in relation to women. It is unfortunate that our compre-hension of the female offender is dramatically limited when anomalous cases are ignored and the assailant is viewed myopically from one perspective. We clearly challenged this orientation, exploring instead the experiences, thoughts, feelings, and behaviors of one woman who did not fit society's stereotypes of women or the predatory homicide of-fender. We hope that our treatment of this phenomenon will broaden the knowledge base of clinicians who work directly with these disturbing women.

Preventing Women Diagnosed with ASPD (Psychopathy) from Committing Crime

Another important implication emerging from this study involves prevention. As the mo-tives, feelings, and thoughts of women diagnosed with ASPD (psychopathy) who commit predatory homicide increasingly become understood by psychologists and criminologists, there is a stronger likelihood that other, similar women will be identified before they en-gage in violence, including murder. Currently, ASPD is infrequently detected in outpa-tient settings. However, people with ASPD regularly have mental health visits as a result of comorbid psychiatric disorders such as depression (Mulder et al., 1994). Moreover, if the early risk factors, such as symptoms of insecure attachment patterns and attachment disorder are noted, more effective interventions could be implemented in an attempt to thwart the development of psychopathy.

More attention to screening women for ASPD and psychopathy in outpatient set-tings could help to detect some of these women who are susceptible to or at risk for com-mitting murder, prior to the offense's occurring. Given our analysis of Aileen Wuornos and other female serial killers, we encourage clinicians to recognize that those disorders highly correlated with violence, such as ASPD or psychopathy, can be found in women. In addition, the available theories about the development of ASPD and the more serious collection of personality traits (i.e., psychopathy), clearly indicate that women are vul-nerable to committing predatory homicide.

The recognition of ASPD (psychopathy) and therapy designed for the specific com-ponents of this disorder could help prevent a homicide by these women. Although per-sonality disorders are difficult to manage, without their detection or understanding there is no chance to intervene in one's subsequent self-destructive or homicidal behavior. Sound psychological and criminological theories are the foundations of effective testing, therapy, and other treatments. Traditionally, these theories have conceptualized psy-chopathology in women according to gender-based stereotypes. It is regrettable that the overwhelming research on psychopathology in general has been concentrated primarily on men (Rutherford et al., 1995).

Moreover, the issue of psychopathy is rarely addressed in women. Additional qual-itative assessments of female-perpetrated predatory homicide can provide a more robust description of psychopathy in women. Although these individuals may exhibit many char-acteristics of psychopathy, to date only a few studies about them have been conducted. In fact, the Hare Psychopathy Checklist (PCL-R) was created from a population of men. It is well-validated for this constituency; however, scant attention has been directed toward validating this instrument for women (Salekin et al., 1997). Future research can continue to expand the use of this assessment tool in ways that are relevant to the experiences of women.

We also note that a richer comprehension of the attachment patterns that form the interpersonal relationships (physical, emotional, behavioral) that emerge, and other related facets of a woman's identity will facilitate the development of a more meaningful articulation of the psychopathy construct for women. Not only that, the diagnosis of ASPD was created from studies about men (Robins, 1966, 1978). Our point is that women—even those who commit homicide—need to be understood on their own terms if prevention efforts are to have any chance of success. This study demonstrated the need for psychologists to develop diagnostic and psychometric instruments that acknowledge the characteristics unique to women, especially mindful of avoiding gender-role stereotypes.

Recognizing how a woman experiences her crime and whether or not ASPD played a role in it is particularly relevant for forensic psychologists. Indeed, if some women with ASPD or psychopathy are not being identified, they may be taking part in therapy that is inappropriate or ineffective relative to their issues. Moreover, if forensic and clinical psychologists misdiagnose ASPD or psychopathy, they may impede the progress of their clients. For instance, psychologists employed within correctional institutions are responsible for rendering mental health services to those prisoners requiring therapeutic assistance. Groups created for women who kill their abusers are a different cohort from those who engage in predatory homicide. Thus, psychologists need to recognize that therapeutic interventions administered to one group may be antitherapeutic if administered to the other.

Another important implication for mental health professionals is the development of treatment modalities tailored to the unique needs of psychopathic women. Clinicians in correctional institutions find that the limitations of time, resources, and training required to conduct therapy with ASPD-diagnosed women make efficacious treatment virtually impossible. However, we note that this problem could be addressed with the support of correctional policy makers and administrators. Accordingly, future research must continue to examine the special needs of this difficult population of offenders, demonstrating when and how targeted interventions would meaningfully attend to the clinical issues posed by women killers.

As our in-depth analysis and interpretation of Aileen Wuornos documented, it possible to access the behavioral, emotional, and cognitive forces at work that establish attachment disorder in childhood, giving rise to ASPD (psychopathy) in adulthood. As such, our naturalistic generalizations were intended to assist psychologists to determine how best to respond to the needs of female killers as we discussed them. Of note is the Simon (1998) suggested that for male offenders diagnosed with ASPD or psychopathy cognitive behavioral methods are far more effective than the more psychodynamic methods of psychotherapy. However, the paucity of research regarding women diagnosed with these disorders renders assertions of this sort in relation to women completely unreliable and unknowable. For that reason it is essential to elucidate the characteristics and motivations of ASPD (psychopathic) female killers. Prospects for effective therapy depend such clarifications.

The effects of diagnosing someone with ASPD or psychopathy on treatment and cidivism also are significant. Indeed, clinicians must be certain whether they are diagno ing solely on the basis of antisocial behavior or on the basis of psychopathic traits as well. We note that the prognosis for a psychopathic individual is far worse than for someone with antisocial personality disorder. However, current treatment efforts for ASPD are only marginally successful (Shipley & Arrigo, 2001; Simon, 1998). Psychologists working inside and outside the prison milieu need to research psychopathy. Understanding what it is and how it operates in relation to women will make prospects for effective treatment that much more likely.

In addition, clinicians must be willing to treat the population of women with ASPD (psychopathy). Forensic and correctional psychologists should be at the forefront of developing intervention programs that address this particular type of offender. Thus far, traditional psychotherapies have not been very effective. However, the theories from which these various psychotherapies were derived did not have in mind the characteristics of a psychopathic individual (Arrigo & Shipley, 2001). Although the prevalence rates for psychopathy are relatively low, these offenders are responsible for a disproportionate amount of crime. Successful prevention intervention strategies regarding psychopathy could have a significant impact, forestalling or abating criminal victimization. For that reason, clinicians must be prepared to work with this population of female offenders.

Diagnostic Clarification with ASPD and Psychopathy

Our inquiry further explained the differences between antisocial personality disorder and psychopathy, thereby impacting the domain of applied forensic psychology. Indeed, the continuum that represents these two disorders is often misunderstood (Arrigo & Shipley, 2001; Gacono, 2000). For instance, many psychologists refer to one psychiatric condition while describing the other. In other cases, psychologists overdiagnose ASPD in forensic populations by meeting the criteria for it using only behavioral standards.

The following scenario illustrates the problem with using only the behavioral criteria of ASPD as constitutive of the diagnosis. Individuals who engage in criminal behavior as adults are more likely by far to have engaged in defiant, delinquent, or unlawful behavior as children or adolescents. Moreover, the person who dropped out of school or obtained a juvenile record might have a more difficult time securing a job as an adult (Robins, 1978). It follows, then, that as an adult, the same individual would have a more difficult time maintaining employment or avoiding criminal conduct as a means of self-support (Robbins, 1978). However, these series of behaviors do not speak to the individual's *personality*. In addition, the behavioral criteria of ASPD include a majority of people in prison; however, psychopathy is evidenced in a small percentage of those incarcerated (Gacono, 2000; Hart & Hare, 1998). Given these observations, critics of ASPD have argued that it has become so diluted from the psychopathy construct that it does little more than the obvious: to identify behaviors that violate social norms and legal conventions (Arrigo & Shipley, 2001).

A forensic psychologist's ability to correctly identify a psychopathic individual can be critical to such matters as future or present dangerousness, recidivism, empathy, and the person's ability to learn from the consequences of an action. As clinicians and lay professionals (e.g., lawyers, judges, correctional administrators) continue to confuse ASPD and psychopathy, false applications of the latter or misdiagnoses of the same regrettably will attach to many undeserving offenders.

The deleterious consequences of being identified with psychopathic characteristics require that clinicians more carefully diagnose, write about, and speak of this disorder as separate from ASPD. Sustaining the confusion between these two psychiatric conditions serves only to diminish the clinician's ability to communicate effectively with other mental health professionals. The preceding investigation more fully explained the continuum and diagnostic criteria of ASPD and psychopathy. We contend that understanding this continuum will enable psychologists to more responsibly diagnose each of these disorders, positively impacting the lives of those who suffer uniquely from them.

Furthermore, forensic psychologists must be aware of their own biases and sensibilities when confronted with ASPD and psychopathic clients. Diagnoses such as these must not arise capriciously or arbitrarily, or otherwise be based on a therapist's countertransference with a difficult prisoner (Shipley & Arrigo, 2001). These diagnostic labels can have severe adverse implications, affecting the duration of a person's life. For example, a psychological evaluation that includes ASPD or psychopathy for an offender being considered for parole can substantially decrease the chances of early release. Accordingly, clinicians have a responsibility to be well-educated about the diagnostic criteria, the current research, and the psychometric instruments used to assess for psychopathy, before diagnosing women with this disorder.

In a similar way, children with insecure attachment patterns are often described as hostile, aggressive, apathetic, and difficult. Therapeutic work with these children is challenging and often not immediately gratifying. This notwithstanding, the inclination to punish rather than treat must be resisted. Continuing to reject these children and failing to address their attachment needs will lead only to disastrous consequences.

In addition, the distinction between reactive attachment disorder (RAD) and attachment disorder as defined by the Attachment Center in Evergreen, Colorado, is worth noting, given its implications with respect to diagnostic clarification. Although these disorders overlap, the severity and breadth of symptoms do vary. Randolph (1997) continues to work with a Diagnostic and Statistical Manual (DSM) committee, endeavoring to develop and revise a RAD diagnosis that better reflects behavioral specificity. In the meantime, however, diagnostic confusion may persist, especially with clinicians uncertain about the differences between the current diagnostic nomenclatures. These disorders are delineated on a continuum of severity. They are not synonymous. Research is needed on the traits and behaviors of attachment disordered children, and DSM diagnostic categories should be configured in ways that are more relevant to clinical practice.

With respect to adult diagnoses, confusion is not limited merely to the ASPD/psychopathy continuum. Indeed, although a great deal of comorbidity exists between personality disorders, traditionally gender has dictated what primary diagnosis an individual received (Kaplan, 1983a, 1983b). Currently, the ASPD diagnosis is almost exclusively reserved for men, whereas personality disorders such as histrionic personality disorder and borderline personality disorder (BPD) are much more frequently found in women. Some researchers suggest that symptoms diagnosed as ASPD in men are routinely diagnosed as BPD in women (Kaplan, 1983a, 1983b). Crucial for clinicians is their ability to understand the differences between the disorders and their capacity to recognize that women might have a condition that is contrary to gender-role stereotypes.

Expert Testimony, ASPD, and Predatory Homicide

Another relevant implication linked to female-perpetrated predatory homicide for ASPD women, is expert testimony. Forensic psychological testimony on this matter should meet the highest standards and should be empirically and clinically based (Zinger & Forth, 1998). Because a finding of psychopathy has the potential to increase the severity of sentencing, careful, prudent, and responsible decision making by the clinician is necessary. Forensic psychology is not an exact science, and the limitations pertaining to our current knowledge of and instruments for tendering expert opinions must be recognized, especially in areas such as predicting future dangerousness. Indeed, an ASPD diagnosis can further exacerbate an already perilous situation for the female offender on trial for murder. Our assessment of the Aileen Wuornos case was designed to inform the reader about predatory homicide and the characteristics of the female serial killer. As such, it illustrated the need for psychologists to be cautious about and well-informed in their forensic assessments and diagnoses that are tendered in a court of law.

Furthermore, forensic psychologists also provide recommendations at parole board hearings. Many factors are considered with respect to a prisoner's release. For example, a genuine display of remorse for one's crimes and the absence of future societal harm are critical variables assessed by clinicians. The convict's perception of her crimes is a crucial component of her treatment plan while incarcerated, as well as a significant dimension of her possible release from confinement. Thus, clinical and forensic insight into the experiences of women who commit predatory homicide would be invaluable, enabling the evaluator to understand the offender's capacity for victim empathy, remorse, and dangerousness. Each of these factors is critical when determining whether a prisoner is or is not suitable for parole.

Psychological and Related Research on Women and Predatory Homicide

The foregoing investigation was relevant for furthering our understanding of female-perpetrated predatory homicide. As we explained, both the diagnosis of ASPD and the traits of psychopathy in women, especially those who commit murder, are inconsistent with gender-role expectations and stereotypes. Predatory homicide is rarely seen in humans (Meloy, 1992). However, in other species, predatory killing is a natural response necessary for the acquisition of food. Exploration into the phenomenon of predatory homicide provides important and useful data about a type of murder uncharacteristically attributed to women. This treatment has occurred because conventional social mores assign affective states such as fear, anxiety, guilt, and remorse to women, believing that these emotions are intrinsically a part of feminine identity. Thus, the calculated nature of serial killing seems antithetical to the nurturing qualities expected from females. However, as we have argued, exploring the view of self and other in women who commit predatory homicide could provide much needed insight into their capacity to represent a different type of female offender.

We note that the recent trend in female-perpetrated homicide emphasizes the experience of women who kill their batterers. However, studies investigating the life histories, attachment patterns, emotional states, social conditions, physical dimensions, personality features, and behavioral aspects of predatory female killers also are sorely needed. As psychological and related research of this sort materializes, we can begin to examine much more systematically the differences and similarities between victim-precipitated female murder and predatory homicide. We submit that our instrumental case study analysis of Aileen Wuornos moved us one step closer to initiating qualitative inquiries in this direction.

In addition, society is prone to relegating women to the role of victim. Clearly, this is appropriate in a number of (if not the majority of) instances. However, the detailed life history and experiences of Aileen Wuornos as we chronicled them deepened our understanding of the victim-offender relationship with respect to female homicides. Indeed, Aileen's perceptions of her victims, as delineated through her interviews, confession, and court testimony, told us a great deal more about how female serial killers understand those they murder than previously identified. An exploration of these data provides valuable information to law enforcement personnel regarding the motive for the crimes. For instance, if the murderess viewed the victim as an object with little meaning or significance, her reason for killing would be substantially different from that of a woman who was terribly afraid. Murder committed in an emotional frenzy is differentiated from predatory murder (e.g., affective versus predatory violence; Meloy, 1992). Future research along these lines could help expand our criminological and psychological knowledge of women who kill and the theories pertaining to this behavior.

IMPLICATIONS FOR LAW AND PUBLIC POLICY

Interest Balancing

Law and policy analysts addressing pressing issues at the crossroads of criminal justice and mental health must understand the way in which law and psychology operate in order to establish meaningful, necessary change. For example, statutory regulations affecting the liberty interests of mentally disordered violent offenders must be balanced against the rights of the public to be safe and secure. Women diagnosed with ASPD (psychopathy) who commit predatory homicide pose many difficult questions for society, implicating policy making at the law-psychology divide. For instance, should women convicted of these crimes receive lighter, harsher, or equivalent sentences as compared with their male offender counterparts? The preceding analysis raised a number of important and unresolved issues relative to gender-role stereotyping, especially in relation to female versus male criminality, mental illness and crime, and women serial killers with ASPD or psychopathic traits. Aileen Wuornos was executed for her crimes. However, what was the penological basis on which this decision was based? Indeed, if women's experiences of committing crime are different from those of men, then should the punishment that is meted out also be different? This is an area that warrants more detailed and thoughtful exploration as law and public policy analysts endeavor to protect the liberty interests of offenders while simultaneously ensuring the rights of an organized society.

Advocacy and Programming

Another implication for the law and policy analyst involves his or her role as an advocate. We note that our inquiry has potential for backlash against women who kill a batterer who murder in self-defense or in defense of a child. Most assuredly, this backlash was not the expressed or implied purpose of our instrumental case study assessment. Indeed, women who engage in victim-precipitated homicide are subjected to unique and troubling life circumstances that must be carefully evaluated by the court system. In short, women who are viciously and repeatedly abused by a partner should not be expected to endure revictimization at the hands of the criminal justice apparatus. Advocates should help these women to have a powerful voice in the system, and they should endeavor to establish laws that affirmatively affect their fate in society. The present analysis did not review female criminality of this sort.

As academicians and clinicians alike begin to recognize that some, albeit few, women are capable of predatory homicide, law and policy makers have a responsibility to identify, promote, and sponsor programs that treat ASPD or psychopathy for women in outpatient and inpatient settings. Potential violence must not be overlooked on the basis of gender. As such, not only is it important to establish and fund initiatives that benefit the victim (e.g., of domestic violence), but also other efforts are needed that are focused specifically on the female homicidal offender of the sort that we have described.

As previously indicated, this study illustrated the need for prevention and intervention programs for at-risk children. Attachment patterns form in infancy and childhood, and they are difficult to change. Schools and other institutions must be responsive to early escapist and destructive behaviors in girls as well as boys. Children should be given ample opportunities to make meaningful attachments with nurturing adults. The negative consequences of inhibited bonding are many and, in extreme cases, can contribute to psychopathy and predatory homicide in adulthood. Law and pubic policy decision brokers must recognize and advocate for infancy, childhood, and adolescent programs, developed through local schools and communities that squarely address the needs of children whose healthy nurturing is not being met at home. Aileen's behavior was unquestionably problematic. Although it caught the attention of several school personnel and of individuals living in her neighborhood, no one intervened with her family to stop the abuse or to provide Aileen with a sense of self-worth.

Criminal Justice and Mental Health Reform

In addition, policy makers also must consider the potential escalation of female delinquency. More longitudinal studies are needed (including life-course or developmental investigations) that evaluate female juvenile offenders for conduct disorder and that follow them into adulthood in order to assess the potential onset and maintenance of ASPD. Not all female juvenile offenders will eventually find themselves in a women's prison for drugs or prostitution. Some women commit predatory homicide. Along these lines, policy makers should consider the implications of the statistical reporting offered in the first several chapters of this book. Although homicide rates committed by adult women have not increased in recent years (FBI, 1997), a rate of increase was noted for homicides committed by female juvenile offenders. Historically, the more violent behaviors (e.g., fire setting, cruelty to animals, etc.) included in the DSM-IV's criteria for conduct disorder described the behavior of boys, whereas conduct such as running away or theft described that of girls (Salekin et al., 1997). We hope that this trend in more violent behaviors by juvenile girls will not result in more predatory homicides by women. Policy makers must carefully monitor such trends and must advocate and promote change where appropriate, including reform within the juvenile and criminal justice systems.

Society, moreover, must come to appreciate that a woman need not be psychotic or out of touch with reality in order to commit a heinous crime like murder. The notion that women who commit such crimes are mentally ill and therefore less culpable has impacted public perception and policies affecting women in the past. Appropriate policies affecting this type of violent female offender must be based on accurate psychological and related research about the unique experiences of these women. We note that although most women are incapable of murder for personal or material gain, it is quite possible for other women. Criminal justice and mental health policy must reflect the appropriate provision of care and treatment for this less common type of female homicide offender.

Consistent with this call for reform, policy makers must make mental health services more accessible to psychiatrically disordered offenders in correctional facilities. This pursuit could include institutional policies regarding targeted mental health training for appropriate staff. For example, enrichment programming relevant to the psychopathic personality should be planned and implemented in order to promote safety among staff and other prisoners. Moreover, program evaluation efforts should be conducted as more clinicians strive to create more effective treatment initiatives for the psychopathic offender.

IMPLICATIONS FOR CRIMINAL JUSTICE ADMINISTRATION AND MANAGEMENT

Policy Implementation

Criminal justice, mental health, and social service administrators are responsible for implementing policy in their respective institutions. Indeed, policy changes are meaningless if administrators fail to enforce or promote identified reforms in the workplace. For instance, prison administrators would be responsible for orchestrating staff training regarding psychopathic and other psychiatrically disordered offenders. Administrators would be involved in the hiring of additional mental health professionals with specialty skills in this area. In addition, these correctional personnel would have some direct influence over the newly established institutional programming.

Management Strategies

Coid (1991) stressed the fact that some psychopaths have such severe psychopathology that they represent a safety risk to other prisoners. Information such as this is crucial to institutional planning, staffing, and management, especially with respect to facility security and personnel safety. In addition, Coid (1991) indicated that staff members in correctional settings usually do not understand that many disruptive behaviors of psychopathic offenders are outward symptoms of their personality pathology. Continued punitive actions may do nothing to deter such conduct.

Moreover, the most seriously psychopathic offenders may refuse treatment or be a danger to the staff providing it. In these situations, an institutional administrator could employ situational and environmental manipulation (Coid, 1991). Indeed, the suggestion here is that rather than change the personality pathology, the offender's behavior could be more effectively controlled or neutralized by altering the containment space. For instance, moving a particularly violent offender to another institution with more structure and better programming could positively affect behavior.

The criminal justice system's paternalistic attitude toward women is evident even in the more modern prisons constructed for them. In most female facilities, maximum- and minimum-security prisoners share the same quarters. The layout of the prisons themselves is less ominous than that of their male facility counterparts, with more relaxed security standards. The "victim" role that women are often thought to fill make them less of a threat. Moreover, prospects for escape by incarcerated women or for violence directed toward correctional officers is not common. However, these characteristics do not account for all female offenders, and some imprisoned women might not fit this pattern at all. Criminal justice administrators need to be well educated about their diverse female occupants. This is especially the case for women who commit predatory homicide. Indeed, this level of pro-active management is necessary in order to run an efficient and a safe facility, and to effectively train staff to work with this type of offender.

Staff Training and Program Development

Administrators of prisons that house predatory homicide offenders must consider many legal and psychological issues. Programs must be implemented to meet the intentions of the law. At the same time, existing or new initiatives must remain cognizant of the offender's civil liberties. For example, housing arrangements, overcrowding, institutional violence, and convict safety all must be considered. Accordingly, administrators need to be well versed in the unique problems posed by female serial killers, especially those women with ASPD and psychopathic traits. The facility manager or warden must consider how much focus is on treatment versus incapacitation in his or her institution, while following the relevant law.

The vast amount of time and personnel resources required to provide meaningful psychotherapy for individuals with ASPD or psychopathy makes it virtually inconceivable in most prison environments today. However, the consistent recycling of the same offenders makes it increasingly obvious that greater attention to genuine rehabilitation efforts is needed if crime is to be abated. For those women who commit other offenses prior to homicide, appropriate therapy while in prison may help to prevent the escalation of their more murderous impulses. Aileen Wuornos had numerous contacts with the criminal justice system, including a short prison term prior to committing seven acts of predatory homicide. For those women incarcerated for life because of predatory homicide, therapy may increase the safety of other prisoners, as well as correctional and mental health staff who come into contact with these offenders. Correctional administrators must assess what type and level of staff training and program development would be needed in order to promote sorely needed therapeutic opportunities for these very troubled and dangerous female offenders.

CONCLUSIONS

This book explored the extant literature regarding female criminality, women and murder, antisocial personality disorder and psychopathic traits in women, ASPD (psychopathy) and female-perpetrated predatory homicide, and attachment theory. Much of what we know about these areas is vastly underdeveloped, remains in its infancy as it is based on our comprehension of offending in males, or is simply nonexistent. What we found was that many stereotypes and myths surround female criminality. For example, women who kill or engage in other gender-incongruent acts are frequently thought of as mentally ill. To dispel this notion, we reported the actual prevalence rates of female criminality and the impact that psychiatric disorders have on their criminal actions.

More generally, however, the extent of female crime, including relevant statistics regarding the crime rates of women versus men as well as the rate of property offenses versus violent crimes committed by female offenders, was given. Theories of female criminality were described. Biological, socioeconomic, psychological, and feminist perspectives of the female offender were offered. Theories of aggression pertaining to women and their impact on violence and on female criminality were examined. In addition, other factors affecting female offenders, including childhood victimization, broken homes, substance abuse, race/ethnicity, and PMS, were delineated. The nature of female homicide was elucidated, and a profile of the female offender was presented. Moreover, the role of drugs and alcohol in female-perpetrated homicide was discussed, and the impact of ecological circumstances was explained. Offender typologies also were supplied. The role that mental disorders play in female-perpetrated homicide was explained. Gender-role stereotypes and bias in diagnosing were highlighted. As we concluded, women historically have been pathologized for their role in crime.

The female homicide offender with ASPD traits/diagnosis and psychopathic personality also was examined. Both ASPD and psychopathy were explained, and their relationship was analyzed. The historical development of psychopathy as a construct and ASPD as a diagnosis were summarized. The diagnostic criteria and confusion between the two disorders were explored. Gender differences in the presentation of the disorders were detailed. Various studies were summarized describing these findings, critiquing the validity of DSM diagnoses of ASPD in women. The role of ASPD (severe) and psychopathy in female-perpetrated homicide was reviewed. As we noted, the female homicide offender's role as the perpetrator rather than the victim of crime was the focus of our inquiry.

Before turning to our instrumental case study of Aileen Wuornos, attachment theory, beginning with the work of Bowlby (1969), was examined. The theory was described and the categories of childhood attachment styles developed through the seminal work of Ainsworth et al. (1978) were discussed. Research on adult attachment patterns was presented. The differences between adult and childhood attachment were delineated. Empirical and related investigations demonstrating the relationship between adult attachment and psychopathology, particularly personality disorders, were explored. The connection between insecure attachment patterns (i.e., avoidant) and psychopathy was illustrated. The DSM-IV's reactive attachment disorder (RAD) and attachment disorder as defined by the Attachment Center in Evergreen, Colorado, were summarized. Along these lines, the Randolph Attachment Questionnaire and the Attachment Disorder Checklist were outlined. A brief review of the neurobiology of attachment concluded the chapter.

We then turned our attention to the case of Aileen Wuornos. Because she was a noted serial killer, we relied on her life story, as culled from various sources, to address the issues of attachment, psychopathy, and female-perpetrated predatory homicide. An instrumental case study was conducted, given the paucity of empirical information about this small cohort of offenders. Aileen's story was selected on the basis of a population of cases of women with ASPD/psychopathy who had committed predatory homicide. As we explained, the phenomenon observed in this case represented the phenomenon by and large; however, given the uniqueness of Aileen's life events, the case also offered an important opportunity to learn (Stake, 1998). The methodology we employed was modeled after the work of Stake (1995). By applying attachment theory to archival data, we presented an interpretation of the way she perceived others, particularly her victims. For purposes of our inquiry, the life of Aileen Wuornos was chronicled from infancy until her incarceration for the homicide of Richard Mallory. On the basis of the compilation of case study materials and our careful reflection upon them, a number of assertions and interpretations were made with respect to the specific issues under consideration.

Our narrative account began with a vignette, describing the time, place, and physical description of Aileen's childhood home. An extensive description outlining Aileen's story and its relevant contexts were presented. The data collected came from books, taped interviews, television reports, court records, and various other sources of print media. The narrative consisted of a chronological reporting of her life events, emphasizing Aileen's attachment styles, personality development, and descent into predatory homicide. Her relationships with primary attachment figures were illustrated, as were her attachment patterns.

Following the presentation of Aileen's life story, a few key issues were developed that were based on our analysis and interpretation of the case and what we learned from it. The narrative was explored in a manner mindful of the research question. The assertions we made about Aileen's story were processed, consistent with relevant psychometric and related research on attachment disorder, psychopathy, and predatory aggression. Naturalistic generalizations also were developed.

The real value of any study is linked to its capacity to influence or promote needed change. Along these lines, we examined a series of compelling, provocative, and practical solutions to the problems posed by female killers diagnosed with ASPD or who possess psychopathic traits. Specifically, we considered what work remained for forensic and correctional psychologists, highlighting prevention, treatment, diagnostic clarification, expert testimony, and future research. In addition, we assessed the role of the law and public policy analyst, outlining several strategies related to interest balancing, advocacy and programming, and criminal justice and mental health reform. Finally, we reviewed several efforts relevant to criminal justice administration and management. In particular, we stressed efforts targeting policy implementation, management strategies, and staff training and program development.

Although certainly suggestive, our instrumental case study inquiry did not directly examine how the criminal justice and mental health apparatuses contributed to, rather than neutralized prospects for, Aileen's intensified illicit behavior. This is a question of complicity, that is, a matter of evaluating the extent to which who Aileen Wuornos became (i.e., a predatory homicidal offender) was an outgrowth of how she was mishandled by the systems ostensibly in place to help her. We take this to be a question of ethics, and it is the subject of this book's final chapter.

11

Epilogue

Reflections on Ethics, Crime, Mental Illness, and Justice

❖

INTRODUCTION

On October 9, 2002, Aileen Wuornos was put to death by lethal injection at Broward Correctional Institution in Pembroke Pines, Florida. She chose to go to her death, firing her attorneys and opposing appeals made on her behalf. At the court hearing, in order to put her execution on a fast pace, she stated, "There's no sense in keeping me alive. This world doesn't mean anything to me (Schneider, 2002)." Clearly, these were sobering comments from a woman whose life had been marred by untold physical, emotional, and sexual abuse.

Chapter 10 explored the attachment patterns and life history of Aileen Wuornos, illustrating how the psychopathic mind can foster and subsequently lead to murder. Our inquiry focused principally on the individual, while exploring the impact that primary attachment figures can have on the development of "self" and "other," and the way that a person interfaces with the world. We traced a life within the context of family and immediate relationships; however, we did not examine this phenomenon as a product and reflection of society. In short, we put Aileen Wuornos under a microscope to better understand psychopathy in women and the disorder's connection to predatory homicide. As such, we were passive observers of a tragic life, just as pedestrians fix their gaze upon a traffic accident with a morbid curiosity that may stem from the fear of their own unmistakable mortality.

It is interesting that many authors view crime as a social problem (e.g., Arrigo, 1999; Snyder, 2001). In the case of Aileen Wuornos, she was scrutinized by the courts, the media, and several institutional facets of society (i.e., the mental health and criminal justice apparatuses). However, we want to critically examine, at least provisionally, the systems that may have contributed to her eventual demise. Indeed, was the execution of Aileen Wuornos the best that we collectively could have done for her? When someone commits crimes as heinous as multiple murders, we tend to breathe a shared sigh of relief following a death sentence. The crimes are so devastating and the offender so dangerous that our response, perhaps somewhat justified, prevents us from pausing and taking a closer look at society at large, as well as at those systems and institutions that constitute it. This notwithstanding, as researchers we are obligated to assess the social forces impacting or otherwise contributing to the offender's behavior. This assessment includes the case of Aileen Wuornos.

Accordingly, in this chapter, we tentatively raise a number of ethical issues linked to crime, mental illness, and justice. Implicated in this assessment are the criminal justice system and the mental health apparatus. In order to explore the ethical dynamics of Aileen's disturbing life circumstances and society's "official" response to them, we consider the extent to which Marxist criminology and restorative justice principles shed additional light on female killers in situations in which issues of poor attachment in childhood and antisocial personality disorder (psychopathy) in adulthood eventually lead to predatory homicide. Our commentary here is not exhaustive or definitive. In short, although we take seriously the murderous behavior of Aileen Wuornos, we ponder whether or not the systems in place to address this troubled woman's needs failed her, thereby contributing to the predatory homicides she most assuredly and regrettably committed.

At the outset we note that society has a growing, prurient interest in people at its fringes, specifically horrific offenders whose monstrous acts relegate them the status of less than or not fully human. Indeed, as a culture, we possess a morbid fascination for the unspeakable and for those who act upon it. Predatory homicide falls so far beyond our own sense of reality or propriety that, for many of us, it simply is not possible to fathom how such individuals can be even remotely linked to our own species. It is notable, though, that we have an insatiable appetite for who these "objects" of alternating attraction and scorn are, as we self-righteously renounce them for their vile and despicable conduct.

The details of the crimes intrigue us. Indeed, as is the case with serial murder, it becomes a spectator sport by way of movies, television, video games, and the Internet (Egger, 2002). We are morosely captivated by the homicides that are committed, find that it takes more and more glamorized reports to shock us, and delight in the capture and punishment of those accused. The awesome and frightening often displaces the uplifting and inspiring, and nowhere is this tendency more evident than in our news media (Kelleher & Kelleher, 1998). It is this institution that increasingly sensationalizes and feeds our obsession with crime. By desensitizing us to the vile nature of the offender's actions through repeated exposure to criminal events, we are led to categorize dismissively the offender as less than or other than fully human, thereby readily endorsing society's taken-for-granted, "throw-away" approach to its disenfranchised (e.g., the poor, the mentally ill, minorities). We are all socialized into this culture of violence. As researchers, we are not immune to this phenomenon. The violent criminal offender is transformed into an entity "outside the purview of God's grace, fallen from the image of God and therefore inferior in the order of things" (Snyder, 2001, p. 43). Some argue that these offenders are objectified into nonpersonhood, as demonstrated by the criminal justice and mental health systems, and by the public's response to criminals. We agree. The question, then, is what role do these institutional entities play in the construction of offenders, including the psychopathic predator who kills repeatedly?

With these thoughts in mind, several issues are speculatively investigated in this final chapter. What role did larger societal factors play in the constitution of Aileen Wuornos? Was the only recourse available to Aileen and to society her execution? Do psychopathic offenders have different options than nonpsychopathic offenders? If current psychological/psychiatric interventions for this criminal can report no or minimal treatment success outcomes, does this make capital punishment a viable alternative? Is the death penalty a "necessary evil": a correctional practice essential to generate and maintain social order, to repair the imbalance created by criminal behavior, and to provide the "greatest good for the greatest number" (Sullivan & Tifft, 2001, p. 31)? Or, is the administration of violence (i.e., the death penalty) always an unacceptable response to the presence of violence in society?

These ethical issues are examined, mindful of the insights of Marxist or radical criminology and restorative justice. Marxism explores how crime, law, and social control develop within a given political economy (Lynch, Michalowski, & Groves, 2000). Restorative justice considers society's collective responsibility and redemptive capacity, activities from which we all potentially benefit (Sullivan & Tifft, 2001). These two conceptual prisms help us understand the actions of people at society's fringes, including those who engage in acts of serial murder.

THE CASE OF AILEEN WUORNOS: REFLECTIONS FROM MARXISM AND RESTORATIVE JUSTICE

An unsettling and pervasive ethical dilemma exists when attempting to balance the demands of society and its citizens who seek safety, security, and freedom from harm, against the rights and interests of those convicted of crime, including murder. Victims and their families demand justice, at times insisting that it be meted out violently (e.g., the death penalty) (Arrigo & Williams, 2004). However, most offenders do not emerge upon the scene absent some physical, economic, political, and emotional scarring, wrought by the very people and systems from which we *all* expect some modicum of support, guidance, or protection. Thus, it follows that if the offender is to be held responsible for his or her decision making, shouldn't society (and its institutions) similarly be held accountable when blindly and woefully failing its people? Indeed, as Snyder (2001, p. 65) observed, "Placing all responsibility for sin upon the individual is a convenient denial of the larger community's complicity—its choices, policies, and structures."

We take the position that a person does not descend into the abyss of murder in a complete and unmitigated vacuum. There are a myriad of factors that can help to bring about this calamity, and this fact has been made abundantly clear by both criminological and psychological research (e.g., Arrigo, 2003). Thus, although punishment ultimately may be necessary for the most violent of offenders, the denial of the larger community's contribution to the criminal event seems rather naive. Indeed, as the case of Aileen Wuornos vividly demonstrated, individual *and* societal factors were interactively at work, transforming her into a predatory serial killer.

Radical criminology views crime as a social construction, built from and around its economic, political, and social systems. In this way, crime and delinquency are not just the responsibility of the offending party. Informed by the insights of Karl Marx, radical criminology takes the position that in order to prevent crime and to establish justice, society must abate or neutralize harmful, debilitating conditions of oppression and victimization (Lynch & Stretesky, 1999). As a sophisticated critique, the radical agenda points out how prevailing criminological theories neglect the role that "inequality and exploitation play in the formation of crime, law, and punishment . . . , expos[ing] the class bias of criminology (Lynch, Michalowski, & Groves 2000, p. 8). Thus, consistent with Marxism (e.g., Quinney, 1970), radical criminology examines the capitalist economic order, arguing that it is a major force in our culture of violence and punishment (for a review in psychology, law, and crime, see, Arrigo, 2003).

Adopting this orientation, Lynch, Michalowski, and Groves (2000) ask the following question: "How can a person find support to heal amid social arrangements that have little or no ability to meet personal needs, indeed, that are structured to deny the meeting of essential needs?" (p. ix). Advocates of the radical paradigm stress the importance of comprehending the history of our social systems in an attempt to better understand the causes of and possible solutions to our current problems. In particular, they draw attention to the division of social class, wherein the powerful seek to maintain relationships that preserve their position of advantage, while the disempowered try to find ways to resist and rectify this inequality (Arrigo, 2002).

Moreover, most people uncritically accept the norms and values of the status quo. Our society maintains religious, educational, political, economic, and related institutions that promote this socialization. However, Marxism explains that the dominant culture becomes so powerful that even those marginalized by its superordinate values accept interpretations of reality that favor and worsen their own subjugated status (Arrigo & Bernard, 1997; Lynch, Michalowski, & Groves, 2000). In addition, our laws and their enforcement agents serve to further promote and maintain the interests of the powerful. It is not surprising, then, that society's values influence the types of behaviors defined as criminal (Quinney, 1970). However, Marxism demands that equitable policies be formed on behalf of those who possess less bargaining power in society where access to economic and political resources are distributed more fairly and where oppression and exploitation stemming from gender, race, or class inequalities are eliminated (Arrigo, 1999).

Many of the preceding observations are relevant to an assessment of Aileen Wuornos and her predatory serial killing. Throughout history, women have been systematically excluded from economic, social, and political power (e.g., Jurik, 1999). Consistent with this exclusion, some radical criminologists argue that capitalism prevents entire groups or classes of people from forming meaningful attachments to societal institutions (Lynch, Michalowski, & Groves, 2000; Spitzer, 1975). Without any attachments to encourage conformity, these individuals are likely to engage in criminal behavior (Arrigo, 2004; Arrigo & Bernard, 1997). We note that the radical criminological view is much broader than attachment theory as discussed elsewhere in this book; however, the same principles apply. As previously delineated, Aileen Wuornos did not have strong, healthy attachments to her primary attachment figures (e.g. parents and grandparents). However, from a Marxist perspective, we are drawn to the economic, political, and societal conditions that contributed to her broken home, the criminal behavior of her biological father, and the lack of social service and related interventions tendered on her behalf.

Radical criminologists maintain that family disorganization is a crucial variable in crime causation (Hirschi, 1983). Indeed, according to Lynch, Michalowski, and Groves (2000, p. 93), "Socialization experiences are 'positive' in that children have 'initial bonds of high intensity' to the family unit." It follows, then, that a Marxist-based critique of the case of Aileen Wuornos would carefully assess the impact that her family dynamics and lower socioeconomic status had in her decision to engage in prostitution, theft, and murder. Although well beyond the scope of our intentions with this chapter or book, the insights of Marxism and radical criminology remind us that crimes like those committed by Aileen Wuornos simply do not and cannot occur in a vacuum.

Notwithstanding the Marxist concerns for inequality stemming from class, race, and gender differences, the criminal justice system executed Aileen Wuornos because she was convicted of a crime (i.e., first-degree murder) for which the death penalty was imposed. However, even if we can justify society's response to violent criminals, what responsibility, if any, does it have to interpret and remedy the circumstances that give rise to such vile criminal actions? Commenting on this very matter, Snyder (2001, p. 101) indicated that "our nation seems fixated on the notion that if we can remove the offending persons from society, we will have taken care of the sickness." However, given the Marxist critique that we have very tentatively sketched here, can it be that our nation's desensitization to violence, including execution, serves only to perpetuate a flawed cycle of redress for harms caused?

Certainly, Aileen Wuornos met and exceeded the criteria for psychopathy. She very callously took the lives of seven people, leaving a trail of victimization and devastation behind her. If she was incorrigible and unsalvageable when executed, was there ever a point in her life when she could have been saved? Alternatively, could any response have been too punitive? In the face of having been abandoned (mostly) by her family and community, to what extent did an absence of adolescent mental health treatment affect Aileen's choice of conduct as an adult? In short, where did society *really* break down and fail her, helping to fashion (unknowingly) a person of awesome violence and terrible destruction?

These questions are not easily answered. Psychopaths are not sympathetic characters. The crimes they commit are most assuredly reprehensible. However, perhaps some indication of how best to proceed is located within restorative justice.

A more humanitarian view of justice comes from the restorative model of reconciliation and mediation (Sullivan & Tifft, 2001). As both philosophy and practice, restorative justice focuses on the healing of individuals and communities, rather than on retribution or punishment. Restorative justice proposes that responding to violence with violence escalates the process of destruction and alienation. Proponents of restorative justice programs, especially those who rely on methods that are standard practice in dispute resolution and conflict mediation, strive first to engage *all* parties impacted by harm to take an active role in helping one another cope with their loss and to heal as a community (Bazemore & Schiff, 2001; Van Ness & Strong, 1997).

There are many differences between retributive and restorative justice. For example, the retributive approach centers on punishment, the maintenance of power, and counter-violence. Conversely, the restorative model focuses on redemption, the balance of power, and making peace with crime. As a society, however, we are "driven to retaliate" when inflicted with pain by others (e.g., the loss of a child through violence) and to equalize the harm with counterharm (Sullivan & Tifft, 2001, p. 2). This response is particularly salient when the offender expresses no remorse, as is frequently the case with the psychopathic offender. Aileen Wuornos showed no repentance; instead, she blamed the victims and proclaimed that the families of those slain owed her an apology for the harm done to her by their loved ones.

Regrettably, we live in a culture that takes as accepted practice the administration of penal harm (including capital punishment), following the experience of personal victimization. However, restorative justice focuses on healing all injured parties, including the victim, the offender, and the community of which both are a part. The maintenance of relationships, the involvement of the community, the role of mediation, the attention to nonpunitive sanctions, and the provision of reparations are all essential components of this perspective (Umbreit, 1995). In this way, "Healing is a circular process, and all dimensions of the circle must be attended to in order for healing to occur" (Snyder, 2001, p. 82). Following this perspective, the actions of every person have meaningful effects on others, since all life is perceived as interconnected. As such, a collective responsibility to sustain, rather than to terminate, life principally exists.

The methods of our criminal justice system, including capital punishment, represent rationalized counterviolence. However, reactive violence does not heal all parties involved (Bazemore & Schiff, 2001; Zehr, 1990). In fact, it does nothing more than foreclose opportunities for genuine self-discovery, empathy, and forgiveness (Arrigo & Williams, 2003). In describing the ethos of punishment so ingrained in the fabric of our culture, Snyder (2001, p. 143) observed that "Violence is at the heart of our society—the violence that produces the conditions for crime, the violence of the criminal act, and the violent responses to crime. Our prisons only reinforce the violence of the soul." Capital punishment, then, is a vivid reminder of how the soul is territorialized and vanquished by the system.

But the problem identified by restorative justice advocates is not limited to the execution of convicts. Indeed, proponents of restorative justice point out that prisons dehumanize their occupants by isolating and reducing them to a number that is restricted by time, space, and protocol (Snyder, 2001). Prisons are rampant with violence, including assaults, murders, and rapes (Clear, 1994). Offenders are often housed in tiny cells, where they defecate and urinate only inches from where they sleep. The prison industrial complex is a modern-day, revolving-door gulag, where treatment initiatives are terminated, forestalled, or underfunded (Christie, 1993; Ross & Richards, 2002). Rather than providing hope and rehabilitation for less violent offenders, prisons have become a training ground for criminal versatility, especially for poor ethnic minorities (Reiman, 2001).

Given our very speculative comments on restorative justice and harm, we are led to ask in what way capital punishment or sustained incarceration addresses the criminal actions of persons like Aileen Wuornos? We note that the nature of psychopathy and predatory homicide is such that the death penalty poses no deterrent effect for these individuals because they assume that they will not be caught or confined (Hickey, 1997). Moreover, as we previously explained, the psychopathic offender is impervious to the thought of personal consequence (Shipley & Arrigo, 2001). Indeed, their narcissistic view of self often leads them to believe that they are smarter than everyone else and above the law. Then, too, success outcomes for the correctional treatment of psychopaths are not very promising (Gacono, 2000). Thus, we wonder what the purpose of execution or long-term penal confinement is for the psychopathic offender if healing and redemption are to be achieved along with the victim, the victim's family, and the community to which all belong?

In addition, we note that gender inequality is also evident within our justice system (Jurik, 1999). The emphasis given to power, force, and weapons reflects a male-centered approach to social control (Lynch, Michalowski, & Groves, 2000). In addition, women tend to be protected from harsher punishments when their crimes are congruent with gender-role stereotypes, especially when defined as the weaker sex. However, females experience more severe punishments when their crimes are antithetical to their statuses as mothers, nurturers, or sexual objects. We are not surprised, therefore, that the heinous and cold-blooded nature of Aileen Wuornos's murders made her an obvious candidate for capital punishment. In situations such as this, it appears as if the application of restorative justice principles is simply unrealizable.

However, why would it have been so impractical to utilize this philosophy and practice prior to Aileen's murderous actions? Both the mental health and the criminal justice systems had ample opportunities to assist her. For example, Aileen's school counselor and several of her other educators raised concerns about her deviant and delinquent conduct. Yet, no system helped Aileen. No professional intervened on her behalf. Although the healing process is multifaceted, by and large the community must first acknowledge what has happened, and sociostructural change must occur. Individual therapeutic intervention is insufficient to fix the problem (Snyder, 2001). Regrettably, the cause of Aileen Wuornos was neither championed by systemic intercession nor by agents representing these entities.

As a society, we should be responsible for creating a social environment that takes into account the needs of all its members; an environment in which young people are taught to respect and to develop personal character and moral aptitude (Coles, 1997). Indeed, restorative relationships should begin at the most personal and basic levels, including with families and in schools, in order to prevent the destruction of the community. Unfortunately, Aileen Wuornos's family and community further alienated her. She was homeless as a teenager and was not offered assistance from her neighbors. Communities are responsible for the restoration of their own neighborhoods. The idea of community is central to restorative justice approaches. "Community is not something that is created when people come together and live together, rather it is something that is preexistent and we can awaken to that experience of communion" (Community Directory, 1995, p. 36).

Having questioned the efficacy of capital punishment, long-term incarceration, and the sentencing process for psychopathic female serial killers, we recognize that not all things can be neatly and cleanly forgiven. It is shortsighted to think that the individual and collective pain that follows in the wake of predatory serial murder could be undone by the mere expression of absolution. According to psychotherapist Judith Herman (1992, p. 190), "The fantasy of forgiveness can be a cruel torture, because it remains out of reach for most ordinary human beings. . . . And even true forgiveness in most religious systems is not unconditional. True forgiveness cannot be granted until the perpetrator has sought and earned it through confession, repentance, and restitution." But here, too, we wonder what systemic efforts could have been taken to create the necessary conditions within which Aileen Wuornos could have explored a basis for genuine contrition.

Harm to another is a unilateral act in which the other's rights and needs are disregarded (Sullivan and Tifft, 2001). Proponents of restorative justice maintain that the criminal justice system dehumanizes and disregards the offender in much the same way as the offender disregarded his or her victims. Capital punishment and sustained imprisonment are clear examples of this. Psychopathic individuals have no authentic sense of other, and they systematically violate the rights and needs of people for their own personal gain or amusement. Often, their actions toward and treatment of others are a function of their deeply rooted personality structure rather than a situational cause for which we should be sympathetic. However, as we have argued, the successful application of restorative justice principles to the case of predatory homicide offenders must weigh both offender and societal forces in the calculus of criminal accountability.

CONCLUSIONS AND SUMMARY

Although crime is a collective problem, Aileen Wuornos faced a very individual death. In response to the news of her impending execution, Circuit Judge C. McFerrin Smith stated, "The loss of any human life is sad. The public will be indifferent because she did so many terrible acts. She earned the public's indifference" (Frederick, 2002). Moreover, many would correctly and fairly assert that despite her childhood experiences, Aileen Wuornos possessed free will and the ability to choose her path. Thus, in the final analysis, this deeply tormented woman who engaged in murderous actions needed to be removed from society, preventing her from preying upon other, unsuspecting citizens.

Yet, we are still troubled by the fact that it is the United States that fosters the greatest number of violent criminals, including serial killers, and the most heinous of crimes (Egger, 2002; Sullivan & Tifft, 2001). Society's outrage at the notion of cold-blooded murder and murderers merely creates tunnel vision. We focus on the offenders and conclude that they must be some kind of monster, an anomaly to humanity. If we slay the monster, the problem will be solved.

This approach is as misguided as it is shortsighted. Increasingly, our desensitization to violence keeps us that much more removed from a solution to physical, emotional, and sexual abuse. For each killer we execute, there are many more to take the person's place on death row. And although there are certainly some individuals who are so dangerous to others that they should not be allowed to freely roam the streets, this execution/confinement approach misses the macrological context in which crime and victimization occur (Lynch, Michalowski, & Groves, 2000). Indeed, in some meaningful respects, the distinction between "victim" and "offender" is rendered irrelevant, especially when larger political, economic, and social forces thwart and undermine the human potential of both, repeatedly and directly.

To be clear, we are well aware that there is an absence of efficacious treatment for the most violent of offenders (i.e., the psychopath) populating our prisons today. Thus, when an individual descends into the murderous depths of serial killing wherein social scientists or policy experts conclude that the person deserves rehabilitation, no reliably effective tools presently exist to treat the offender. Indeed, it is simply not yet possible to "reprogram" a mind that knows little, if any, conscience, empathy, or consequence. While the mental health community has become much more skilled in evaluating and identifying psychopathy (Gacono, 2000), much of what it offers the offender is reactive and does little more than to label the individual in question, after a crime has been committed. And herein lies the rub: if we have nothing to avail the person by way of meaningful treatment, are we not required to protect society from a predatory murderer through life imprisonment or even execution?

In response, we do find it quite difficult to ignore the pain and anguish of the victim's family. Moreover, the exceptionally violent offender cannot be placed neatly into a "healing paradigm," because this solution is based on the premise of empathy, a capacity to form a conscience, and a willingness to help in the healing of the person or parties harmed. These principles seem to have enormous utility for the vast majority of offenders. Indeed, statistically speaking, most offenders are not psychopathic and do not commit serial murder. In the case of Aileen Wuornos, however, the critical periods of moral development and attachment to others had long since passed by the time she was sentenced to death. At the time of her execution, she was so damaged and so dangerous to society that the only other option was a life sentence, without the possibility of parole. In fact, at the hearing to waive her remaining appeals for execution, Aileen Wuornos stated, "I killed those men, robbed them cold as ice. And I'd do it again, too. . . . There's no chance in keeping me alive or anything, because I'd kill again. I have hate crawling through my system" (Zarrella, 2002). Aileen had no ties to the community, to her family, or to social institutions. Her motivation to change or to heal seemed completely out of intellectual and emotional reach. Perhaps, then, the choice of what to do in her case was clear.

However, this outcome does not absolve the systems to which she was connected. Both the criminal justice and the mental health apparatuses failed her. To this extent, we cannot help but wonder what would have become of Aileen Wuornos had they addressed her specific needs in a timely fashion. Indeed, unless we effect some substantial social changes, including a more collective responsibility for the welfare of others, we will remain ill-equipped to prevent the development of the most violent and morally bankrupt of offenders. Early intervention would likely have had some impact on who Aileen Wuornos became; and rehabilitation, if provided much earlier in her life, might have eliminated her tendency to act explosively, violently, murderously. Had Aileen's family and community protected her as a child, she probably would have matured into a much different adult. Regrettably, this was not her fate.

This book explored many individual and family specific events; however, we hope that this chapter shed some additional light on several collective, societal responsibilities, bringing the problem of predatory female killing and psychopathy into sharper focus. In brief, this chapter speculatively examined a number of matters linked to ethics, justice, and accountability for how persons with mental illness are dealt with by systems entrusted with their care and treatment. The case of Aileen Wuornos raises many troubling concerns about her overall life, implicating mental health, criminal justice, and related social service agencies.

The possibility for more effective, pro-active intervention regarding the ethical dilemmas we described lies in our understanding of the broader social context in which (predatory) homicide occurs. When Aileen Wuornos murdered, she acted alone in the dark of night. She met her personal needs for revenge, power, and material possessions. She felt entitled to these things and did not consider the consequences of her behavior. However, the society that had virtually ignored and discarded her from birth stood up and took notice. By this time, though, it was too late to heal her wounds.

As a society, we take little responsibility for our part in developing a culture of violence or for seeding a criminal mind. We fail to appreciate our shared identity as a community and the primacy of humane treatment for all people. We value our individual economic growth more than we value an equitable and fair distribution of life chances for all citizens, including the poor, women, race and ethnic minorities, and other disenfranchised groups. Rather than exploring how principles of restorative justice might promote healing and advance peace, our approach to violent crimes and criminals, including the growing number of serial killers among us, is to support stricter correctional sentences, especially capital punishment, and to incarcerate more individuals than any other industrialized nation in the world (Snyder, 2001). As researchers and practitioners, we do not believe that this is the best that we can or should do. The troubling case of Aileen Wuornos painfully reminds us of this fact.

It seems simple to put our blind faith in the existing system, when the popular mantra is to "get tough" on crime. We spend millions of dollars to warehouse criminals but are unwilling to invest in prevention and in the scores of lives that might be saved rather than avenged. If as authors of this book we could honestly conclude that society had exhausted all available and tangible resources for this very worthwhile purpose, particularly for those children victimized or objectified, we might be inclined to regard the death of Aileen Wuornos and others like her as tragic but understandable. Unfortunately, this level of support for our youth remains woefully inadequate in the United States.

Aileen Wuornos was a product of her own machinations, forged in the crucible of parental neglect and abuse, and was a recipient of institutional malaise, ensconced in the politics of criminal justice and mental health abandonment and indifference. Although she was most assuredly responsible for her criminal behaviors, the systems in place to help Aileen failed her with impunity. In this way, the cycle of violence into which she plummeted was complete. Her personal victimization as a child was externalized in adolescence and adulthood, resulting in the deaths of seven men. Unable to secure much-needed assistance for her unfathomable torment, Aileen was punished for her serial killings. She was the source and product of violence: rejected/detached, unlovable/unloving, and predatory/psychopathic. On the fringes of society, she struggled to survive, until she met her ruinous conclusion.

More than providing a provocative illustration of predatory homicide in psychopathic women, we hope that our analysis produces some much-needed reflection. The disciplines of psychology and criminal justice must reevaluate their individual and collective understanding of female killers. Indeed, the lives of far too many citizens have become the needless casualties of institutional myopia and inertia on this topic. Accordingly, we invite researchers, policy analysts, and educators to examine more closely the issues entertained throughout this book. The fate of people like Aileen Wuornos and of those whom these psychopathic offenders harm clearly depends on it.

References

ADLER, F. (1975). *Sisters in crime: The rise of the new female criminal.* New York: McGraw-Hill.

ADLER, F., & SIMON, R. (Eds.) (1979). *The criminology of deviant women.* Boston: Houghton Mifflin Company.

A & E. (1998). American Justice: Death Row Prostitute: Aileen Wuornos.

AHERNS, A. (2001). A biography of Aileen Wuornos.
    http://www.courttv.com/onair/shows/mugshots/indepth/wuornos. html

AINSWORTH, M. D. S. (1969). Object relations, dependency, and attachment: Theoretical review of infant-mother relationship. *Developmental Psychology, 40,* 969–1025.

AINSWORTH, M. D. S. (1982). Attachment: Retrospect and prospect. In C. M. PARKES & J. STEVENSON-HINDE (Eds.), *The place of attachment in human behavior* (pp. 3–30). New York: Basic Books.

AINSWORTH, M. D. S., BLEHAR, M. C., WATERS, E., & WALL, S.(1978). *Patterns of attachment: A psychological study of the strange situation.* Hillsdale, NJ: Erlbaum.

ALEXANDER, P. C. (1993). The differential effects of abuse characteristics and attachment in the prediction of long-term effects of sexual abuse. *Journal of Interpersonal Violence, 8,* 346–362.

AMMEN, S. (1990). A phenomenological hermeneutical investigation of Maturana's biological systems theory and its implications for the theories of family therapy. *Dissertation Abstracts International, 51,* 1483B.

AMERICAN PSYCHIATRIC ASSOCIATION. (1952), *Diagnostic and statistical manual of mental disorders.* Washington, DC: Author.

AMERICAN PSYCHIATRIC ASSOCIATION. (1968). *Diagnostic and statistical manual of mental disorders (Rev. Ed.).* Washington, DC: Author.

AMERICAN PSYCHIATRIC ASSOCIATION. (1980). *Diagnostic and statistical manual of mental disorders* (3rd ed.). Washington, DC: Author.

AMERICAN PSYCHIATRIC ASSOCIATION. (1987). *Diagnostic and statistical manual of mental disorders* (3rd revised ed.). Washington, DC: Author.

AMERICAN PSYCHIATRIC ASSOCIATION. (1994). *Diagnostic and statistical manual of mental disorders* (4th ed.). Washington, DC: Author.

ARNOLD, R. (1990). Processes of victimization and criminalization of black women. *Social Justice, 17,* 153–166.

ARRIGO, B. A. (2000). *Introduction to forensic psychology: Issues and controversies in crime and justice.* San Diego: Academic Press.

ARRIGO, B. A. (2002). The critical perspective in psychological jurisprudence: Theoretical advances and epistemological assumptions. *International Journal of Law and Psychiatry, 25,* 151–172.

ARRIGO, B. A. (2003). Psychology and the law: The critical agenda for citizen justice and radical social change. *Justice Quarterly, 20,* 399–444.

ARRIGO, B. A. (2004). *Criminal behavior: A systems approach.* Belmont, CA: Wadsworth.

ARRIGO, B. A. (Ed.). (1999). *Social justice/criminal justice: The maturation of critical theory in law, crime, and deviance.* Belmont, CA: Wadsworth.

ARRIGO, B. A., & BERNARD, T. J. (1997). Postmodern criminology in relation to radical and conflict criminology. *Critical Criminology: An International Journal, 8,* 39–60.

ARRIGO, B. A., & PURCELL, C. E. (2001). Explaining paraphilias and lust murder: Toward an integrated model. *International Journal of Offender Therapy and Comparative Criminology, 45,* 6–31.

ARRIGO, B. A., & SHIPLEY, S. L. (2001) The confusion over psychopathy I: Historical considerations. *International Journal of Offender Therapy and Comparative Criminology, 45,* 325–344.

ARRIGO, B. A., & WILLIAMS, C. R. (2003). Victim voices, victim vices and restorative justice: Rethinking the use of impact evidence in capital cases. *Crime & Delinquency, 49.*

The Attachment Center. (2001). What is attachment disorder?
http://www.attachmentcenter.org/whatisit.htm

BASKIN, D. R., & SOMMERS, I. (1993). Females' initiation into violent street crime. *Justice Quarterly, 10,* 559–581.

BAZEMORE, G., & SCHIFF, M. (Eds.). (2001). *Restorative community justice: Repairing harm and transforming communities.* Cincinnati: Anderson Publishing.

BELL, C., & FOX, M. (1996). Telling stories of women who kill. *Social & Legal Studies, 5,* 471–494.

BERKOWITZ, L. (1964). Aggressive cues in aggressive behavior and hostility catharsis. *Psychological Review, 71,* 104–122.

BETTENCOURT, B. A., & MILLER, N. (1996). Gender differences in aggression as a function of provocation: A meta-analysis. *Psychological Bulletin, 119,* 422–447.

BJORKQVIST, K. (1994). Sex differences in physical, verbal, and indirect aggression: A review of recent research. *Sex Roles, 30,* 177–188.

BLACKBURN, R. (1969). Sensation seeking, impulsivity, and psychopathic personality. *Journal of Consulting and Clinical Psychology, 33,* 571–574.

BLACKBURN, R. (1998). Criminality and the interpersonal circle in mentally disordered offenders. *Criminal Justice and Behavior, 25,* 155–176.

BLUM, A., & FISHER, G. (1978). Women who kill. In I. L. Kutash, S. B. Kutash, & L. B. Schlesinger (Eds.), *Violence: Perspectives on murder and aggression* (pp. 463–474). San Francisco: Jossey-Bass.

BOWLBY, J. (1969). *Attachment and loss: Vol. 1. Attachment.* New York: Basic Books.

BOWLBY, J. (1973). *Attachment and loss: Vol. 2. Separation: Anxiety and anger.* New York: Basic Books.

BOWLBY, J. (1980). Attachment and loss: Vol. 3. Loss: *Sadness and depression.* New York: Basic Books.

BRENNER, C. (1973). *An elementary textbook on psychoanalysis.* (Rev. ed.). New York: International Universities Press.

BROWNSTEIN, H. H., SPUNT, B. J., CRIMMINS, S., GOLDSTEIN, P. J., & LANGLEY, S. (1994). *Changing patterns of lethal violence by women: A research note, 5,* 99–118.

BUNCH, B. J., FOLEY, L. A., & URBINA, S. P. (1983). The psychology of violent female offenders: A sex-role perspective. *Prison Journal, 63,* 66–79.

CAMPBELL, A., MUNCER, S., & GORMAN, B. (1992). Sex and social representation of aggression: A communal-agentic analysis. *Aggressive Behavior, 19,* 125–135.

CHESNEY-LIND, M. (1998). *The female offender: Girls, women, and crime.* Thousand Oaks, CA: Sage.

CHESNEY-LIND, M., & SHELDON, R. (1992). *Girls, delinquency, and juvenile justice.* Pacific Grove, CA: Brooks/Cole.

CHODOFF, P. (1982). Hysteria and women. *American Journal of Psychiatry, 139,* 545–552.

CHRISTIE, N. (1993). *Crime control as industry: Towards gulags western style?* New York: Routledge.

CICCHETTI, D., & TOTH, S. L. (1995). Child maltreatment and attachment organization. In S. Goldberg, R. Muir, & J. Kerr (Eds.), *Attachment theory: Social, developmental, and clinical perspectives* (pp. 279–308). Hillsdale, NJ: Analytic Press.

CLEAR, T. (1994). *Harm in American penology: Offenders, victims, and their communities.* Albany: State University of New York Press.

CLECKLEY, H. (1941). *The mask of sanity* (1st ed.). St. Louis: Mosby.

CLECKLEY, H. (1950). *The mask of sanity* (2nd ed.). St. Louis: Mosby.

CLECKLEY, H. (1982). *The mask of sanity* (7th ed.). St. Louis: Mosby.

CLONINGER, C. R., & GUZE, S. B. (1970a). Female criminals: Their personal, familial, and social backgrounds. *Archives of General Psychiatry, 23,* 554–558.

CLONINGER, C. R., & GUZE, S. B. (1970b). Psychiatric illness and female criminality: The role of sociopathy and hysteria in the antisocial woman. *American Journal of Psychiatry, 127,* 303–311.

COID, J. W. (1991). Psychiatric profiles of difficult/dangerous prisoners. In K. Bottomley & W. Hay (Eds.), *Special units for difficult prisoners* (pp. 132–148). Hull, England: Centre for Criminal Justice, University of Hull.

COLE, K. E., FISHER, G., & COLE, S. S. (1968). Women who kill: A sociopsychological study. *Archives of General Psychiatry, 19,* 1–8.

COLES, R. (1997). *The moral intelligence of children.* New York: Random House.

COLLINS, N. L., & READ, S. J. (1990). Adult attachment, working models, and relationship quality in dating couples. *Journal of Personality and Social Psychology, 58,* 644–663.

COMER, R. J. (1995). *Abnormal psychology* (2nd ed.). New York: Freeman.

Community Directory (1995). *A guide to cooperative living.* Langley, WA: Fellowship for Intentional Community.

COTE, G., & HODGINS, S. (1992). The prevalence of major mental disorders among homicide offenders. *International Journal of Law and Psychiatry, 15,* 89–99.

Court TV. (1992). The trial of Aileen Wuornos.

Court TV. (1999). Mugshots: Aileen Wuornos.

CRESWELL, J. W. (1998). *Qualitative inquiry and research design: Choosing among the five traditions.* Thousand Oaks, CA: Sage.

CRONIN, T. (1996, May). *Criminal personality profiling.* Lecture at Northwestern University Traffic Institute. Chicago.

DAHL, A. A. (1993). The personality disorders: A critical review of family, twin, and adoption studies. *Journal of Personality Disorders,* Supp. (*1*), 86–99.

DALTON, K. (1961). Menstruation and crime. *British Medical Journal, 2,* 1752–53.

DALTON, K. (1982). Violence and the premenstrual syndrome. *Police Surgeon, 21,* 8–15.

DALY, K., & CHESNEY-LIND, M. (1988). Feminism and criminology. *Justice Quarterly, 5,* 497–538.

DANIEL, A. E., & HARRIS, P. W. (1982). Female homicide offenders referred for pre-trial psychiatric examination: A descriptive study. *Bulletin of the AAPL, 10,* 261–269.

DATESMAN, S. K., SCARPITTI, F. R., & STEPHENSON, R. M. (1975). Female delinquency: An application of self and opportunity theories. *Journal of Research in Crime and Delinquency, 12,* 120.

DIBBLE, U., & STRAUS, M. A. (1980). Some social structure determinants of inconsistency between attitudes and behavior: The case of family violence. *Journal of Marriage & the Family, 42,* 71–80.

DINGES, N. G., ATLIS, M. M., & VINCENT, G. M. (1998). Cross-cultural perspectives on antisocial behavior. In D. M. STOFF, J. BREILING, & J. D. MASER (Eds.), *Handbook of antisocial behavior* (pp. 463–473). New York: Wiley.

DOBASH, R. E., & DOBASH, R. (1979). *Violence against wives.* New York: The Free Press.

D'ORBAN, P. T. (1979). Women who kill their children. *British Journal of Psychiatry, 134,* 560–571.

D'ORBAN, P. T., & O'CONNOR, A. (1989). Women who kill their parents. *British Journal of Psychiatry, 154,* 27–33.

EAGLY, A. H., & STEFFEN, V. J. (1986). Gender and aggressive behavior: A meta-analytic review of the social psychological literature. *Psychological Bulletin, 100,* 309–330.

EDWARDS, S. S. M. (1986). Neither bad nor mad: The female violent offender reassessed. *Women's Studies International Forum, 9,* 79–87.

EGELAND, B., & FARBER, E. A. (1984). Infant-mother attachment: Factors related to its development and changes over time. *Child Development, 88,* 753–771.

EGGER, S. A. (2002). *The killers among us: An examination of serial murder and its investigation* (2nd ed.). Upper Saddle River, NJ: Prentice Hall.

ELICKER, J., ENGLUND, M., & SROUFE, L. A. (1992). Predicting peer competence and peer relationships in childhood from early parent-child relationships. In R. Parke & G. Ladd (Eds.), *Family-peer relations: Modes of linkage* (pp. 77–106). Hillsdale, NJ: Erlbaum.

ERICKSON, M., SROUFE, L., & EGELAND, B. (1985). The relationship between quality of attachment and behavior problems in preschool in a high-risk sample. In I. Bretherton & E. Waters (Eds.), *Growing points of attachment theory and research: Monographs of the Society for Research in Child Development, 50,* 147–166.

ERONEN, M. (1995). Mental disorder and homicidal behavior in female subjects. *American Journal of Psychiatry, 152,* 1216–1218.

FARR, K. A. (1997). Aggravating and differentiating factors in the cases of white and minority women on death row. *Crime & Delinquency, 43,* 260–278.

Farrington, (1991). Antisocial personality from childhood to adulthood. *The Psychologist, 4,* 389–394.

FBI (Federal Bureau of Investigation). (1997). *Crime in the United States: Uniform crime reports.* Washington, DC: U.S. Department of Justice.

FIRESTONE, P., BRADFORD, J. M., GREENBERG, D. M., & LAROSE, M. R. (1998). Homicidal sex offenders: Psychological, phallometric, and diagnostic features. *Journal of the American Academy of Psychiatry and the Law, 26,* 537–552.

FLOWERS, R. B. (1994). *Female criminals, crimes, and cellmates.* Westport, CT: Greenwood Press.

FONAGY, P. (1999). Points of contact and divergence between psychoanalytic and attachment theories: Is psychoanalytic theory truly different? *Psychoanalytic Inquiry, 19,* 448–480.

FONAGY, P., TARGET, M., STEELE, M., & STEELE, H. (1997). The development of violence and crime as it relates to security of attachment. In J. Osofsky (Ed.), *Children in a violent society* (pp. 263–281). New York: The Guilford Press.

FORD, M. R., & WIDIGER, T. A. (1989). Sex bias in the diagnosis of Histrionic and Antisocial Personality Disorders. *Journal of Consulting and Clinical Psychology, 57,* 301–305.

FORTH, A. E., & MAILLOUX, D. (2000). Psychopathy in youth: What do we know?. In C. B. Gacono (Ed.), *The clinical assessment of psychopathy: A practitioner's guide* (pp. 25–54). Mahwah, NJ: Erlbaum.

FREDERICK, H. (2002). Convicted serial killer Aileen Wuornos granted death wish. http://njcnt1.news-jrnl.com/cgi-bin/.pl

FREUD, S. (1933/1968). Some psychical consequences of the anatomical distinction between the sexes. In S. Freud, *Sexuality and the psychology of love.* New York: Collier Books.

FRODI, A., MACAULAY, J., & THOME, P. R. (1977). Are women always less aggressive than men? A review of the experimental literature. *Psychological Bulletin, 84,* 634–660.

FRY, D. P., & GABRIEL, A. H. (1994). On aggression in women and girls: Cross cultural perspectives. *Sex Roles, 30,* 165–167.

GABBARD, G. O. (1990). *Psychodynamic psychiatry in clinical practice.* Washington, DC: American Psychiatric Press.

GACONO, C. B. (ed.). (2000). *The clinical and forensic assessment of psychopathy: A practitioner's guide.* Mahwah, NJ: Erlbaum.

GACONO, C. B., & MELOY, J. R. (1994). *The Rorschach assessment of aggressive and psychopathic personalities.* Hillsdale, NJ: Erlbaum.

GACONO, C. B., MELOY, J. R., SHEPPARD, K., & SPETH, E., et al. (1995). A clinical investigation of malingering and psychopathy in hospitalized insanity acquittees. *Bulletin of the American Academy of Psychiatry and the Law, 23,* 387–397.

GEBERTH, R. VERNON, J., & TURCO, R. N. (1997). Antisocial personality disorder, sexual sadism, malignant narcissism, and serial murder. *Journal of Forensic Sciences, 42,* 49–60.

GIORGI, A. (1994). A phenomenological perspective on certain qualitative research methods. *Journal of Phenomenological Psychology, 25,* 190–220.

GODWIN, R. (1978). *Murder U.S.A.: The ways we kill each other.* New York: Ballantine Books.

GOETTING, A. (1986). Correlates of prisoner misconduct. *Journal of Quantitative Criminology, 2,* 49–67.

GOETTING, A. (1987). Homicidal wives: A profile. *Journal of Family Issues, 8,* 332–341.

GOETTING, A. (1988a). Patterns of homicide among women. *Journal of Interpersonal Violence, 3,* 3–19.

GOETTING, A. (1988b). When females kill one another. *Criminal Justice and Behavior, 15,* 179–189.

GOETTING, A. (1989). Patterns of marital homicide: A comparison of husbands and wives. *Journal of Comparative Family Studies, 20,* 341–354.

GOLDBERG, S. (1991). Recent developments in attachment theory and research. *Canadian Journal of Psychiatry, 36,* 393–400.

GORDON, P. (1988). *Heroes of their own lives: The politics and history of family violence.* London: Virago.

GREENSPAN, S. I. (1981). *Psychopathology and adaptation in infancy and early childhood.* New York: International Universities Press.

GRINSPOON, L., & BAKALAR, J. B. (1978). Drug abuse, crime, and the antisocial personality: Some conceptual issues. In W. H. Reid (Ed.), *The psychopath: A comprehensive study of antisocial disorders and behaviors* (pp. 234–243). New York: Brunner/Mazel.

GROSSMAN, K. E., & GROSSMAN, K. (1991). Attachment quality as an organizer of emotional and behavioral responses in a longitudinal perspective. In C. M. Parkes, J. Stevenson-Hinde, &

P. Marris (Eds.), *Attachment across the life cycle* (pp. 93–114). London: Tavistock/Routledge.

GUNN, J. (1993). Lecture: Epidemiology and forensic psychiatry. *Criminal Behaviour and Mental Health, 3,* 180–193.

HAMBURGER, M. E., LILIENFELD, S. O., & HOGBEN, M. (1996). Psychopathy, gender, and gender roles: Implications for antisocial and histrionic personality disorders. *Journal of Personality Disorders, 10,* 41–55.

HAMILTON, S., ROTHBART, M., & DAWES, R. (1986). Sex bias diagnosis in DSM-III. *Sex Roles, 15,* 269–274.

HARE, R. D. (1980). A research scale for the assessment of psychopathy in criminal populations. *Personality and Individual Differences, 1,* 111–119.

HARE, R. D. (1991). *The Hare psychopathy checklist–revised.* Toronto, Canada: Multi-Health Systems.

HARE, R. D., & HART, S. D. (1993). Psychopathy, mental disorder, and crime. In S. Hodgins (Ed.), *Mental disorder and crime* (pp. 104–115). Newbury Park, CA: Sage.

HARE, R. D., HART, S. D., & HARPUR, T. J. (1991). Psychopathy and the DSM-IV criteria for antisocial personality disorder. *Journal of Abnormal Psychology, 100,* 391–398.

HART, S. D., & HARE, R. D. (1998). Psychopathy: Assessment and association with criminal conduct. In D. M. Stoff, J. Breiling, & J. D. Maser (Eds.), *Handbook of antisocial behavior* (pp. 22–35). New York: Wiley.

HAZAN, C., & SHAVER, P. R. (1994). Deeper into attachment theory. *Psychological Inquiry, 5,* 68–79.

HEWITT, J. D., & RIVERS, G. A. (1986, October). *The victim offender relationship in convicted homicide cases.* Paper presented at the annual meeting of the Academy of Criminal Justice Sciences, Boston.

HICKEY, E. (1991). *Serial killers and their victims.* Pacific Grove, CA: Brooks/Cole.

HICKEY, E. (1997). *Serial killers and their victims* (2nd ed.). Pacific Grove, CA: Brooks/Cole.

HILLBRAND, M., KOZMON, A. H., & NELSON, C. W. (1996). Axis II comorbidity in forensic patients with antisocial personality disorder. *International Journal of Offender Therapy and Comparative Criminology, 40,* 19–25.

HIRSCHI, T. (1969). *Causes of delinquency.* Berkeley: University of California Press.

HIRSCHI, T. (1983). Crime and the family. In J. Q. WILSON (Ed.), *Crime and public policy.* San Francisco: ICS Press.

HODGINS, S. (1992). Mental disorder, intellectual deficiency, and crime: Evidence from a birth cohort. *Archives of General Psychiatry, 49,* 476–483.

HOLMES, R. M., & HOLMES, S. T. (1994). *Murder in America.* Thousand Oaks, CA: Sage.

HUESMANN, L. R., ERON, L. D., LEFKOWITZ, M. M., & WALDER, L. O. (1984). Stability of aggression over time and generations. *Developmental Psychology, 20,* 1120–1134.

HYDE, J. S. (1984). How large are gender differences in aggression? A developmental meta-analysis. *Developmental Psychology, 20,* 722–736.

JORDAN, B. K., SCHLENGER, W. E., FAIRBANK, J. A., & CADDELL, J. M. (1996). Prevalence of psychiatric disorders among incarcerated women. *Archives of General Psychiatry, 53,* 513–519.

JURIK, N. (1999). Socialist feminism, criminology, and social justice. In B. Arrigo (Ed.), *Social justice/criminal justice: The maturation of critical theory in law, crime, and deviance* (pp. 313–350). Belmont, CA: Wadsworth.

KAGAN, J. (1986). Rates of change in psychological processes. *Journal of Applied Developmental Psychology, 7,* 125–130.

KAPLAN, M. (1983a). The issue of sex bias in DSM-III: Comments on the articles by Spitzer, Williams, and Kass. *American Psychologist, 38,* 802–803.

KAPLAN, M. (1983b). A woman's view of DSM-III. *American Psychologist, 38,* 786–792.

KASHANI, J. H., ORASCHEL, H., ROSENBERG, T. K., & REID, J. C. (1989). Psychopathology in a community sample of children and adolescents: A developmental perspective. *Journal of the American Academy of Child and Adolescent Psychiatry, 28,* 701–706.

KELLEHER, M. D., & KELLEHER, C. L. (1998). *Murder most rare: The female serial killer.* Westport, CT: Praeger.

KENNEDY, D. (1992). *On a killing day.* Chicago: Bonus Books.

KERNBERG, O. F. (1992). *Aggression in personality disorders and perversions.* New Haven, CT: Yale University Press.

KLEIN, D. (1973). The etiology of female crime: A review of the literature. *Issues in Criminology, 8,* 3–30.

LAHEY, B. B., & LOEBER, R. (1998). Attention deficit/hyperactivity disorder, oppositional defiant disorder, conduct disorder, and adult antisocial behavior: A life span perspective. In D. M. Stoff, J. Breiling, & J. D. Maser (Eds.), *Handbook of antisocial behavior* (pp. 51–59). New York: Wiley.

LEAFF, S. (1978). The antisocial personality: Psychodynamic implications. In W. H. REID (Ed.), *The psychopath: A comprehensive study of antisocial disorders and behaviors* (pp. 79–118). New York: Brunner/Mazel.

LEVENSON, M. R. (1992). Rethinking psychopathy. *Theory and Psychology, 2,* 51–71.

LEVY, K. N., & BLATT, S. J. (1999). Attachment theory and psychoanalysis: Further differentiation within insecure attachment patterns. *Psychoanalytic Inquiry, 19,* 541–575.

LEVY, T. M. (1993, May). *Adult attachment styles and personality pathology.* New research presented at the 1993 American Psychiatric Association Annual Meeting, San Francisco.

LEVY, T. M. (1996). Attachment: Biology, evolution and environment. www.attachmentcenter.org/articles/article007.htm

LEWIS, M. (1992). *Shame: The exposed self.* New York: The Free Press.

LEWIS, M., & FEIRING, C. (1991). Attachment as personal characteristic or a measure of environment. In J. L. Gewirtz & W. M. Kurtines (Eds.), *Intersections with attachment* (pp. 3–21). Hillsdale, NJ: Erlbaum.

LILIENFELD, S. O., VAN VALKENBURG, C., LARNTZ, K., & AKISKAL, H. S. (1986). The relationship of histrionic personality disorder to antisocial personality and somatization disorders. *American Journal of Psychiatry, 43,* 718–722.

LINK, B. G., ANDREWS, H., & CULLEN, F. T. (1992). The violent and illegal behavior of mental patients reconsidered. *American Sociological Review, 57,* 275–292.

LINK, B. G., & STUEVE, M. (1994). Psychotic symptoms and the violent/illegal behavior of mental patients compared to community controls. In J. Monahan & H. Steadman (Eds.), *Violence and mental disorder: Developments in risk assessment* (pp. 137–159). Chicago: University of Chicago Press.

LINNOILA, M. (1998). On the psychobiology of antisocial behavior. In D. M. Stoff, J. Breiling, & J. D. Maser (Eds.), *Handbook of antisocial behavior* (pp. 336–340). New York: Wiley.

LUNTZ, B. K., & WIDOM, C. S. (1994). Antisocial personality disorder in abused and neglected children grown up. *American Journal of Psychiatry, 151,* 670–674.

LYKKEN, D. T. (1995). *The antisocial personalities.* Hillsdale, NJ: Erlbaum.

LYNCH, M. J., MICHALOWSKI, R., & GROVES, B. (2000). *The new primer in radical criminology: Critical perspectives on crime, power, and identity.* Monsey, NY: Criminal Justice Press.

LYNCH, M. J., & STRETESKY, P. B. (1999). Marxism and social justice: Thinking about social justice, eclipsing criminal justice. In B. A. Arrigo (Ed.), *Social justice/criminal justice: The maturation of critical theory in law, crime, and deviance* (pp. 14–29). Belmont, CA: Wadsworth.

MAIN, M. (1995). Recent studies in attachment. In S. Goldberg, R. Muir, & J. Kerr (Eds.), *Attachment theory: Social, developmental, and clinical perspectives* (p. 471). Hillsdale, NJ: The Analytic Press.

Main, M., Kaplan, N., & Cassidy, J. (1985). Security in infancy, childhood, and adulthood: A move to the level of representation. In I. Bretherton & E. Waters (Eds.), *Growing points of attachment theory and research: Monographs of the Society for Research in Child Development, 50,* 66–104.

Mann, C. R. (1986, October). *Getting even? Women who kill in domestic encounters.* Paper presented at the annual meeting of the American Society of Criminology, Atlanta.

Mann, C. R. (1990). Black female homicide in the United States. *Journal of Interpersonal Violence, 5,* 176–201.

Mann, C. R. (1996). *When women kill.* Albany: State University of New York.

Martze, J., Swan, C. S., & Varney, N. R. (1991). Posttraumatic anosmia and orbital frontal: Neuropsychological and neuropsychiatric correlates. *Neuropsychology, 5,* 213–225.

Matas, L., Arend, R. A., & Sroufe, L. A. (1978). Continuity of adaptation in the second year: The relationship between quality of attachment and later competence. *Child Development, 49,* 547–556.

McClain, P. D. (1982). Black female homicide offenders and victims: Are they from the same population? *Death Education, 6,* 265–278.

Meloy, J. R. (1992). *The psychopathic mind: Origins, dynamics, and treatment* (2nd ed.). Northvale, NJ: Aronson.

Messerschmidt, J. (1986). *Capitalism, patriarchy, and crime: Toward a socialist feminist criminology.* Totowa, NJ: Rowan & Littlefield.

Messerschmidt, J. (1997). *Crime as structured action: Gender, race, class, and crime in the making.* Thousand Oaks, California: Sage.

Millon, T., Simonsen, E., & Birket-smith, M. (1998). Historical conceptions of psychopathy in the United States and Europe. In T. Millon, E. Simonsen, M. Birket-Smith, & R. D. Davis (Eds.), *Psychopathy: Antisocial, criminal, and violent behavior* (pp. 3–31). New York: The Guilford Press.

Monahan, J. (1998). Major mental disorders and violence to others. In D. M. Stoff, J. Breiling, & J. D. Maser (Eds.), *Handbook of antisocial behavior* (pp. 92–100). New York: Wiley.

Moustakas, C. (1994). *Phenomenological research methods.* Thousand Oaks, CA: Sage.

Mulder, R. T., Wells, J. E., Joyce, P. R., & Bushnell, J. A. (1994). Antisocial women. *Journal of Personality Disorders, 8,* 279–287.

Naffine, N. (1987). *Female crime: The construction of women in criminology.* Boston: Allen and Unwin.

Offord, D. R., Adler, R. J., & Boyle, M. H. (1986). Prevalence and sociodemographic correlates of conduct disorder. *American Journal of Social Psychiatry, 6,* 272–278.

Offord, D. R., Boyle, M. H., & Rancine, Y. A. (1991). The epidemiology of antisocial behavior in childhood and adolescence. In D. J. Pepler & K. H. Rubin (Eds.), *The development and treatment of childhood aggression* (p. 470). Hillsdale, NJ: Erlbaum.

O'Keefe, M. (1995). Predictors of child abuse in martially violent families. *Journal of Interpersonal Violence, 10,* 3–25.

Pajer, K. A. (1998). What happens to "bad girls"?: A review of the adult outcomes of antisocial adolescent girls. *American Journal of Psychiatry, 155,* 862–870.

Patterson, G. R. (1986). Performance models for antisocial boys. *American Psychologist, 41,* 432–444.

Perry, B. D. (1997). Incubated in terror: Neurodevelopmental factors in the "cycle of violence." In J. Osofsky (Ed.), *Children in a violent society* (pp. 124–149). New York: The Guilford Press.

Phillips, D. (1990). Subjectivity and objectivity: An objective inquiry. In E. Eisner & A. Peshkin (Eds.), *Qualitative inquiry in education* (pp. 19–37). New York: Teachers College Press.

Phillips, D. M., & DeFleur, L. B. (1982). Gender ascription and stereotyping of deviants. *Criminology, 20,* 431–448.

POLLACK, O. (1950). *The criminality of women.* Philadelphia: University of Philadelphia Press.

POLLOCK, J. M. (1999). *Criminal women.* Cincinnati: Anderson.

QUINNEY, R. (1970). *The social reality of crime.* Boston: Little, Brown, & Company.

RAFTER, N. H. (2000). *Encyclopedia of women and crime.* Phoenix: Oryx Press.

RAINE, A. (1998). Antisocial behavior and psychophysiology: A biosocial perspective and a pre-frontal dysfunction hypothesis. In D. M. STOFF, J. BREILING, & J. D. MASER (Eds.), *Handbook of antisocial behavior* (pp. 289–303). New York: Wiley.

RANDOLPH, L. (1997). *Randolph attachment disorders questionnaire.* Evergreen, CO: Attachment Center at Evergreen, Inc.

RANDOLPH, L., & MYEROFF, R. (1998). Does attachment therapy work?: Results of two prelimi-nary studies. www.attachmentcenter.org/ranmyer.html

REIGER, D. A., BOYD, J. H., BURKE, J. D., RAE, D. S., MYERS, J. K., KRAMER, M., ROBINS, L. N., GEORGE, L. K., KARNO, M., & LOCKE, B. Z. (1988). One-month prevalence of mental disorders in the United States. *Archives of General Psychiatry, 45, 977–986.*

REIGER, D. A., MYERS, J. K., KRAMER, M., ROBINS, L. N., BLAZER, D. G., HOUGH, R. I., EATON, W. W., & LOCKE, B. Z. (1984). The NIMH epidemiologic catchment area (ECA) program: Historical context, major objectives, and study population characteristics. *Archives of General Psychiatry, 41, 934–941.*

REIMAN, J. (2001). *The rich get richer and the poor get prison: Ideology, class, and criminal jus-tice* (6th Ed.). Needham Heights, MA: Allyn and Bacon.

RENKEN, B., EGELAND, B., MARVINNEY, D., MANGELSDORF, S., & SROUFE, L. A. (1989). Early childhood antecedents of aggression and passive-withdrawal in early elementary school. *Journal of Personality, 57, 257–281.*

RICE, M. E., & HARRIS, G. T. (1997). The treatment of mentally disordered offenders. *Psychology, Public Policy, and Law, 3, 126–183.*

ROBINS, L. N. (1966). *Deviant children grown up.* Baltimore: Williams & Wilkins.

ROBINS, L. N. (1978). Aetiological implications in studies of childhood histories relating to antiso-cial personality. In R. D. Hare & D. Schalling (Eds.), *Psychopathic behavior: Approaches to research* (pp. 255–271). Chichester, England: Wiley.

ROBINS, L. N., & REGIER, D. A. (1991). *Psychiatric disorders in America: The epidemiologic catchment area study.* New York: Free Press.

ROBINS, L. N., TIPP, J., & PRZYBECK, T. (1991). Antisocial personality. In L. N. Robins & D. A. Regier (Eds.), *Psychiatric disorders in America: The epidemiologic catchment area study* (pp. 258–290). New York: Free Press.

ROSENBAUM, M. (1987). Social control, gender, and delinquency: An analysis of drug, property, and violent offenders. *Justice Quarterly, 4, 117–132.*

ROSENSTEIN, D. S., & HOROWITZ, H. A. (1996). Adolescent attachment and psychopathology. *Journal of Consulting and Clinical Psychology, 64, 244–253.*

ROSS, J. I., & RICHARDS, S. C. (2002). *Convict criminology.* Belmont, CA: Wadsworth.

ROSTORW, A. (October 9, 2002). *Florida executes killer Aileen Wuornos.* www.planetout.com/news/article.html?date=2002/10/09/1

ROTHBARD, J. C., & SHAVER, P. R. (1991). *Attachment styles and the quality and importance of at-tachment to parents.* Unpublished manuscript, State University of New York at Buffalo.

ROTHBARD, J. C., & SHAVER, P. R. (1994). Continuity of attachment across the life span. In M. B. Sperling & W. H. Berman (Eds.), *Attachment in adults: Clinical and developmental perspec-tives* (pp. 31–71). New York: The Guilford Press.

RUSH, G. E. (1991). *The dictionary of criminal justice* (3rd ed.). Guilford, CT: Dushkin.

RUSSELL, S. (1992). *Damsel of death.* London: BCA.

RUTHERFORD, M. J., ALTERMAN, A. I., CACCIOLA, J. S., & SNIDER, E. C. (1995). Gender differ-ences in diagnosing Antisocial Personality Disorders in methadone patients. *American Journal of Psychiatry, 152, 1309–1316.*

RUTTER, M. (1998). Antisocial behavior: Developmental psychopathology perspectives. In D. M. Stoff, J. Breiling, & J. D. Maser (Eds.), *Handbook of antisocial behavior* (pp. 115–123). New York: Wiley.

SALEKIN, R. T., ROGERS, R., & SEWELL, K. W. (1997). Construct validity of psychopathy in a female offender sample: A multitrait-multimethod evaluation. *Journal of Abnormal Psychology, 106,* 576–585.

SALEKIN, R. T., ROGERS, R., USTAD, K. L., & SEWELL, K. W. (1998). Psychopathy and recidivism among female inmates. *Law and Human Behavior, 22* 109–128.

SCHNEIDER, M. (2002). Florida judge clears the way for female serial killer who wants to be executed. http://www.marcodailynews.com/01/07/florida/d654902a.htm.

SCHORE, A. (1991). Early superego development: The emergence of shame and narcissistic affect regulation in the practicing period. *Psychoanalysis and Contemporary Thought, 14,* 187–250.

SCHORE, A. (1994). *Affect regulation and the origin of the self: The neurobiology of emotional development.* Hillsdale, NJ: Erlbaum.

SCHURMAN-KAUFLIN, D. (2000). *The new predator: Women who kill, profiles of female serial killers.* New York: Algora.

SCULL, A. T. (1989). *Social order/mental disorder: Anglo-American psychiatry in historical perspective.* Berkeley: University of California Press.

SEGALL, W. E., & WILSON, A. V. (1993). Who is at greatest risk in homicides?: A Comparison of victimization rates by geographic region. In A. V. Wilson (Ed.), *Homicide: The victim/offender connection* (pp. 132–152). Cincinnati: Anderson.

SERIN, R. C. (1991). Psychopathy and violence in criminals. *Journal of Interpersonal Violence, 6,* 423–431.

SHAH, S., & ROTH, L. (1974). Biological and psychological factors in criminality. In D. Glasser (Ed.), *Handbook of Criminology* (pp. 58–81). Chicago: Rand McNally.

SHIPLEY, S. L., & ARRIGO, B. A. (2001). The confusion over psychopathy (II): Implications for forensic (correctional) practice. *International Journal of Offender Therapy and Comparative Criminology, 45,* 407–420.

SHIPLEY, S., & ARRIGO, B. (2004). *The female homicide offender: Serial murder and the case of Aileen Wuornos.* Upper Saddle River, NJ.: Prentice Hall.

SHOWALTER, E. (1985). *The female malady: Women, madness, and English culture (1830–1930).* Boston: Little, Brown and Company.

SIMON, L. M. J. (1998). Does criminal offender treatment work? *Applied and Preventative Psychology, 7,* 137–159.

SIMON, R. J. (1975). *The contemporary woman and crime.* Washington, DC: U.S. Government Printing Office.

SIMON, R. J. (1976). Women and crime revisited. *Social Science Quarterly, 4,* 658–663.

SMART, C. (1976). *Women, crime, and criminology: A feminist critique.* London: Routledge.

SMART, C. (1977). The new female criminal: Reality and myth. *British Journal of Criminology, 19,* 50–59.

SNYDER, T. R. (2001). *The Protestant ethic and the spirit of punishment.* Grand Rapids, MI: William B. Eerdmans Publishing Company.

SPERLING, M. B., BERMAN, W. H., & FAGEN, G. (1992). Classification of adult attachment: An integrative taxonomy from attachment and psychoanalytic theories. *Journal of Personality Assessment, 59,* 239–247.

SPITZER, S. (1975). Toward a Marxian theory of deviance. *Social Problems, 22,* 638–651.

SPUNT, B., BROWNSTEIN, H., CRIMMINS, P, & LANGLEY, S. (1997). American women who kill: Self-reports of their homicides. *International Journal of Risk, Security, and Crime Prevention, 4,* 62–81.

SROUFE, L. A. (1983). Infant-caregiver attachment and patterns of adaptation in preschool: The roots of maladaptation and competence. In M. Perlmutter (Ed.), *Minnesota Symposia in Child Psychology, 16,* 41–83.

SROUFE, L. A., & FLEESON, J. (1996). Attachment and the construction of relationships. In W. W. HARUP & Z. RUBIN (Eds.), *Relationships and development* (pp. 51–71). Hillsdale, NJ: Erlbaum.

STAKE, R. E. (1995). *The art of case study research.* Thousand Oaks, CA: Sage.

STAKE, R. E. (1998). Case studies. In N. K. DENZIN & Y. S. LINCOLN (Eds.), *Strategies of qualitative inquiry* (pp. 86–109). Thousand Oaks, CA: Sage.

SULLIVAN, D., & TIFFT, L. (2001). *Restorative justice: Healing the foundations of our everyday lives.* Monsey, NY: Willow Tree Press.

SUTKER, P. B., ALLAIN, A. N., & GEYER, S. (1978). Female criminal violence and differential MMPI characteristics. *Journal of Consulting and Clinical Psychology, 46,* 1141–1143.

SWANSON, J., HOLZER, C., GANJU, V., & JONO, R. (1990).Violence and psychiatric disorder in the community: Evidence from the epidemiologic catchment area surveys. *Hospital and Community Psychiatry, 41,* 761–770.

TEPLIN, L. A., ABRAM, K. M., & McCLELLAND, G. M. (1996). Prevalence of psychiatric disorders among incarcerated women. *Archives of General Psychiatry, 53,* 505–512.

THIBAULT, E. A., & ROSSIER, J. (1992, October). *Misframed family violence issues.* Paper presented at the annual meeting of the American Society of Criminology, Atlanta.

THOMAS, W. I. (1923/1969). *The unadjusted girl.* Montclair, NJ: Patterson Smith.

TIIHONEN, J., ERONEN, M., & HAKOLA, P. (1993). Criminality associated with mental disorders and intellectual deficiency. *Archives of General Psychiatry, 50,* 917–918.

TOCH, H. (1998). *Violent men: An inquiry into the psychology of violence.* Chicago: Aldine.

TOTMAN, J. 1978). *The murderers: A psychosocial study of criminal homicide.* San Francisco: R and E Research Associates.

UMBREIT, M. (1995). *Mediating interpersonal conflict: A pathway to peace.* West Concord, MI: CPI Publishing.

U.S. Department of Justice. (1992). *Women in jail 1989.* Washington, DC: Author.

U.S. Department of Justice. (1994). *1991: Women in prison.* Washington, DC: Author.

VAILLANT, G. E. (1994). Ego mechanisms of defense and personality psychopathology. *Journal of Abnormal Psychology, 103,* 44–50.

VAN NESS, D., & STRONG, K. H. (1997). *Restoring justice.* Cincinnati: Anderson Pubishing.

VOLD, G. B., BERNARD, T. J., & SNIPES, J. B. (1998). *Theoretical criminology* (4th ed.). New York: Oxford University Press.

VORMBROCK, J. K. (1993). Attachment theory as applied to wartime and job-related marital separation. *Psychological Bulletin, 114,* 122–144.

WARNER, R. (1978). The diagnosis of antisocial and hysterical personality disorders: An example of sex bias. *The Journal of Nervous and Mental Disease, 166,* 839–845.

WATERS, E., WIPPMAN, J., & SROUFE, L. A. (1979). Attachment, positive affect, and competence in the peer group: Two studies in construct validation. *Child Development, 50,* 821–829.

WEISHEIT, R. A. (1984). Women and crime: Issues and perspectives. *Sex Roles, 11,* 567–581.

WEISS, R. S. (1982). Attachment in adult life. In C. Parkes & J. Stevenson-Hinde (Eds.), *The place of attachment in human behavior* (pp. 171–184). New York: Basic Books.

WEKERLE, C., & WOLFE, D. A. (1998). The role of child maltreatment and attachment style in adolescent relationship violence. *Development and Psychopathology, 10,* 571–586.

WEST, M., & KELLER, A. (1994). Psychotherapy strategies for insecure attachment in personality disorders. In M. B. SPERLING & W. H. BERMAN (Eds.), *Attachment in adults: Clinical and developmental perspectives* (pp. 313–330). New York: The Guilford Press.

WIDIGER, T. A., & SPITZER, R. L. (1991). Sex bias in the diagnosis of personality disorders: Conceptual and methodological issues. *Clinical Psychology Review, 11,* 1–22.

WIDOM, J. (1998). Child abuse, neglect, and witnessing violence. In D. M. Stoff, J. Breiling, & J. D. Maser (Eds.), *Handbook of antisocial behavior* (pp. 159–170). New York: Wiley.

WILBANKS, W. (1983). Female homicide offenders in the U.S. *International Journal of Women's Studies, 6,* 302–310.

WILCZYNSKI, A. (1997). Mad or bad? Child-killers, gender and the courts. *British Journal of Criminology, 37,* 419–436.

WILCZYNSKI, A., & MORRIS, A (1993). Parents who kill their children. *Criminal Law Review, 2,* 31–36.

WILLIAMS, J. B. W., & SPITZER, R. L. (1983). The issue of sex bias in DSM-III: A critique of "A woman's view of DSM-III" by Marcie Kaplan. *American Psychologist, 38,* 793–798.

WILSON, W. (1991). *Good murders and bad murders: A consumer's guide in the age of information.* Lanham, NC: University Press of America.

WOLFGANG, M. E. (1958). *Patterns in criminal homicide.* Philadelphia: University of Pennsylvania Press.

WONDERS, N. (1999). Postmodern feminist criminology and social justice. In B. Arrigo (Ed.), *Social justice/criminal justice: The maturation of critical theory in law, crime, and deviance* (pp. 111–130). Belmont, CA: Wadsworth.

YARVIS, R. M. (1995). Diagnostic patterns among three violent offender types. *Bulletin of the American Academy of Psychiatry and the Law, 23,* 411–419.

ZARRELLA, J. (2002). Wuornos' last words: I'll be back.
http://www.cnn.com/2002/LAW/10/09/wuornos.execution/

ZEHR, H. (1990). *Changing lenses.* Scottsdale, PA: Herald Press.

ZELNICK, L., & BUCHHOLZ, E. S. (1990). The concept of mental representations in the light of recent infant research. *Psychoanalytic Psychology, 1,* 29–58.

ZINGER, I., & FORTH, A. E. (1998). Psychopathy and Canadian criminal court proceedings: The potential for human rights abuses. *Criminology, 40,* 237–276.

ZOCCOLILLO, M. (1993). Gender and the development of conduct disorder. *Development & Psychopathology, 5,* 65–78.

Index

❖